AMONGST
THE RUINS

AMONGST THE RUINS

*Why Civilizations Collapse
and Communities Disappear*

JOHN DARLINGTON

YALE UNIVERSITY PRESS
NEW HAVEN AND LONDON

p. 13: Quotes from both *The Tollund Man* and *Bogland* by Seamus Heaney, from *New Selected Poems 1966–1987* © The Estate of Seamus Heaney. Used by permission of Faber and Faber Limited. Used by permission of Farrar, Straus & Giroux, LLC, http://us.macmillan.com/fsg. All rights reserved

p. 13: © George Barnett, 1965, *The Beaghmore Stone Circles* from his collection of poems *The Wee Black Tin*, by kind permission of Graham Mawhinney

p. 36: By kind permission © Nicholas Comfort 1994 *The Lost City of Dunwich* published by Terence Dalton, Ltd

p. 156: Permission granted by Zehao Zhou to quote from his dissertation *The Anti-Confucian Campaign during the Cultural Revolution*, August 1966–January 1967 © Zehao Zhou

p. 180: © Bobby Troup/Warner Chappell Sync

p. 184: From *The Grapes of Wrath* by John Steinbeck published by Penguin Classics. Copyright © John Steinbeck 1939. Reprinted by permission of Penguin Books Limited. Copyright renewed © John Steinbeck 1967

p. 257: By kind permission © Graham Fairclough 2009

For information about this and other Yale University Press publications, please contact:
U.S. Office: sales.press@yale.edu yalebooks.com
Europe Office: sales@yaleup.co.uk yalebooks.co.uk

Set in Linotype Sabon by Tetragon, London
Printed in Great Britain by Gomer Press Ltd, Llandysul, Ceredigion, Wales

Library of Congress Control Number: 2022948965

ISBN 978-0-300-25928-5

A catalogue record for this book is available from the British Library.

10 9 8 7 6 5 4 3 2 1

CONTENTS

PREFACE

The best of Prophets of the future is the Past.

LORD BYRON; DIARY EXTRACT, 28 JANUARY 1821

Or alternatively:

Those who cannot remember the past are condemned to repeat it.

GEORGE SANTAYANA

Study the past, if you would divine the future.

CONFUCIUS

The past resembles the future more than one drop of water resembles another.

IBN KHALDUN

At times it feels like the past is filled with a cacophony of voices warning about how important it is to learn from the past. Indeed, there are at least 300 familiar quotations which champion the relevance of history to the future.

However, there is a counterview that it is impossible, fruitless even, to try to treat what has happened previously as a useful barometer for what will happen next:

If men could learn from history, what lessons it might teach us! But passion and party blind our eyes, and the light which experience gives us is a lantern on the stern which shines only on the waves behind.

SAMUEL TAYLOR COLERIDGE

That men do not learn very much from the lessons of history is the most important of all the lessons of history.

ALDOUS HUXLEY

And, of course, there is always the ever-quotable Mark Twain, who remarked, 'The past does not repeat itself, but it rhymes.' My favourite, however, and a reason for writing this book, is from an anonymous source: 'History repeats itself because no one was listening the first time.' Clearly, I am firmly in the camp that claims there are valuable lessons to learn, it's all about asking the right question. How can we train ourselves to pay better attention to those voices of yesteryear, particularly during times of collapse and crisis, or ahead of them?

This book explores some of the ways that we can draw from the past, both philosophically and practically, to help plan for and guide the future.

AMONGST THE RUINS

THE ANATOMY OF LOSS

Ruins lie at the heart of this book. Mutely eloquent reminders of our immortality, they are memento mori on the grandest scale. They are the architectural car crashes of the past which we rubberneck from the present, whispering 'there but for the grace of God go I . . .'. Ruins represent our failures: civilizations that have collapsed, communities who moved out or were forced to move on, or the abandoned dreams of despots, democrats and the divine. But, given that time is relative, and *all* buildings will eventually end as dust, they are also our successes, notices marking the extraordinary achievements of humankind. Ruins prompt questions: what person visiting the red sandstone facades of Petra's Treasury would not ask why or how? Machu Picchu, Chichen Itza and Angkor Wat inspire because we want to know more about the people who built them. And, while they signify lives lived long ago, they also tell us something about where we are heading. Ruins are libraries, abandoned books that divulge stories about what happened decades, centuries or millennia ago, and which are repeated today. The outcome may not be the same, but we would be arrogant to ignore the lessons of history.

This book is a search for the present and future in the past. In it we will explore the loss of ancient civilizations, the collapse of ruling elites and the disappearance of more recent communities.

This is a vast subject. Edward Gibbon needed six volumes for his *History of the Decline and Fall of the Roman Empire* (1766–89), which has now been reprinted countless times. A search of the internet using the phrase 'fall of empire' will bring up thousands of books, videos and films documenting the stumble, trip and sprawl of the powerful, from the Aztecs and Incas through to the empires of the British, Soviets and Americans. Flick through the pages of any atlas of world history and be overwhelmed by the growing bloom and subsequent shrivelling of colours depicting the tread of ancient Mesopotamians, Mongols, Umayyads, Spaniards and Portuguese, amongst many, many others. The last imperial Chinese dynasty stretched over nearly 15 million square kilometres at its greatest extent (the Qing Dynasty in 1790 CE), and doubtless more still will be written about modern China, the twenty-first-century global superpower, when its time has passed.

These are fascinating approaches, but I am interested in the explanations that underpin why ancient and more recent civilizations disappeared. How did we reach the ruin? What are the reasons behind the fall, or the shrinking frontiers in the atlas? And, as importantly, is there a commonality to that loss that might help us today?

In response to that challenge, I have selected seventeen places from across the globe that illustrate specific stories of decline and

Fig. 1 'Destruction' by Thomas Cole from *The Course of Empire* series, 1836. This, the fourth in a series of five paintings on the subject of the rise and fall of civilizations, shows barbarians sacking a classical city. It is followed by 'Desolation'.

collapse. Some will be recognizable and well known, but most have been chosen to touch on the fascinating variety of heritage across the world and the connections between people and disappearance. The book is divided into five organizing themes which seek to corral the causes of loss: climate change, natural hazards, economics, human frailty and war. Selected because they are the most cited reasons for collapse, the categories overlap, with human decision-making influencing them all. Critically, there is rarely a single explanation for why civilizations fail. The cumulative impact of multiple causes is acknowledged from the outset, where one disaster compounds another, often leading to a catastrophic downward spiral. Some stories will speak solely to the organizing theme, but where there are multiple causes, the theme may be the most significant, or the trigger for decline, or will introduce an important and interesting line of discussion.

My scope is broad. Our raw materials are the physical remains of architectural and archaeological heritage, but I touch on intangible cultural traditions, particularly in the last chapter where I explore the inevitability of future loss in which it may be impossible to retain even the ruins of the past. Here, taking the past with you in the form of *the activity*, be it an idea, a function, a dance, recipe or song, as opposed to bricks and mortar, becomes an important option.

My chronology and geography are wide-ranging too, with some stories sealed under 3,000-year-old peat and others that are told through the carcasses of twentieth-century buildings. I take in most of the world's continents, from the ice of the Arctic fringe, through to the desert landscapes of North Africa, by way of South America's high mountains and Southeast Asia's urban sprawl. Not all the tales are told at the same speed. Some are about instant catastrophe, the minutes it might take an earthquake to destroy a place; others are about a gentle implosion, the architectural equivalent of taking an undercooked soufflé out of the oven; yet more still are about a decline which is so slow that those living through it are not even aware of it. But importantly, all the stories contain lessons that are applicable well beyond the sight of their tumbled walls or abandoned landscapes.

Nor are all the stories told at the same scale. Sometimes the headline is about a civilization – the Sumerians, for example, who once dominated what is now southern Iraq. Here, through the lens of the abandonment of the city of Girsu, we will explore the impact of salinification on a sophisticated agricultural system that once supported a large population. Alternatively, the story might focus on a stratum of society as told through the loss of a single building – Beaudesert Hall: the fall from power of the landed 'gentry' in England due to taxation, economics and changing social attitudes. Or it might be about the loss of a community because the raison d'être of that community has disappeared, as in the case of Humberstone in Chile, which was abandoned when the saltpetre mined there was rendered obsolete by new materials manufactured elsewhere.

A depressing subject? If this book were a film, it might be introduced by credits warning '*May contain scenes of doom, death, decline, disaster . . .*' – a decidedly downbeat alliteration. At first glance the topic *is* all about failure: our overexploitation of the earth's natural resources, our response to the inevitable impact of building homes on the slopes of a volcano and in the places where tectonic plates collide, or our tribal urge to destroy the neighbours. The body count adds up. There is definitely an element of schadenfreude in the telling of these stories, but we should not enjoy them as tales of horror, something which happened a long time ago that is somehow detached and irrelevant today. This feels like sitting in an idling car and complaining about the traffic jam – we are the traffic. The fact is that many of the stories concern trends and patterns that are present, if not amplified, in our current world.

But I also don't want to paint a picture that is all doom and gloom. Human ingenuity in the face of adversity is inspirational and is told in part here, as are the multiple adaptations to changes that made life more difficult for ancient peoples across the world. Run out of water? Use technology to search for it deeper in the earth or dam valleys to capture it in the winter for use in the hotter summer months. Too much water? Build above it, divert it or use windmills to pump it elsewhere. The geography of the 17 per cent of the Netherlands that has been reclaimed from the sea is founded on just such ingenuity. There are limits to where humankind can and cannot live, but these have always changed. What worshipper of Luna, Khonsu, Artemis, Máni, Chandra, Tsukuyomi-no-Mikoto or Metztli – gods and goddesses of the moon from across the world – would conceive we could land on its stony surface and succeed in returning to the mortal world?

There is also that question of timescale. For example, to view the decline of the Roman Empire as a long and relentless progression of disasters ignores both its peaks and the positives. And that is if we can agree what triggered it, and when, and what marked its final dying breath. Gibbon's classic, *Fall of the Roman Empire*, covered a period of 1,500 years, and he firmly fired the starting gun for the crisis in 376 CE when large numbers of Gothic peoples began crossing the Rhine. Most mark 476 CE to be the death knell, when the barbarian king Odoacer overthrew the teenage Romulus Augustus, the last emperor of the Western Empire, and the Senate sent the imperial insignia to Flavius Zeno, his counterpart in the Eastern Empire. But of course, the collapse of the Western Roman Empire was then succeeded by the flourishing of the East: 'Rome did not fall in the fifth or sixth centuries. It changed and multiplied itself . . . It may have been a chameleon, but it was certainly no phoenix, because there were no ashes.'[1] Others see the origins of decay much earlier, in the loss of power of the Republican democratic institutions, the moment Augustus declared himself *princeps civitas*, first amongst the people, in 27 BCE.[2] Still more point to the Muslim conquests of the eighth century as the beginning of the end.[3]

Perspective is important too: using the same example, who suffered from Rome's decline? Certainly not the Gothic peoples who had been pushed out of their lands by the Huns, nor perhaps many of the people working on the trading routes of the Mediterranean, where the short-term interruption of political events could be overridden by the need for bread, wine and oil. Many now see this period of Late Antiquity as a time of change between the classical and medieval worlds, with plenty of continuity in everyday life, interspersed by events that impacted dramatically on the political and religious leadership.

The point is that the concept of decline is a moving target, sometimes clear-cut – the break-up of the Soviet Union, the fall of Nazi Germany or the collapse of the British Empire – but often the path to ruination is uneven, messy and complex.

A final point on the tone of this exploration into the loss of civilizations is that it is written from an archaeological perspective.

What does that mean? It means that archaeologists have a long body clock. We work not to years nor decades, but to centuries and millennia. Ours is a slow heartbeat, where the important issues of each era are filtered out from the day-to-day by the inevitable reckoning of time. Consequently, we see change as the only constant in history. And in the context of such a long view of the past, every civilization will eventually turn to dust. To continue our Roman analogy, we are blessed with some remarkable monuments dating to the period: from the Colosseum in the imperial capital, through to Baalbek's temples, Ephesus's Great Theatre and Hadrian's Wall. But these monuments are the stubborn survivors of literally millions of buildings that once existed, the tiniest fraction of an architectural heritage that has entirely disappeared. The others, which ranged from simple wooden homes to stone-built palaces, have either decayed or have been demolished, reused or built over. Nothing lasts forever. One day, ideally in the unimaginable distance of the future, the Pantheon will eventually succumb to the ageing process of time. If a similar prognosis is offered for *all* our physical cultural legacy, then immortality is born of the passing on of ideas. We celebrate the architecture of the past in our own moments, seek to conserve that which we value now and, at the same time, try to predict what future generations will cherish.

CHAPTER 1

CLIMATE CHANGE

GIVEN THE URGENCY of the current climate crisis, we tend to frame change in the present or the recent past, and on our own actions that have accelerated or will slow it. But, regardless of the undeniable impact of human influence, the planet's climate has been changing since before humans walked the earth. Four stories of the disappearance of historic cultures are presented here, which each explore how communities have responded to climatic conditions that have been getting incrementally cooler, wetter, warmer or drier.

First, we step back to the Bronze Age and see the impact of climate change on the pastoral Bronze Age peoples who inhabited the slopes of the Sperrin Mountains in Northern Ireland. Here at places like Beaghmore and Copney a remarkable assemblage of stone circles, alignments, avenues and cairns are to be found hidden underneath the moorland peat, symbols of a wider hidden landscape lost to the onset of the wetter, colder climatic conditions of the Late Bronze Age (1200–650 BCE). How did this happen, what was our human contribution, and how did we respond?

Next, we will turn to Herschel Island (Qikiqtaruk) off the Yukon coast of Canada, where a warming climate rather than a cooling one is the issue. Used as an Inuvialuit hunting base for centuries, and more recently established as a commercial whaling station, Herschel was all but abandoned after the market for whale oil collapsed in 1907. Now increased global temperatures are presenting new challenges to preservation, with rising sea levels sweeping away both European and earlier culture, and thawing permafrost accelerating the discovery and destruction of once frozen archaeology. Permafrost covers almost a quarter of the Northern Hemisphere, including Alaska, much of Canada, and Siberia. It contains within it the remarkably preserved remains of earlier peoples: evidence that is desiccated and lost as the permafrost disappears. This will be one of the biggest and least appreciated losses of global cultural heritage in future times.

Coastal climate change is graphically illustrated in our third story, using the example of Dunwich off England's Suffolk coast. Listed in the Domesday Book of 1086 as one of the ten largest towns in the country, Dunwich once had a population of over 5,000 people and eighteen churches and religious institutions. Now, just two churches remain, and fewer than 200 residents, the remainder of the town being lost to the sea. Again, the question is asked, how did the people of Dunwich respond to the slow death of their town?

From too much water, to drought, the final story under the theme of climate change describes the equally destructive impact of a warming, drier environment on heritage. The Garamantes' empire once stretched for 647,500 square kilometres in the Saharan area of Libya and North Africa. Originating from Berber tribes in the Iron Age (200 BCE) and rising to regional prominence in the second century CE, the Garamantes were described by Herodotus as 'a very great nation'. Despite Roman propaganda which sought to depict the Garamantes as barbarians, they inhabited a powerful and sophisticated kingdom with a capital that was home to 10,000 people. The Garamantes' success was built on their sophisticated water management system, but in the fourth century CE a drying climate, coupled with the overexploitation of a diminishing supply of water and the increasing numbers of slaves required to maintain it, led to their slow decline and eventual disappearance. Depleting water supplies, or their salinification, and the loss of civilization to sand, is a little-told story that can be repeated across the desert regions of the world.

Climate change will be the biggest global driver of loss of heritage over the coming decades, whether through inundation by water, sand and salt, or because places that were once inhabitable are no longer so, leading to their abandonment. These four stories underpin the importance of learning from the past in the face of a changing climate, or as expressed in this adapted version of a Native American proverb: 'We not only inherit the land from our ancestors, we borrow it from our children.'

The Stone Circles of the Sperrin Mountains, Northern Ireland

Lost worlds have always captured the imagination, whether the mythological romance of Atlantis and Eldorado or the extraordinary revelations of new technologies, which allow us to see the true extent of the Angkor Archaeological Park in Cambodia under its thick canopy of trees and Dunwich in the murky water on the edge of the North Sea (see below). However, there is another lost landscape that we often miss because it is covered not by water, plants or volcanic debris, but by peat. Globally this inland 'sea' covers 4.2 million square kilometres,[1] the equivalent of seventeen times the land area of the United Kingdom. Peat is slow to grow, accumulating at approximately one millimetre each year, and has featured in our

Fig. 2 Beaghmore circles from the air showing a variety of stone circles, cairns and alignments. The contrast between the remaining russet-covered peat and green grass of the excavated area is stark.

landscapes since the end of the last glaciation some 15,000 years ago; from a modern perspective it therefore has the appearance of permanence, a soft version of geology. But it is inextricably linked to humans who lived before its formation, and whose world lies buried under its dense brown blanket.

Fortunately, a bog is a goldmine for archaeologists because it locks in so much information not only about its own origin and growth, but also about what went on in the wider landscape. Any water-saturated deposits have the potential to preserve evidence from the past that desiccates, disintegrates and disappears elsewhere. The cold, wet and oxygen-lite nature of peat slows down the rate of decay of organic matter, so preserving many things that fall within its damp, fibrous grasp. It is estimated that archaeologists working in peatlands may find up to 90 per cent of the material culture of ancient communities contained within it, as opposed to 10 per cent of those working on dry land.[2] A peat bog can therefore be a library of the past holding airborne pollen that precisely documents changes to the surrounding vegetation; seeds and plant material telling us about diet and materials; the wooden posts and platforms of ancient homes; even the bodies of people themselves, often beautifully preserved but disconcerting victims of prehistoric ritual. The carbon in the peat gives us dates, while the identifiable marks of bog growth and contraction tell us something about the climate over millennia. But peat is selective, in overly acidic conditions the soil can quickly eat away bone and antler and destroy certain metals, particularly if they are subjected to repeated wetting and drying.

Bogs don't just appear, they are living things, requiring the right combination of wet, cold and poor drainage, and the right type of wet – in this case acid rich and nutrient poor, mainly falling as rainfall. There are several different types of peat bog in the UK and Ireland and their growth is complex, but they may be simplified according to how they form. Raised bogs, as seen in the west of Ireland, tend to form from the slow infill of lakes where marginal plants slowly decompose to slowly choke and absorb the water body. Sphagnum moss gradually takes over, growing and dying back annually, with new sphagnum mounting the rotting but partially preserved former growth. Raised bogs or fen peat can be as much as ten metres deep, many forming at the end of the last Ice Age around 8000 BCE. Blanket bogs on the other hand are often younger and shallower-growing during the Neolithic and the Bronze Age. They were created as a result of tree clearance which, with high rainfall, led to increased impoverishment of the soils. Minerals, particularly iron, washed through the soil horizon, forming a hard, impenetrable pan that trapped water above. Trees struggled to regrow in this soggy new environment, but marsh vegetation thrived, including the ubiquitous bog-forming sphagnum.

Ireland is renowned both for its raised and blanket bogs, which by turn contain a rich reservoir of archaeological sites. The Irish Archaeological Wetland Unit identified 3,462 sites in 45,000 hectares of peat bog, equating to 7.7 sites per square kilometre,[3] a figure that is far higher than English counterparts and likely to be an underestimate. The peat, and things contained within it, were a consistent theme for the poet Seamus Heaney, who grew up on a farm near bog country in Northern Ireland. Aside from arguably his most famous poem, 'Digging' (1966), he frequently returned to this subject, writing of the 'Trove of the turfcutters'/Honeycombed workings' ('The Tollund Man', 1972), inspired by the discovery of a bog body in Denmark in 1950, where 'Every layer they strip/Seems camped on before' ('Bogland', 1969). George Barnett, a slightly less celebrated poet, was fascinated by the same:

> Around by Blackrock in the County Tyrone,
> Are numbers of circles and big standing stones,
> At Michael McMahon's they stand by the score,
> About his wee farm, around by Beaghmore.
>
> The stones were set up before any peat grew,
> And just have a look and you'll find it is true,
> The most of them's neatly set up on their end,
> And some people say, by the bold 'Beaker-Men!'[4]

Barnett, an amateur archaeologist and folklorist, first drew attention to the stone circles of Beaghmore, County Tyrone, in Northern Ireland, during the 1930s. As today, local people on the fringes of the Sperrin Mountains have long held rights of turbary – originally medieval entitlements to cut peat for fuel – from the blanket bog, and it was while out observing this traditional practice that Barnett identified what was to turn out to be one of the most extensive prehistoric landscapes in Ireland.

After Barnett's initial identification, Northern Ireland's state heritage service commissioned a series of investigations to understand more about the site. Excavations from 1945 to 1949, and again in 1965, slowly uncovered not one but seven stone circles hidden under the peat. These represented a Neolithic and Bronze Age world that clearly pre-dated the damper, wetter conditions which prompted the growth of the blanket bog.

The first signs of human activity at Beaghmore belong to the Neolithic, 5,250 years ago, when people cleared small patches in the native birch, willow, pine and hazel woodland and settled in the area. They were early farmers, probably living in seasonal camps and making the most of the easily cultivated sandy soils for simple cultivation alongside a largely pastoral existence. Most likely they hunted, fished and foraged too, making the most of the wild resources as well as benefiting from early domestication. We don't know a great deal about them, except they used stone tools, cooked in hearth pits and divided up the land into fields, marked by boundaries made from stones cleared from the area. They abandoned the hillside at Beaghmore by the early third millennium and there was a hiatus before the arrival of the stone circle builders after *c*. 1500 BCE.[5] We know much more about these new settlers because they left behind a ceremonial landscape that bears comparison with similar sacred places in Scotland, Wales, Southwest England and Brittany. These Bronze Age folk were part of a migration of people or ideas (there is a lively and continuing debate as to which – the joy of archaeology is that our documents are the material cultures of the past, which leave enormous scope for disagreement!) that originated in eastern Europe, bringing distinctive types of pottery, funerary traditions and new metalworking skills in copper, bronze and gold.

At Beaghmore we have no sight of the houses that the new settlers lived in, nor their farms and industries; instead, we have their spectacular sacred place. Stones gathered locally were used to create ceremonial circles, either by placing them on the ground or setting them upright in simple foundation pits. These are not of the same scale as the great circles at Avebury in Wiltshire, or Brodgar on the

Isle of Orkney, ranging between 11 and 18 metres in diameter, and even the largest standing stone is around 1.2 metres high, but they are unique and highly distinctive.

Six of the seven circles were paired, and all of them were associated with smaller burial cairns, made from stone rubble, again collected from nearby. The cairns were kerbed with small boulders and most contained cremated human remains. The single circle is markedly different from all the twins: it is larger, both in diameter (18 metres) and in the size of the principal stones, some of which stand up to 1.2 metres high, and the whole of its interior is filled with 884 smaller stones, each set upright. As ever, there is much speculation about the purpose of the 'dragon's teeth', as the smaller stones are known, with the most likely explanation being that they prevented people accessing burials placed at the centre of the circle.

Stretching out from the stone circles and cairns were at least ten alignments of standing stones, some made up of numerous small stones which extended 50 metres into the unexcavated peat and were paired with a shorter row of larger stones. Four of the rows led

Fig. 3 Beaghmore circle and cairns. Here two sets of twinned stone circles have a cairn in between each pair, and both large and small stone alignments running in short and longer lines from them. In the background is the 'dragon's teeth', a circle filled with nearly 900 smaller stones.

directly from the burial cairns and were all parallel, each pointing from the cairn towards the northeast horizon.

When Beaghmore was first excavated, the presence of stone circles in Ireland was limited, and Beaghmore's dragon's teeth circle was believed to be a one-off. However, research conducted over the second half of the twentieth century and the beginning of the twenty-first century, has revealed that Barnett's discovery on the fringes of the Sperrins was not an isolated example.

On Copney Hill, ten kilometres southwest of Beaghmore, a further nine stone circles, possibly ten, were found following identification in 1979.[6] Known by local turf-cutters, who recognized the tops of the taller stones peeping through the peat, part of the site was cleared of peat in 1994, and three of the largest circles were excavated a year later. The ambition was to open the site to the public. Underneath the turf, all of the excavated circles revealed more sophisticated versions of Beaghmore's dragon's teeth, with the largest stones on the perimeter and interiors filled with smaller standing stones. In two of the circles, the inner stones were set in

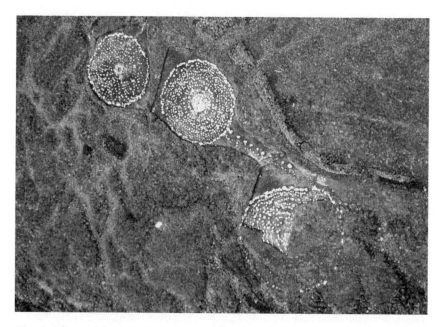

Fig. 4 Three of Copney's nine stone circles and a double stone alignment revealed underneath the peat after excavation. Each circle has a central burial cairn and an interior filled with smaller upright stones reminiscent of Beaghmore's dragon's teeth.

AMONGST THE RUINS

ever decreasing circles and culminated in a central burial cairn, as if focusing on a bullseye. In the other circle, the inner stones radiated out in semi-straight lines from another centrally placed cairn. The six unexcavated circles are much smaller, none being greater than 10 metres in diameter, compared to the largest which stood at 24 metres. A double alignment connected two of the excavated circles, with one row made of smaller stones next to a larger neighbour, exactly as at Beaghmore. Interestingly, the alignment of the row to the southwest was not the same as its counterparts to the northeast.

Beaghmore and Copney are the most impressive complexes discovered in Northern Ireland to date, but they are not the only ones. More circles, cairns and stone rows are to be found across the region. Moymore, also in County Tyrone, has at least nine circles, all clustered together, with two stone alignments at right angles to one another, one typically consisting of a double row of smaller and larger stones. The Northern Ireland Sites and Monuments Record (NISMR) lists over 110 circles from seventy-nine separate sites, many small at around ten metres in diameter and all made up of low stones rather than large monoliths, although there are occasionally larger separate 'sentinel' stones overlooking their smaller collected companions. Interestingly, there are almost no other stone circle complexes of this type – small, modest and in multiples with rows and cairns – found in the rest of Ireland – the tradition appears to be one centred on Counties Tyrone and Derry/Londonderry in the north.[7]

So, what are they? The joy of prehistory is that there is no documentary record to conclusively prove or disprove theories of past use, so we are reliant on the science and imagination of archaeologists to unravel the past. An archaeologist's raw ingredients are the material remains that we humans leave behind. This includes everything from the ruins of our ancestors' temples and the stained ground of a disintegrated building to the fragments of shattered cooking pots or the dead sparks of hammer-scale that once flew from a blacksmith's forge. But such evidence is ephemeral and highly selective: wood rots, metal decays, even stone fractures, delaminates or is carried away for reuse; and so the archaeologist is left to decipher a jigsaw in which most of the pieces are missing. If human material remains are the raw ingredients in the archaeological cookbook, then the techniques that convert them to the food of theory include non-intrusive fieldwork, often carried out at a landscape scale to map the 'lumps and bumps' of mute earthworks; buildings recording, essentially archaeology on the vertical scale; and an increasingly large armoury of scientific techniques that aid everything from dating using tree-rings through to determining the original source of stone axe, quern (hand-grinding stone) or menhir (a large, upright standing stone). Excavation is usually seen as the signature technique of the archaeologist, but in reality it is often the final resort, notably because it is expensive and its very act destroys the evidence it seeks. Excavation dismantles the chronology of a place, peeling back and removing layers of activity to find and record that underneath. It is the equivalent of tearing pages out of a precious but incomplete book and attempting to reconstruct its story through the memory of snatched phrases, occasional paragraphs and rare pages. The digging archaeologist is therefore a masseur of earth, a rigorous copyist and the ultimate slash-and-burn scientist. And archaeological excavation can only ever be a translation of a copy . . . of a half-truth . . . of an original event from the past that can never be revealed.

Where does this leave our understanding of the stone circles of the Sperrins? All the sites have several critical characteristics in common, which are the anchors for interpretation: firstly, they are consistently associated with burial cairns, places where a few people have been interred, rather than the graveyards of the many. Secondly, there is clearly a deep connection between the cairns, the stone circles and the stone alignments – these are ensemble landscapes, not necessarily designed contemporaneously, but cumulatively, with each phase recognizing and building on its predecessor. There is also a relationship with earlier and later landscapes, in which they 'not only reached back to the Neolithic but foreshadowed others of the Iron Age'.[8] And their conformity of size, construction and materials across an area suggests that their builders were tribes of people, who shared the same values, societal structure and leadership. Thirdly, they all appear in similar geographical locations, almost all above 150 metres (500ft contour) on rough, hilly ground. Fourthly, the stone rows connected the sites with something beyond the horizon, their alignment was an important part of Bronze Age life. And finally, aside from the evidence of earlier Neolithic field systems underneath

AMONGST THE RUINS

the circle-builders, complex, there is no contemporary evidence of domestic living: no homes, hearths or rubbish pits. People were not making things here, nor were they sleeping, cooking, tending animals or trading amongst the stones.

So what were they doing? There is a longstanding joke amongst (and about) archaeologists, in that we cry 'ritual' when we come across anything that we do not understand. But this is undoubtedly a ritual landscape. Its defining attributes allow us to fashion a story of mid-to-late Bronze Age peoples using the marginal semi-uplands of the Sperrins as spaces for veneration. This was a setting for burial, a sacred place strongly associated with the seasons, a place to connect with the ancestors, a place to meet and remember the past, and maybe to make decisions about the future.

George Barnett, the champion of Beaghmore, felt that the circles and alignments there were part of an astronomical calendar. He even built a replica in his garden to test the theory – a model that he later replaced in 1962 with a full-size replica of Stonehenge, made of wood and painted blue and white.[9] There is a consistent orientation between some of the rows, the cairns and the winter solstice,[10] but the relationship between the circles, their interior variations and the outlying dolmens is unproven, and probably unprovable.[11] A further challenge to this theory is that while there is some consistency of alignment at individual places, the same is not necessarily true between them: for example, at Beaghmore the rows align northeast from the cairns, whereas at Copney they align southeast. It follows that they were unlikely to be pointing at the same thing. However, on a broader scale, the role of the seasons and the course of the sun and moon must have had a significant impact on Bronze Age peoples. What other way would there be to measure the day, the agricultural calendar or the passing of the years? Synchronization with the sun is reflected elsewhere in the architecture of Bronze Age society – the doors of the domestic round houses of the era found elsewhere consistently face the south side of the buildings to catch the sun, while sleeping areas are most often to the north and east, the side of darkness and first awakening. The same position is reflected in Bronze Age burials.

So, the stone circles of the Sperrins were sacred places of burial and veneration, but they were not places of habitation. Their placement was conscious, seemingly away from the homes of their builders on marginal land in open landscape, giving long views. This is a common Bronze Age characteristic in which ceremony and ritual took place in transient zones – marshes, lakes, tidal foreshores and boggy hillsides – separate places on the edge of the living. The next research objective must be to find evidence of the everyday to complement the stony ritual landscape of the circle builders.

The liminal nature of these Bronze Age ceremonial landscapes gives a hint to the next episode in this story of loss – changes that marked the difference between marginal and uninhabitable, leading to abandonment of the sites. The key to understanding is the wetter, colder conditions that led to the arrival of peat and the long boggy invasion that was to eventually hide the earlier prehistoric landscapes.

What happened to the Bronze Age ceremonial landscapes in the foothills of the Sperrin Mountains? An early theory pointed to a very direct correlation between clearance, climate and abandonment. Bronze Age farmers continued to clear the land of trees for growing crops

Fig. 5 Reconstruction of a late Bronze Age landscape in Northern Ireland showing ceremonial landscapes of stone circles, alignments, burial cairns, barrows and henges on cleared tracts of upland, with villages and farmed land on lower ground.

AMONGST THE RUINS

and grazing, which eventually led to soil exhaustion and hastened – by a colder, wetter climate – the irreversible formation of peat. The reality is a little more subtle. Evidence from Beaghmore suggests that the climate was already deteriorating before the circle builders erected their stones and placed some of them over their dead, with the mountainside location already being seen as marginal land. Their final departure, probably sometime in the eighth century BCE, may have been hastened by societal change, exacerbated by a changing climate and exhausted soil conditions. It is easy to see how all three factors can be interrelated, with climate and soil pressures on food supply impacting upon social hierarchies, leading to conflict, migration and abandonment.

Once the peat started to form it built a thick blanket that slowly consumed first the lowest monuments, growing until in some places even the tallest stones were covered. That landscape remains true today, excepting where it has been reclaimed in pockets for agriculture or converted to a crop of coniferous forest, both of which would require draining, or more recently, where it has been harvested as a garden conditioner and for fuel on a commercial scale. Of course, peat cutting by individual families is evident throughout the area, and in a sense it is this that brings us full circle, because the vast majority of discoveries of the Sperrins' prehistoric landscape has initially come to light when local turf-cutters have come across the buried arrangement of stones.

The story of the stone circles of the Sperrins is not over. The presence of this prehistoric landscape has only been given away by the tops of the tallest stones peeping above the peat, like the highest peaks in a mountain range showing through the cloud, or revealed by the serendipitous slice of the turf-cutter's *tairsgeir* (spade). We are only seeing a fraction of what is possible. More circles, cairns and rows will lie under the brown refuge of the peat awaiting discovery. Advances in archaeological prospecting using geophysical techniques, especially ground penetrating radar, may be a key to unlocking this hidden world. Science that allows us to see through the peat without excavating it, and to identify the contrasting pre-bog land surface with its stone-built ceremonial landscape, would significantly increase our understanding of the Bronze Age in Northern Ireland.

Ironically, there is an advantage in not physically revealing more of the Sperrins' circles. The Copney site was excavated in 1995. Since then, the exposed stones, particularly the smaller ones, have shown signs of deterioration.[12] Recent frost action, causing the stones to crack and spall, may be added to the negative weathering effects of being buried in an acidic soil. That decay may slow down as a new outer edge hardens on the stones, but is unlikely to stop.[13] Unwitting accident, blundering livestock, vandalism and the action of rogue vehicles are equally good arguments for leaving the heritage in the soil, but these threats are surely trumped by allowing the public to experience something of the spirit of the place that our ancestors felt over 3,000 years ago.

A far bigger threat to these sites, and all the heritage held or covered by the peat, is climate change. Some of the raised bogs and peat moorland of Ireland and the United Kingdom have been in place for over 10,000 years. Global warming could change that, reversing peat growth and thereby releasing millions of tons of trapped methane into the atmosphere, contributing another greenhouse gas to an already devastating mix.

In the lee of the Sperrin Mountains, the impacts of a warming world could re-expose a prehistoric landscape that was lost in the past, in part, due to climate change. Such a 'reveal' would be an equally catastrophic portent for the future of our own civilization.

Herschel Island–Qikiqtaruk, Canada

Communities at the edge of the world are the most vulnerable to change. Those that live on the margins of land and water, or at the extremes of human habitation, will always be the first to see the future. One such group is the Inuvialuit people, an indigenous Inuit group living on the fringes of frozen earth and an ice-clad sea on Canada's northern arctic coast. This is a story of a warming climate and its impact on the Inuvialuit and later European and North American settlers. As with so many of these stories, there is no single reason for change and abandonment, so our main focus here is on the slow thawing of the permafrost, a ground condition that covers almost a quarter of the northern hemisphere, and its implications for cultural heritage.

AMONGST THE RUINS

The earliest occupation of what is now Alaska and northwest Canada was by palaeo-arctic peoples who migrated across the land-bridge that connected with Siberia from *c.* 12000 BCE. Later, after ice-age meltwaters flooded the link to Russia, the area saw the arrival of successive cultural groups such as the Dorset (800 BCE–1300 CE) and Thule peoples (900–1700 CE), the latter migrating along Canada's arctic coast from Western Alaska from around 1000 CE. The Thule are the direct antecedents of today's Inuvialuit.

The area of northern Canada stretching from Herschel Island–Qikiqtaruk in the Yukon to the Mackenzie River Delta in the Northwest Territories is the historic heartland of the western Inuvialuit. By the nineteenth century they were divided into eight distinctive regional groups, each exploiting slightly difference resources and each focused on a central winter village. To the west, off Herschel (Qikiqtaruk), the Inuvialuit sought the bowhead whales, while in the east the communities of the Mackenzie Delta targeted beluga whales who favoured the shallow, warmer and less salty estuarine waters to moult, feed and give birth. The importance of the whale to the indigenous people of the area cannot be underestimated. A single bowhead yearling could provide up to 10,000 kilograms of

Fig. 6 A mid-nineteenth-century painted wooden plaque showing Inuvialuit hunting beluga whales. Three men in kayaks drive a pod of whales into shallow water, with one preparing to use a harpoon.

meat, blubber and skin, as well as a significant quantity of baleen and bone which could be used for tools, buildings, sledges, art and artefacts.[14] They also hunted and trapped a range of other animals including seals, caribou, moose, a huge assortment of fish (fifty-five varieties including arctic char, cod, cisco, whitefish, trout and salmon), waterfowl, muskrat and arctic fox.

For the majority of these communities there was a seasonal rhythm to life, with groups coming together in the late summer and early autumn for the whaling season. Afterwards most would move inland to hunt migrating caribou, returning to their homes to see out the dark days of winter. With the return of longer days, groups would move out onto the sea ice in search of seals, living in snow houses or caribou-skin tents. One thousand years of occupation by the Inuvialuit and their forebears has left a fascinating material culture, particularly from the fifteenth century onwards. The remains of half-sunken buildings, constructed into a slope and covered with sods, are the most substantial reminders of Inuvialuit life – indeed they are the largest buildings belonging to the Inuit cultures of the Arctic. Made of wooden planks and driftwood logs, these *igluryuaq*, or winter houses, were often cruciform in plan with three raised benches or chambers leading off a central space. The smaller benches would be used for working or eating, while the larger platforms were also for sleeping. Sometimes an additional chamber would lead off the central one, and was used as a kitchen. The *igluryuaq* were entered by a long (often up to eight metres) access tunnel that at first sunk into the ground before rising into the central chamber, and acted as a 'lock' against the cold outside. Inside, a fire could be lit and extended families (up to six in the larger *igluryuaq*) could hunker down during the colder winter months. Other buildings included *qadjgiq* (also known as *karigi* or *qargi*), large communal subterranean structures, used mainly by men as a mixture of council house, sweat lodge, dance hall and schoolroom. Typically, these were 15–20 metres long, and again made of timber, or occasionally whale ribs, and covered in turves. As with the *igluryuaq*, oil lamps would light and warm the interiors. Waste middens, hearths, working areas and storage buildings would typically complete the ensemble of village structures.

While the Inuit of Canada and Alaska and their predecessors had encountered European, American and Russian settlers – not least through the Norse settlement of Greenland from the tenth to the fifteenth centuries CE – it wasn't until the early nineteenth century that regular connections were made along the north Arctic coast. From the interior white trappers and their parent companies sought their skills in the fur trade, but it was a series of expeditions by the Royal Navy searching for the Northwest Passage that literally put the region on the map. Captain John Franklin's second expedition in 1825–7 set out to explore the coast from the Mackenzie River, heading westwards towards Alaska and the Bering Sea. The expedition was one of several commissioned by Sir John Barrow, Second Secretary to the Admiralty, to explore new territories across the world: part post-Napoleonic War job-retention scheme for the Royal Navy, and part imperial quest for discovery.[15] Many such undertakings ended in disaster, including Franklin's earlier expedition in 1819–22 in which eleven of the twenty members died. The Mackenzie River Expedition was, however, a success. With twenty-eight men and three small boats, the largest being eight metres long, Franklin managed to map approximately half of the continent's arctic coast. On the way, his team frequently came across the Inuvialuit, recording their way of life. The party reached Qikiqtaruk, which Franklin renamed after the preeminent Herschel family of scientists (Babbage, Buckland, Conybeare and Gilbert, also scientists, had rivers and mountains named in their honour) on 17 July 1826:

> At the conclusion of this conference, our visitors assured us, that having now become acquainted with white people, and being conscious that the trade with them would be beneficial, they would gladly encourage a further intercourse, and do all in their power to prevent future visitors from having such a reception as we had on our arrival in these seas. We learned that this island, which has been distinguished by the name of Herschel, is much frequented by the natives at this season of the year, as it abounds with deer, and its surrounding waters afford plenty of fish.[16]

Franklin's party did not quite succeed in completing the western route of the Northwest Passage, turning back just six days short of meeting another expedition coming from Alaska because of high winds and

Fig. 7 The old whaling station at Pauline Cove, Herschel Island, Qikiqtaruk Territorial Park, Canada. Fragmented sea ice can be seen in the background.

sea ice. However, his discoveries inevitably led to further exploration, including his last in 1845–7 in which he died aged sixty-one, when his two ships HMS *Erebus* and HMS *Terror* became icebound.

Increased contact between the Inuvialuit and westerners brought trade, but also disease, alcohol and severe depletion of natural resources. Throughout the nineteenth century American and British whalers sought new sources of prey as Atlantic coastal stocks became exhausted. Demand was driven by the need for whale products: from baleen for umbrella spokes and knife handles, to lamp oil and spermaceti candles for lighting before electricity. American whalers followed the bowhead whales to their summer grounds in the Beaufort Sea, reaching Point Barrow on the north coast of Alaska by 1854. In 1890 the steamboats *Mary D. Hume* and *Grampus* arrived from San Francisco, and for the first time wintered on Herschel Island, which soon became the base for the area's whaling operations – a 'virtual American colony on the Canadian arctic coast'.[17] The summer whaling season was short, so by overwintering at Herschel the whalers could gain a significant advantage, even if it meant ten months on the island. *Grampus* returned south with twenty whales in 1891,

AMONGST THE RUINS

while *Hume* overwintered again, returning the following year with thirty-seven whales worth $400,000 – one of the most profitable voyages in American maritime history.[18] Other expeditions followed in the wake of such early successes, with over 500 whalers and fifteen boats overwintering during the settlement's heyday in the late 1890s.

To service the fleet, timber-framed buildings were constructed on the island: storehouses for blubber and bone, a community house containing offices and a billiard room (later used for church services), ice houses, a mission house, and a graveyard for those who would not return home. Most whalers would live on board the ships, but come the summer months when the boats would be out to sea, those left behind, including women, would camp in tents on the island. The American and Canadian communities lived alongside the Inuvialuit, some of whom were employed by the whalers, or came to trade with them, in particular through provisioning furs from the coastal interior.

With the fleet icebound for most of the year, life on Herschel was not easy, combining hardship with boredom. Repairs, the collection of freshwater ice and fuel, and hunting on the mainland for food, offered welcome respite from cabin fever, as would a perpetual round of entertainment in the form of dances, parties and theatrical performances which largely took place on the boats. The trading of alcohol, or the raw materials required to make it, brought new vices to the Inuvialuit. Missionaries, such as the Anglican priest Isaac Stringer and his wife, Sadie, sought to redress the balance, preaching Christianity to the Inuvialuit and the evils of drink: 'I fully believe that a few years will see the salvation or the ruin of the Eskimo [*sic*] at Herschel Island . . .'[19] And, as with so many other relatively remote and closed communities (see chapter 4), western whalers and trappers brought with them western diseases, to devastating effect. A succession of major outbreaks of smallpox, measles, scarlet fever and typhus during the 1860s had a disproportionate impact on the Inuvialuit, made worse by more regular contact after 1890. Measles struck again in 1900 and 1902, leading to the abandonment of some of the major villages of the Mackenzie Delta to the east, including Kukpak and Kittigazuit. A stable population of around 2,500 in the early 1800s was reduced to just 150 in 1910.[20] Captain Howard, a whaler on Herschel, wrote in 1906:

The Huskies [the Inuit] in this region are diminishing very rapidly, measles cleaning out a whole band a few years ago. They resorted to a sweat bath for a cure, and when in a profuse perspiration went out and rolled in the snow to cool themselves, with the inevitable result, they all died.[21]

The whalers also had a negative impact on bowhead stock. The scale of the American vessels, and new technologies, such as cannon-fired harpoons, drastically reduced the numbers of whales. In the decades from 1890 until the beginning of the First World War, commercial whalers took an estimated 1,500 bowhead whales from the northern arctic coast waters. In reality, this was an industry already in decline due to overfishing and competition from electricity for lighting and other sources of oil, and steel replacing baleen. The last whalers overwintered on Herschel in 1907/8, but the island continued as a focal trading point, whales being replaced by a boom in arctic fox pelts which lasted until the 1940s.[22] While never completely abandoned, particularly by the Inuvialuit, Herschel Island became

Fig. 8 Pauline Cove, Herschel Island, Qikiqtaruk Territorial Park, Canada. Three Inuvialuit settlements existed on the island when it was first discovered by Europeans in 1826. Abandoned by permanent residents in 1987, it is still used by the Inuvialuit and visited by tourists.

AMONGST THE RUINS

no more than a liaison point and a shadow of its former self. The last permanent residents left Herschel in 1987. Today, the island is part of the Inuvialuit Settlement Area and a Yukon Territorial Park. It is now used by the Inuvialuit and Inupiat as a camp and base for hunting, albeit this use is declining, and by tourists, who increasingly stop over for the day on cruise tours. The island receives on average 400–500 visitors a year, who share it with important wildlife, including a rare colony of black guillemots.

So far, the story of Herschel Island and Canada's western arctic region has been about the socio-economic reasons for collapse: disease, old technologies being usurped by new ones, the relentless pursuit of diminishing natural resources and shifting global markets. But there is a further threat to both Herschel's living *and* its abandoned heritage – the increasing consequences of climate change. The Inuvialuit way of life has always been closely tied to the natural world, but the pace of current climate change is beyond the realm of historical experience. Anecdotal evidence from the Banks Island community further to the east of Herschel Island suggests a later freeze and earlier melt of the spring ice, which impacts directly upon the caribou migrations upon which the Inuvialuit have relied.[23] A deepening of the summer thawing into once-frozen ground where meat might traditionally be stored has resulted in spoilage, while supplies of 'drinkable ice' that is salt-free are diminishing. Inland lakes are draining away as the permafrost beneath them melts and travelling to and across the Inuvialuit Settlement Region is increasingly difficult for the same reason. Many of the hunting grounds and techniques used to capture fish and game within them are increasingly difficult to access or apply. In short, the pressure on the Inuvialuit to make adaptations to their traditional way of life is significant, requiring them to move or to change substantially in the face of unprecedented climatic disruption.[24]

In truth a changing climate has always impacted this brutal landscape, exposed as it is to extremes of cold and wind, snow, ice and water. Herschel owes its very existence to climate change: it was born when the snub nose of an advancing glacier pushed up a toe of sea sediment to create the island during the last glaciation. Since that time patterns of global warming and cooling are evidenced by the changing uses and occupation by the Inuvialuit and their forebears.

Most recently there has been another acceleration in the rate of climate change, resulting in increased warming, rising sea levels and a greater number of storm events. The consequences are dramatic. The ancient homes of Inuvialuit and of their predecessors, and those of the whalers which briefly flared into life towards the end of the nineteenth century, are physically disappearing. Both communities looked seawards, locating their villages on the fringe of land and sea, leaving their cultural remains especially vulnerable to these latest climatic changes. And it is a particularly destructive mixture. Settlements that were once high and distant enough to be out of the range of the stormy sea are now exposed, literally washing away in great gouts with each spell of tempestuous weather.

A warmer, rising and more tempestuous sea offers some of the most visceral imagery of the consequences of climate change, but there are other processes at work that are equally destructive to heritage. Permafrost occurs across large parts of the northern hemisphere, from Canada and Alaska through Greenland, northern Scandinavia to Siberia. Typically in these regions, the ground remains frozen the whole year round, save in many places for a thin 'active'

Fig. 9 A research team measure thawing permafrost on Herschel Island (Qikiqtaruk) in 2013. Softened soil collapses and runs into the sea in a 'thaw slump'.

AMONGST THE RUINS

layer on top which softens each spring allowing plants to flourish throughout summer. As global temperatures rise, more and more permafrost is slowly thawing. This has multiple effects, not least in that this releases significant quantities of methane (CH_4), a potent greenhouse gas, into the atmosphere, which contributes towards global warming. When it comes to cultural heritage, organic material previously preserved in the frozen soil becomes exposed to microbiological activity. A clock begins and decomposition processes that had otherwise been held in check turn the rock-hard soils under the active layer into a spongy pulp. Increased decay leads to the slow disintegration of wood, skin and any other organic building materials, and the release of greenhouse gasses. Related processes can further compound the rate of destruction: in some areas exposure to the air can lead to desiccation, with the soil and all it contains literally blowing away; in others, the increased depth of the active layer leads to the movement of soil down a slope, slumping and slipping, sometimes catastrophically. The dynamic nature of these soils, with permafrost sandwiched between the seasonally thawing active layer above and the unfrozen ground (*talik*) below, can also result in a range of geothermal activity that churns the earth, creating extraordinary landscapes of geological features. And, where frozen ground was once load-bearing, now it is not, resulting in damage or loss of existing structures and a reduction of space upon which to build anew. Where the permafrost-bearing-land meets the sea, as with the Canadian arctic – the same zone where peoples have historically settled and live today – all the destructive processes are multiplied.

The effects of a changing climate are writ large on Herschel Island. Here, sea levels have risen by 20 centimetres during the last century, and are predicted to rise a further 50 centimetres during this one. Coastal erosion takes back up to 22 metres of land a year, while thawing permafrost leads to catastrophic slumping and moving ground. So far, the whaler settlement buildings have already been moved on two separate occasions to keep them safe, albeit only temporarily. In the burial ground, grave markers are collapsing, and coffins have been ejected from the ground by the moving soil. Further east down the coast from Herschel on the banks of the Mackenzie Delta, whole Inuvialuit villages such as Nuvugaq have slipped into the sea. To the west, on Alaska's arctic coast, three out of the four known archaeological sites in a 100-kilometre stretch facing the Beaufort Sea have disappeared, with the last in the process of being lost.[25] Multiply such an impact across the 180,000 recorded archaeological and historic sites of the arctic region,[26] be they Inuit or whaler camps on the soft arctic coastline of Alaska and Canada, or mammoths thawing from the permafrost in Siberia, and this becomes a story of loss on an epic scale. And it is a real loss. The heritage of the arctic region is extraordinary for the stories it tells of people living at the extremes of the earth, their early witness to a changing climate, adaptation to it, and use of natural resources. And it's extraordinary because of its survival, where the natural processes of decay, particularly of organic matter, are dramatically slowed by freezing temperatures, leaving a unique record. But it is also a difficult place in which heritage professionals can work: remote, only seasonally accessible and expensive. And, for the same reasons, there is so much that we do not know.

The historic settlement at Pauline Cove on Herschel Island and the traditional Inuvialuit villages of Canada's western arctic coast are no longer solid ground in which to found a building or bury the dead. Nor, for the most part, are they places where preservation of cultural remains *in situ* is realistic. As with much of the region, these are parts of the arctic world where we must accept loss, recording instead what has gone before, transferring important cultural traditions, and finding ways in which to celebrate humankind's ingenuity . . . or to remember our folly.

Dunwich, England

Dunwich is England's muddy, shingle-laden Atlantis. Today the village on Suffolk's coast is home to 200 people, whereas at its height 5,000 would have lived, worked and traded in one of the country's busiest seaports. This is a story about the impact of a changing climate, the forces of nature and the gradual disappearance of a town into the sea.

Inevitably, Dunwich's early history is vague. It appears likely that an Anglo-Saxon town was preceded by a Roman settlement, perhaps a shore fort, but little evidence has yet been found to support it.

Fig. 10 Seal of the City of Dunwich in Suffolk, *c.* 1199. A sailing cog with fore and aft fighting stages is shown with four fishes in the water below, inscribed: 'SIGILL : BVRGI : DE : DONEWIZ'.

Chroniclers have identified it as the post-Roman settlement of *Dummoc*. It may have been the first seat of the Anglo-Saxon bishops of East Anglia, but there is a strong rival for this and their original church, which was dedicated to Saint Felix, in the eponymously named Felixstowe further down the coast. The earliest reliable record for Dunwich as we know it today is in England's Domesday Book of 1086 CE; the entry is telling:

> Edric of Laxfield held Dunwich in the time of King Edward as one manor; now Robert Malet holds it. Then 2 carucates of land, now one; the sea carried off the other . . . Then 120 burgesses, now 236; and 180 less two poor men. Then one church, now 3 and they pay £4 and 10 shillings. In total, the value is £50 and 60,000 herrings as a gift. In the time of King Edward it paid £10.[27]

The book was primarily a tax survey, recording the land newly acquired by William the Conqueror twenty years earlier from Harold Godwinson, the last Anglo-Saxon king. It documents the transfer of property from Anglo-Saxon landholders to the Norman French. It lists current uses and values and those at the time of King Edward the Confessor, Harold's predecessor and, in William's eyes, the last legitimate King of England. In 1066 Dunwich was already a prosperous town totalling 120 citizens, their families and their entourages – twenty years later that number had doubled, with new churches being constructed and taxation increasing by a multiple of six. With an estimated population of 3,000 people, Dunwich was in the top 20 per cent of settlements recorded in the Domesday Book, and it was already the largest port on the East Anglian coast. Mention of the role of the Church, including other Dunwich land held by the Abbey of Etheldreda in Ely, emphasizes one of two factors contributing towards Dunwich's early growth, the other being fishing. The 'gift' of 68,000 herrings for the king (a further 8,000 herrings are recorded in another Domesday entry), in reality a tax, points to the scale of the town's most significant industry. But the entry also offers a foresight of the future, listing the loss of half Dunwich's farmland to the sea.

Medieval Dunwich grew to be an affluent place. By the early thirteenth century it had all the accoutrements of an important trading town, and ecclesiastical and administrative centre. The Church was well represented: John Stow writing in 1573 noted that, in the past, the town had '. . . 70 pryshe churches, howses of religion, hospitals, and chapelles . . .'.[28] Seventy religious institutions is fanciful, but the point is made that the Church played an influential role in the life of the town. More accurately, Dunwich had eight churches, each with their own defined parish boundaries, which were complemented by three chapels, a cell of Benedictine monks, a Dominican Priory, a Franciscan Friary, and a house of the Knights Templar which was later handed over to the Knights Hospitaller in 1322. There was a leper hospital dedicated to Saint James and the Maison Dieu, a large almshouse devoted to the Holy Trinity.

Secular life was represented by a guild or town hall, and a mint, while the town's mercantile engine focused on the harbour and central marketplace which, even as Dunwich was in decline, was where forty-seven shops were located. The usual array of medieval urban trades such as bakers, butchers and blacksmiths would have worked alongside more specialist professions, making the most of the town's trading opportunities: pykers who sold the fish from the boats, smokers and salters who preserved the raw product, coopers fashioning the barrels to store them, warehousemen, ropemakers and shipwrights. The original Anglo-Saxon town was protected and

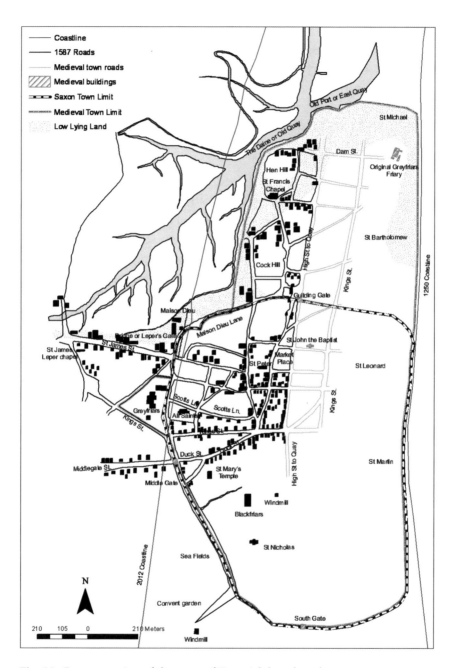

Fig. 11 Reconstruction of the town of Dunwich based on documentary, map and coastal change analysis. The Saxon town limits are speculative but assume a Saxon date for the Pales dyke and its extension to the north and east along the contour line. Lower-lying ground to the north is confirmed by coastal pilot charts, the 1587 map and current topography.

defined by a rampart and a 12-metre wide, 4-metre deep ditch, the *Payles Dyke*, pierced by at least four gates. The later medieval town expanded north beyond the Guilding Gate, continuing a grid of streets that gathered in the two highest parts of the town, Hen Hill and Cock Hill, places where the fishing nets would be laid out to dry or mend after the season. By the beginning of the thirteenth century, Dunwich was over a mile long, north to south, a size similar to that of London at the same time.

The key to Dunwich's success, and failure, was the harbour provided by the estuarine mouth of the River Dunwich where it and the River Blythe fed out to the sea. Here The Haven and The Daine provided sheltered places to draw up ships and land goods, protected by two embracing arms: a gravel spit called Kingsholm to the north, with the town perched on another spit of land to the south. The original attractions were obvious: a safe location close to an abundant supply of fish, with good access by boat up the busy eastern seaboard of the country. The archaeological record, particularly after 950 CE, shows a marked increase in fishbones found in middens all along the East Anglian coast, including Dunwich. This industry boomed due to increased demand from the growing populations in towns across the country, and a strengthening of the Christian tradition of abstaining from meat for as many as 182 days of the year. Dunwich's natural harbour combined with the presence of large shoals of herring, which could be caught from the shore in fish traps and estuarine weirs, or more commonly using smaller boats with weighted seine nets stretched between them, or drift nets.

The prime fishing season was the autumn when the herrings spawn in the warmer southern waters of the North Sea, arriving in great numbers close to the shore. At Dunwich, the shoals would be spotted from wooden towers, or condes, alerting the fishing fleet to their location. Two of these structures survived until at least 1587. A successful herring season was crucial to the town, but it was short, lasting for six intense weeks. During its heyday Dunwich would have been at its busiest from the end of September, with local fishing boats joined by those from all along Britain's east coast. Fresh herring have a short shelf life of just days before they begin to go rancid, so not only was the town busy catching and landing the fish, but also gutting, salting and barrelling them. In this way they could be transported across the country and would stay edible for up to two years. Typically, these 'white' or raw herrings would be packed a thousand at a time in thirty-two-gallon barrels. They were smoked too, resulting in 'red herrings' or kippers, which were hung in reed frames and packed 600-strong in straw. Other fish were caught including sprats and eels, and at times the port also possessed a large offshore fishing fleet, sending twenty barks as part of the Iceland fleet in the late thirteenth century, where they would trade grain and fish for cod, mackerel, sturgeon and whale.[29]

The connection between the fishing industry and Dunwich's ecclesiastical houses was strong. The first recorded church in the town was dedicated to St Michael, a patron saint of mariners, and Michaelmas on 29 September was the official start of the herring season and annual fair. The season concluded at Martinmas on 11 October, and so, unsurprisingly, St Martin's was another of Dunwich's early churches. The first town seal showed a ship and four fishes.[30]

Dunwich was not just a fishing port, but an important place from which to trade with mainland Europe and Iceland. In 1289 '80 great ships' brought wine from Gascony, stone from Caen, steel from Spain, and spices from the Far East by way of the Dutch ports, in exchange for English cloth, grain and salt.[31] Compared with the difficulties of transporting large quantities by road, the sea and rivers of England afforded a relatively easy highway for a range of day-to-day goods required across the country, London in particular. And, because of the burgeoning coastal traffic, piracy was commonplace. In 1282 raiders from Holland '. . . did spoye and robbe whosoever they met, slew many men and carried away not a few shippes with all ye goodes in them'.[32] Not that the people of Dunwich were always the victims; the men of the port were equally well represented in the courts for perpetrating crimes against their neighbours as well as foreign merchants. Conflict with France, Spain or the Dutch also provided a good excuse to get rich. War and piracy ensured that Dunwich played a role, with its vessels either commandeered by the Crown to protect offshore shipping or as a place where ships were built for the royal fleet. The last royal commission was of a pinnace, for Elizabeth I's campaign against the Spanish Armada in 1588. It is a sad reflection of Dunwich's diminished status that this single vessel was the smallest allowed by the Crown for the campaign.

So, what happened? How did a town of 5,000 people become today's village of 200? In macro terms the answer is that the same geomorphological processes that separated the United Kingdom from continental Europe during the last Ice Age remain in play to this day. Shifting tectonic plates and a rising sea level continue to exert a westward pressure on East Anglia's coastline, swapping land for sea. But it is a more localized story of littoral pressure and a shifting sand and gravel shoreline that defined the loss of Dunwich. The same driving combination of tide, wind and current that brought the herrings close to the shore to spawn, began to physically remove the town, and, as importantly, deprive it of its harbour.

The Domesday Book records a process of loss that pre-dated Dunwich's heyday. Clearly the eastern edge of the town was vulnerable both to the slow, inexorable advances of coastal erosion and the dramatic impact of storm surges. Analysis of historic mapping combined with geological and archaeological surveys suggest that Dunwich's pre-Norman shoreline was over 1.2 kilometres further to the east of that today.[33] By the time that Ralph Agas drew his map in 1587, the town had already lost 750 metres to the sea, while by turn, over 75 per cent of the streets and buildings that he depicted are no longer present today. The catastrophically destructive impact of certain storms is well documented. A major gale was recorded in 1287, followed by an even more destructive event in 1328. The latter destroyed churches and either flattened or carried away houses in some of the eastern parishes of the town. In St Nicholas parish, for example, only 30 of its 200 houses survived, while in neighbouring St Martins 75 of its 100 houses were lost. All the seaward parishes suffered in a similar way and the events prompted the Greyfriars to relocate, while St Bartholomew, St Michael and likely several others were lost forever.

Despite these losses of land, property and life, the people of Dunwich adapted to their precarious living at the edge of land and sea. But a more fundamental threat doomed the town. Each passing storm pressed more material between the harbour's protective spit and the sea. This choked the entrance to Dunwich's port, simultaneously pushing the river mouth further north and at the same time causing the river to slow and silt up. The townspeople, realizing the critical importance of the harbour to Dunwich, recut an entrance to the harbour on numerous occasions. Inevitably, nature finally won out. Trapped by the Kingsholm spit, the Dunwich River was forced to join the dominant River Blythe 5 kilometres further to the north between Walberswick and Southwold, and with it went a safe haven and trade. Boats could still draw up on the shingle beach, but such a task was reserved for smaller vessels and made more dangerous by the treacherous stumps of ruined buildings on the seashore.

Since its decline, Dunwich has fascinated many, including Daniel Defoe, the English writer and journalist, who toured Suffolk in 1722:

> The Ruins of Carthage, of the great City of Jerusalem, or of ancient Rome, are not at all wonderful to me; the Ruins of Nineveh, which are so entirely sunk as that it is doubtful where the City stood; The Ruins of Babylon, or the Great Persepolis, and many Capital Cities, which Time and the Change of Monarchies have Overthrown, these, I say, are not at all Wonderful, because being the Capitals of great and flourishing Kingdoms, where those kingdoms were overthrown, the Capital Cities necessarily fell with them; But for a Private Town, a Seaport, and a Town of Commerce, to Decay, as it were, of itself . . . this, I must confess, seems owing to nothing but to the Fate of Things . . . It is true, this Town is manifestly decayed by the invasion of the Waters . . . eaten up by the Sea . . . and the still encroaching Ocean seems to threaten it with a fatal Immersion in a few Years more.[34]

Such fascination has continued into the modern era, where archaeological research has sought to track Dunwich's submerged past. Using a range of remote sensing technologies, alongside traditional fieldwork, the Dunwich Project team explored the seabed, intertidal and marshland areas in and around the current village in a comprehensive attempt to map change.[35] Geophysical survey using magnetometers and sonars has revealed a murky, piecemeal underwater world of scattered churches and scoured-out foundations. The silted harbour may contain the preserved remains of timber wharfage, while new sandbanks almost certainly hide more evidence of this once busy town.

Fig. 12 Ruins of Greyfriars' late fourteenth-/early fifteenth-century refectory, Dunwich. The site, now on the eastern, cliff side of the current village, was originally outside the medieval town walls to the west. It had probably already moved from its original thirteenth-century location, still further to the east, when the latter was damaged by storms.

And, as for the future? Dunwich will continue to change. The dynamic nature of the coast, a strong littoral current combined with ongoing pressure from the east and the rise in storm surges, means that stasis will never be an option. Ultimately nature will win out, it is merely a question of the timeframe. Managing active shorelines is a complex, contentious and emotional business, made more difficult by an acceleration in the rate of change caused by climate change. In the UK, management options range from doing nothing through to the construction of new, hard sea defences. The former acknowledges the primacy of natural processes and the inevitability of loss, the latter prioritizes people's homes and businesses. At Dunwich, the solution is one of managed loss, recognizing that more land will be flooded and buildings destroyed, but allowing it to happen in such a way that gives people time to move on.[36] The likely diagnosis for the remaining historic buildings of Dunwich will be to preserve them by recording them – effectively capturing a facsimile of the real thing before it is lost. Such an approach is not unusual, nor is it restricted to Dunwich; indeed, it is likely to be the second most common form of mitigation of the impacts of climate change for vast swathes of doomed heritage across the world. And the most common? Gradual disappearance without either mention or record. Perhaps, as we begin to understand our own contribution to a changing climate, there is an increasing appreciation of the need to record cultural loss, facilitated by new technologies.

The last word is left to Daniel Defoe, who saw Dunwich as a memento mori – a reminder not only of the temporal existence of humanity, but also of our cultural legacy:

> By Numerous Examples we may see,
> That Towns and Cities Die, as well as we.[37]

The Garamantes, Libya

From too much water to too little, this story, set in the hyper-arid landscape of the Central Sahara, describes the destructive impact of a warming, drier environment on heritage, and the overwhelming importance of water to humankind.

Fig. 13 Garamantian rock painting showing chariot, charioteer and two horses, 500 BCE–500 CE.

Today the region of Fazzān (southwest Libya) is harsh and sparsely populated, with what little settlement there is concentrated in a series of linear depressions sandwiched between arid mountains and desert seas of sand. Rainfall is minuscule, a maximum of 15 millimetres annually in the highest, 'wettest' places, and temperatures regularly reach 50 degrees Celsius. But it was not always like this. Taking a long view over millennia, the region has fluctuated between dry, arid periods and more temperate humid conditions, with the dry phases somewhat counterintuitively corresponding with the global Ice Ages. From around 8000 BCE, Fazzān entered a wet phase, so wet that parts of the area were covered in lakes.[38] Humans exploited the natural resources of fish and game, hunting aurochs, rhinoceros, giraffe, donkey and ostrich, some of which are evocatively illustrated in the rock art of the period. Gradually, following at least two more centuries-long dry phases, a more settled pastoralism emerged, based on summer monsoons and domesticated cattle, sheep and goat herding on the grasses of the plains. Interestingly, the transition from hunter-gatherers to farmers in Libya was not a response to improving climatic conditions, but worsening ones. Diminishing supplies of water made the former more difficult across the increasingly arid uplands, while concentrating people in the depressions where groundwater was more easily accessed, which later developed into oases.[39]

The most recent climatic switch to warmer, drier conditions began around 3000 BCE, a significant trend that continues today. The timescale is important because this is a story of processes played out in slow motion over centuries, rather than those that lead to a quick rise to power and tumultuous collapse. From this long and complex interplay of climate, resources and migration a new power emerged – the Garamantes, who came to dominate this corner of the world from 900 BCE to around 500 CE.

The Garamantian Empire once stretched for 250,000 square kilometres across southwest Libya. They were a powerful and sophisticated autochthonous African kingdom, with a written script, stratified society, kings and luxury goods. Recent archaeological evidence has revealed forts, temples, pyramidal tombs, stone-built palaces and sophisticated towns. At its height, the capital, Garama, was home to 10,000 people. They introduced the camel to the Saharan desert, rode horses and drove chariots. They were engineers, traders and raiders. And yet until recently few have heard of them, or they have been dismissed as barbaric nomads. There are two reasons for this – firstly, their want of recognition is rooted in the propaganda and misunderstanding of their Greek and Roman rivals. Herodotus was the first to chronicle their existence, writing in the fifth century BCE, when he describes the Garamantes as 'an exceedingly great nation' who, memorably, have 'cattle that go backward as they graze, the reason being that their horns curve forward'.[40] He is followed by the great and good of classical authors: Strabo, Virgil, Pliny, Seneca, Ptolemy and Tacitus all comment, some effectively reposting earlier descriptions of the Garamantes that invariably characterize them as nomadic barbarians, war-hungry raiders who live a miserable existence on the fringe of empire. In essence they become the exotic equivalent of anti-civilization, particularly compared to the might and sophistication of Rome. There is a distinct aroma of rivalry here – Rome fought at least three campaigns with the Garamantes, who also had the habit of allying themselves with their enemies. While the Romans might claim the Garamantian territories as their own, the reality is that it was never a permanent part of their empire, nor was such an ambition realistic when set alongside other imperial priorities. Why dedicate resources to holding difficult, inhospitable lands, when it was easier to claim it via treaties and words? Besides, the Garamantes played a pivotal role in the trans-Saharan trade routes that was mutually beneficial, bringing slaves, Garamantian carbuncles (red carnelians), wild animals for the amphitheatres of the empire and sub-Saharan gold to the Mediterranean ports, and receiving oil, wine and other luxury goods in return.

Unfortunately, the tone set by the classical authors persisted into the twentieth century. For example, Sir Mortimer Wheeler, the great archaeologist, in the 1950s dismissed the Garamantes as 'predatory nomads'. More recently, David Mattingly observed that there was no mention of the Garamantes in either the third edition of the *Oxford Classical Dictionary* (2003) or in the *Cultural Atlas of Africa*.[41] These omissions remain today, even in updated versions.

A second reason for the dearth of attention paid to the Garamantes is more pragmatic and is founded on a relative lack of research in

difficult and inaccessible terrain; southwest Libya remains a challenging region to access and the archaeology of Fazzān has historically
attracted less interest than the empires of Egypt, Mesopotamia, Greece
or Rome, nor has it been well travelled by antiquarians.

Fortunately, the reputation of the Garamantes is undergoing
a revival and the academic lacuna is being addressed, particularly through Italian and French scientific missions of the 1930s
and 1940s, and the work of Charles Daniels, the Fazzān Project
(1997–2001)[42] and others, where the multidisciplinary appliance
of science has begun to reveal a fascinating story that was simply
not visible before.

Nowhere is that sophistication more evident than in the now
ruined capital of Garama (modern-day Jerma). Excavations in this
town, which lies buried under its medieval and modern successor,
show that it extended over approximately 9 hectares and contained
a fortified *qasr* at its centre, monumental buildings with colonnaded
courtyards and porches, and a Roman-style bathhouse. Beyond
Garama and other Garamantian towns such as Qasr ash-Sharaba,
recent study of high-resolution satellite imagery has revealed several
fortified villages, each with an associated area of oasis garden.[43]

Fig. 14 Satellite picture showing a fortified village and fort of the late Garamantian
period. Made of mud brick, the inner fortified *qasr* compound is enclosed by a wider
rectangular walled circuit, both reinforced by externally projecting towers. Beyond
is the village and associated oasis garden plot.

The Garamantes' rise to power is inextricably linked to water. Their empire, which reached its peak between 1 and 400 CE, emerged out of the reducing resources of the late Neolithic. Here migrants from oases further to the east arrived, mixing with local groups to form a tribal confederation. The evidence does not tell us if there was conflict, but the appearance of hillforts on Fazzān escarpments and warlike rock-art showing imagery of chariots all suggests that the transition was unlikely to have been peaceful. The result was a blend of influences as befitting Fazzān's geography at a crossroads between the Mediterranean and the sub-Saharan interior, and between the eastern and western kingdoms of northern Africa. The most important influence – indeed the empire-defining one – was the foggara irrigation system. Probably introduced via that east–west corridor from Egypt, a foggara is an underground tunnel, excavated into an escarpment from the valley floor, that links a subterranean water table or aquifer to a lower-lying agricultural area. The tunnel slopes down slightly, allowing a gravity-fed system to tap water off the aquifer before the water table follows the contour. The angle of the tunnel is important – too steep and the flowing water erodes the sides, causing collapse – too shallow and it quickly fills with sediment. Foggaras were constructed using a series of shafts, beginning at the source of the aquifer where a 'mother well' was sunk. Once water was located, tunnelling between the base of adjacent shafts would begin, with the spoil upcast around the shafts marking the way from the mother well to the outlet point. Depending on the terrain, the vertical shafts would be spaced between 5 to 10 metres apart, much closer than those of their Persian counterparts, suggesting use of unskilled, slave labour as opposed to expert classes of builders (*muqanni* in Iran). Using a windlass, a leather bucket for spoil and simple hand tools, the excavated material would be brought to the surface of each shaft and spread out around the perimeter in a characteristic ring. After the foggara was complete the shafts provided access for maintenance, while the spoil ring stopped unwanted material washing into the system. From the air, a single foggara appears like the determined campaign of a giant and unusually direct mole.

Historically, the irrigation system evolved in Iran during the Achaemenid period (*c.* 550–330 BCE), where they are known as

Fig. 15 Foggara with closely spaced access shafts. The circular mounds of spoil around the top of each shaft track the course of the foggara across the countryside.

qanats, and spread from there east to India (as *karez*) and China, and west to Mesopotamia, Egypt and, eventually, the Central Sahara. The advantage of fogaras was that, once constructed, they had the capacity to irrigate a much larger area than water drawn from wells. The disadvantage was that construction and upkeep required huge numbers of people. The oases geography of Fazzān was particularly suited to foggara-fed farming, and the Garamantes made good use of slaves to create and maintain them. Consequently, there are over 600 foggaras in the area, each varying between 500 and 4,500 metres in length, with the tunnel normally limited to 500 millimetres wide and under 2 metres tall: effectively the size of the human required to dig it out.[44] A conservative estimate suggests that there are over 1,200 kilometres of foggaras in Fazzān, and while these would not have been all working at the same time, they gave life to the Garamantian population and underpinned their rise as the dominant Central Saharan civilization.

How did the foggara system work? Water flowed underground from the tapped aquifer along the tunnel into a terminal basin or pond. From there the water could be controlled by way of simple sluice gates to irrigation channels that fed gardens and fields. It is

AMONGST THE RUINS

thought that watering was done at night, both to minimize evaporation and to ensure plants were not dowsed in full sun. Those plants were dominated by the date palm, which offered shade to plants below, but the Garamantes also cultivated figs, grapevines, wheat and barley too, with millet and sorghum appearing in the later stages of their empire.

The social implications of an economy largely supported by foggaras is important. Their construction and maintenance required communal effort – this is not a story of one farmer excavating and using a single well, but of centralized authority and the heavy use of slave labour. The fields watered by the foggaras would also need coordination, with the surplus crops helping to sustain a ruling elite.

Maintaining the foggaras was critical. Sand and gravel brought down by the running water or erosion into the tunnels and access shafts would have to be cleared out regularly. Collapses, particularly through the softer material, would need to be removed for the system to operate effectively. But it's possible to see a greater stress in the system. Fazzān's aquifers are a non-renewable resource effectively created by prehistoric rainfall, so the impact of each foggara tapping into them was to lower the water table. As the aquifers diminished over time, so old foggaras were extended and new ones tunnelled, reaching further and deeper underground. This endless search for precious water is a continuation of the story of a drying climate which began over 5,000 years ago, and is as much at the root of the Garamantes, decline as it is part of their rise to power. 'The Garamantian success in oasis farming is also the root of its own failure.'[45]

The waning of the Garamantian empire was drawn out over centuries and likely rooted in three related pressures – a reducing water supply, disruption to trade and the diminishing authority of the ruling elite. This was a gradual weakening of the social, economic and political fabric, rather than a sudden collapse.

While the decline was slow, at times probably unnoticeable to those living through it, it was accelerated by certain events. During the third century CE the Roman Empire to the north was in crisis. Following the assassination of the emperor, Severus Alexander, in 235 CE, the Roman state fragmented into separate territories each led by competing claimants. Hyperinflation, barbarian attacks on the borders, civil war, plague and the breakdown of trade almost led to the end of empire before the steadying reforms of Emperor Diocletian (r. 284–305 CE). One consequence of this chaotic period was the breakdown of trade resulting in the contraction of Rome's African sea ports, including the three cities of *Oea* (now Tripoli), *Sabratha* and *Leptis Magna*. For the Garamantes the loss of markets, ports and trade must have been sorely felt, in particular the dominant slave trade and the subsequent economic depression had a knock-on impact in Fazzān and on neighbouring kingdoms further to the south. A lack of resources, including the all-important slaves to maintain the foggaras, was a major contributor to the atrophy of the system. All at a time when the prospection for water was increasingly necessary, but more and more difficult because of falling water tables. The tension created by diminishing resources and conflict can also be seen in an increase in defended settlements across Fazzān, reflecting the threats from outside the region and possibly the fragmentation of Garamantian society back into tribal groups and away from an overarching ruling authority.

Another accelerator, or perhaps the final nail in the coffin, was prompted by the Arab conquest of North Africa in the seventh century CE. After the first official invasion in 647 CE of Byzantine territories, inheritors of the former Roman province, Arabic forces conducted raids into Garamantian territory to the south. The campaign of the Arab general Uqba bin Nāfi in 666/7 CE reached Garama, attacking the city and its fortress. By this time the prominence of the foggara system of irrigation was over. Where once the whole of the wadi floor had been cultivated land, a strip 2 kilometres wide and many kilometres long fed by the foggaras, now fields were abandoned, alongside the formerly water-filled ditches and channels. Instead, in the search for deeper water and systems that required less maintenance and reliance on slaves, the foggaras were gradually replaced by individual wells which sought deeper aquifers beneath Fazzān's central depression. Each of these hand- or animal-drawn *khattāra* (a bucket on the end of a counterweighted arm) and *dalw* (a skin bag suspended from a frame on a pulley) wells served a far smaller farmed area. Research suggests that one *dalw* well in the 1930s might water a single garden, compared to twelve irrigated by an average foggara.[46]

The shape of farming shifted too. Instead of extensive foggara-irrigated fields, farming was contained within much smaller oasis areas, with knock-on implications for the number of people that the area was able to sustain. This transition in the search for water from foggara to well, and from an economy that relied on slave labour to one without, marked the disappearance of the Garamantes, and their replacement by other ruling elites from beyond the area.

The best way to see the palimpsest of Fazzān history is from the air. The story of a once fertile region, sandwiched between rock and sand, is clear in the geology: the sand and its saltpans are all that remains of the inland sea that brought life to the region in the palaeolithic and has been disappearing ever since. The later dotted lines of the foggaras and field-systems show something of the extent of the Garamantes' heartland, which by turn is overlain by a contracted landscape of well-irrigated oases. And now there is a new pattern in the arid countryside: serried collections of perfectly circular fields, the largest almost one kilometre in diameter. These gigantic crop circles are the next iteration of the search for water. Motorized pumps, sophisticated deep-drilling equipment and booms which drip water from centrally pivoted pipes, have largely replaced the hand- or animal-drawn wells and now reach over 100 metres deep into the aquifers. The impact is twofold: firstly, the modern artesian wells render older *khattāra, dalw* systems and any surviving foggaras redundant, effectively sucking the water out of their range; and secondly, for the same reason, the traditional pattern of irregular rectangular fields has been either abandoned or overwritten by the large, more efficient circular fields. But aquifers need replenishing, and the combination of deep pumps drawing more water, together with the same trend towards drier, arid conditions that created and ended the foggara landscape, is repeated in the twenty-first century. The desert has repossessed land where centre-pivot agriculture was practised, leaving circular ghost fields of sand where once there had been green crops.

And the future? In truth, it's not bright for the substantive human occupation of this part of the Sahara. The cost of searching for

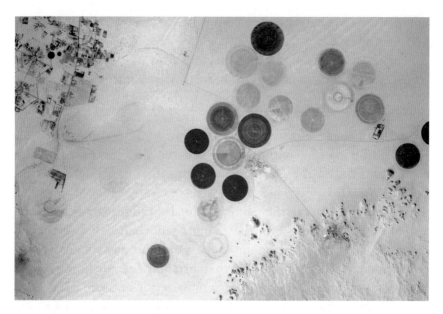

Fig. 16 Modern circular irrigation fields using centre-pivot systems, and the ghosts of former examples disappearing into the sand, Libya.

water is not infinite, no matter the advances in technology. At some stage the expense of extraction will reach the point of diminishing returns and will not be viable. This is not a case of history repeating itself, but of living in the middle of one of history's large turns made worse by our own actions. We are reacting to the repercussions of the same long, drying arc that saw the rise of the Garamantes to regional dominance, and eventually saw them disappear into obscurity.

At its height the Garamantian kingdom had a population of up to 100,000 people.[47] The Italian census of 1936 recorded 33,500, a likely increase on even lower numbers of the post-Garamantian medieval period.[48] Since then the population has increased, but so too has the pressure on water. The forewarning of the inevitable should allow us to plan, but this is difficult if you are a contemporary Fazzān farmer struggling with the daily challenges of making a living and feeding the family. Help – to move away or transition to a different way of life – is most likely to come from outside, but the Libyan state is itself barely functioning in the aftermath of war, and so the future of the inheritors of the Garamantes is uncertain.

History, as told through the archaeological remains of Fazzān, is clear: humans are infinitely inventive, thriving in some of the most difficult landscapes on earth, but in a battle with the forces of nature it is us who must adapt to survive. And sometimes that creativity is simply not enough. The desert, or a version of it, will reclaim most of Fazzān. Until the next cycle.

CHAPTER 2

NATURAL HAZARDS

Earthquake, volcanoes, tsunami, mud and landslip may bring an instant and catastrophic end to communities. Three case studies under the banner of 'Natural Hazards' explore the impact of natural events on heritage, most brought about by the dynamic but devastating nature of the earth's crust.

We begin with the first of two stories from the Caribbean. 'I saw the earth open and swallow a multitude of people; and the sea mounting in upon us over the fortification,' wrote Reverend Emmanuel Heath, a survivor of an earthquake in June 1692 which destroyed Port Royal, Jamaica. Established as a Spanish settlement in 1509, Port Royal went on to become the largest city of the Caribbean by the end of the seventeenth century, and one of the richest in the world. Captured by the English in 1655, it grew as the unofficial capital of Jamaica, defended by five forts and containing over 200 residencies, warehouses and shops. By the latter half of the seventeenth century Port Royal was the principal Caribbean base from which privateers operated. For the same reason, it earned a reputation for high spending, entertainment, drinking and debauchery – the 'richest and wickedest city in the New World'. Immediately before the earthquake the town was home to around 6,500 people, of whom 2,500 were slaves. It had four churches and a cathedral, Governor's House and Court, as well as a predictably large number of taverns, theatres and brothels. When the earthquake struck, two-thirds of the town sank immediately into the sea. It's estimated that between 1,500 and 3,000 people died during the event, while an eyewitness wrote that after 'the Earthquake was a general Sickness, from the noisome Vapours belched forth, which swept away above 3000 Persons'. Today Port Royal is a small fishing village and tourist destination, but the ruined remains of its heyday survive under the sea.

Next, we travel to Ani, in eastern Turkey, which was once the ninth-century CE capital of Armenia, with an estimated population of 100,000 people. Known as 'the City of 1,001 Churches', its prosperity was rooted in its role as an administrative capital and a trading hub with access to the Byzantine and Persian empires. It was sacked by the Mongols in 1236 and decimated by an earthquake in 1319, albeit not completely abandoned until 1735. Rediscovered and romanticized in the nineteenth century, it was then caught up in the First World War and the Armenian genocide. Ani's story of decline begins with the 1319 earthquake, but is brought up to date with a succession of events that make it a surprise that anything remains standing. These include neglect, political wrangling, theft, target practice, poor restoration and further earthquakes in 1832 and 1988. It became a World Heritage Site in 2016.

Pompeii or Herculaneum are well-known motifs for the impact of volcanic activity on historic places, both as examples of the destructive power of volcanoes and, ironically, as an extraordinary means of preservation. For our final story we return to the Caribbean and to Montserrat. Plymouth, the capital city of Montserrat, was subsumed when the Soufrière Hills volcano erupted in 1995 and 1997. Renamed by Christopher Columbus in 1493, Montserrat has a native prehistory that stretches back to 4000 BCE. The first European settlers were Irish Catholics, relocated by the English from neighbouring islands in 1632, and then from colonial Virginia in 1634. Greater numbers arrived after the Battle of the Boyne (1690) as Cromwell expelled Irish Catholics and sent them into indentured service across the Caribbean. The majority of the population thereafter were of African origin and Montserrat, as with nearly all the Caribbean islands, was reliant on a slave economy to produce sugar, the country's dominant export. The heritage of Plymouth and its surrounding area comprised a mix of pre-European archaeological sites with colonial-era buildings, remnants of the sugar industry as well as churches and the institutions of governance. In the 1990s the two catastrophic eruptions of the previously dormant Soufrière Hills volcano devastated parts of the island as pyroclastic flows and volcanic ash killed nineteen people, destroying Plymouth and many other settlements. After the eruptions 8,000 people left the area, and the southern half of the island was declared an exclusion area, as it remains today.

Will Durant, the American author and philosopher, remarked that 'Civilization exists by geological consent, subject to change without notice.' This collection of stories explores the moments when geology issued notice, and civilization had to respond.

Port Royal, Jamaica

> *I saw the earth open and swallow a multitude of people; and the sea mounting in upon us over the fortification . . .*[1]

Archaeologists rely on a range of evidence to date the sites they are working on: scientific techniques such as dendrochronology or Carbon[14] analysis; coins stamped with a known king, queen or

Fig. 17 The earthquake at Port Royal in Jamaica which destroyed the city, by Jan Luyken and Pieter van der Aa I, 1698.

emperor; historic documents or, more commonly, the time-period inferred through different pottery styles and fabric. These offer dating solutions tied to years at best, more likely to the vagueness of decades, centuries or millennia. A brass pocket watch found during an underwater excavation in 1959 in the harbour of Port Royal, Jamaica, stopped at 11.40 a.m. on 7 June 1692.[2] Maybe its owner had forgotten to rewind it or perhaps it had accidentally fallen into the sea – most likely both, as it records a moment when the thriving commercial capital of a Caribbean colony was overwhelmed by a devastating earthquake and subsequent tsunami.

Earlier, on that Saturday morning, the Reverend Emmanuel Heath, Rector of Port Royal, had been persuaded to a glass of wormwood wine after prayers in St Paul's church by John White, acting Governor of Jamaica. New to the island, Heath was naturally alarmed when the ground began 'rowling and moving under my feet, upon which I said, *Lord, Sir, what's this?* He [White] replied very composedly, being a very grave Man, *It's an Earth quake; be not afraid, it will soon be over,* But it increased, and we heard the Church and Tower fall, upon which we ran to save our selves.'[3] Heath went on to describe in graphic detail how Port Royal was reduced to a place of mayhem, destruction and death:

> . . . I found the Sea had entirely swallow'd up the Wharf, with all the goodly Brick houses upon it, most of them as fine as those in Chepside, and two entire streets beyond that.
>
> . . . It is a sad sight to see all this Harbour, one of the fairest and goodliest I ever saw, covered with the dead bodies of people of all conditions, floating up and down without burial; for our great and famous burial place, called the Palisadoes was destroyed by the earthquake; which dashing to pieces the tombs, whereof there were hundreds in that place, sea washed the carcasses of those that were buried out of their graves . . .
>
> . . . But no place suffered like Port Royal; where the streets (with Inhabitants) were swallowed up by the opening of the Earth, which then shutting upon them, squeezed the People to Death. And in that manner several were buried with their heads above Ground; only some Heads the Dogs have eaten; others are covered with Dust and Earth, by the people who yet remained in the Place, to avoid the Stench.[4]

AMONGST THE RUINS

Other eyewitness accounts gathered by Hans Sloane for the Royal Society, who had earlier lived in Jamaica and witnessed the regularity of earthquakes there, echo the tragic detail of lives lost and property ruined.[5] Water flew upwards from the wells, houses were swallowed or thrown down in heaps, sand rose 'like waves in the Sea'. When the earthquake struck, two-thirds of the town sank immediately into the ocean, sand liquefied taking buildings with it, and twenty ships capsized with one, the frigate *Swann*, lifted over rooftops by the subsequent tsunami. In a period of over three minutes, Port Royal went from being the busiest port on the English-held islands of the Caribbean to a disaster zone.[6] The defended settlement of just over 50 acres, comprising more than 2,000 tightly packed structures at the end of a 10-mile spit of land called the Palisadoes, was immediately reduced to half its size, with whole streets sinking under the sea to a depth of up to 10 metres of water. Major landmarks disappeared in an instant, including five of the port's defensive forts, the Reverend

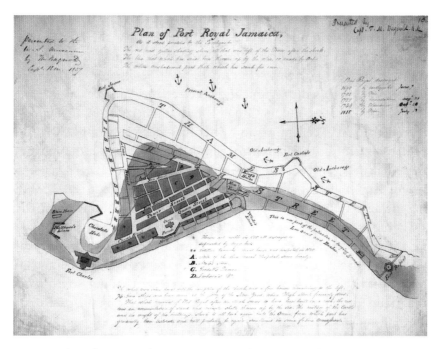

Fig. 18 'Plan of Port Royal Jamaica as it stood previous to the Earthquake', made in 1815. Areas of red and yellow shading show what was left of the town after the 1692 earthquake, the blue depicts land reclaimed from the sea and white is used to show areas that were completely destroyed.

Heath's St Peter's church, as well as numerous merchant houses, taverns and warehouses. Of those buildings left standing, many were reduced to piles of rubble, or would later have to be demolished. Even the graveyard gave up its dead. It is estimated that between 1,500 and 2,300 people died during the event, out of a population of around 6,500.[7] Some 2,000 more died in the aftermath, from disease and injury.

The disaster was, in many ways, inevitable. The English had first arrived on Jamaica in May 1655, led by Admiral William Penn (whose father was the founder of Pennsylvania) and General Robert Venables. The invading fleet was part of Oliver Cromwell's 'Western Design' to oust the Catholic Spanish from the Caribbean, a plan that had gone embarrassingly awry when Penn and Venables were rebuffed during an assault on nearby Hispaniola in April, despite vastly superior numbers. Arriving at Caguaya Bay on the south coast of Jamaica, this time the English forces quickly overran those of the Spanish, taking their capital, Villa de la Vega (later Spanish Town), and establishing themselves as colonists for the next 300 years. While Jamaica did not have the gold reserves that the English had hoped for – or the Spanish before them, hence their concentration on other islands – it was strategically well positioned to overlook trade routes across the region, and between the Americas (north and south) and Europe. And, in Caguaya Bay, anglicized to Cagway Bay, it possessed an excellent seaport offering a deep harbour behind the protective arm of the Palisadoes spit of land. To make the most of these features, Port Royal was built on the end of the Palisadoes, where deep-hulled boats could moor close to the harbourside, negating the need to transfer goods to smaller ships of shallower draught, sheltered from the wind and under the watchful eye of the forts.

The geology of Cagway Bay is important: the long spit was made up of a series of coral islands (cays) linked and supplemented by gravel and sand brought to the sea by rivers running south from the island's mountainous interior, and pushed west by the prevailing current and wind. So, while the town was founded to benefit from the natural topography, it was also limited by it. The precious area of relatively solid land afforded by the terminal cay of the Palisadoes was small, and so, as Port Royal thrived, it could only grow upwards or out into the sea. It did both. Such was the success of the town that structures of two or more storeys were commonplace. By the 1680s John Taylor wrote of many houses over four storeys high, 600 of them brick-built, and while the number was probably exaggerated, the presence of tall, heavy European-style buildings attests to the port's burgeoning wealth. Growing upwards, the late eighteenth-century port had an estimated density similar to that of central London during the 1930s.[8] The other option, growing outwards, involved reclaiming land from the sea by driving lines of timber piles into the sand, and filling behind to extend the shorefront wharfage, creating more room for warehouses on top.[9] Add Jamaica's location on the messy fringe of two tectonic plates to Port Royal's densely packed settlement, precariously perched on land half in and half out of the sea, and all the ingredients were in place for the 1692 disaster.

Jamaica sits on the tectonic boundary of the small Gonâve microplate and its Caribbean neighbour to the south, and on 7 June a slip-strike earthquake of around 7.5 magnitude hit the island. The impact was multifold. In the heart of the town, the land 'trembled', 'rowled', and buildings were shaken and shattered to pieces, but the impact was even more devastating in the sea. Here the earthquake had a transformative impact on the sandy fringes of the settlement; sustained vibration and increased water pressure loosened the structure of the water-saturated ground, causing the sand grains to separate, effectively creating quicksand. This liquefaction process was instant. Where once buildings and wharfs had been founded on (relatively) solid ground, now they were not, dropping metres into a catastrophic slurry. And once the earthquake was over, the land froze solid again, holding people and structures in a buried state. And then there was the tsunami. It is estimated by the Earthquake Unit of the University of the West Indies that during the quake the sea in the bay withdrew by almost 300 metres, creating a 1.8-metre-high wave when it returned.[10] Both phenomena explain the graphic accounts of the ground opening to bury people alive, and ships being thrown above the streets of the town.

The disaster didn't end there, but continued via a series of aftershocks for days. After the immediate impact of the earthquake, the death toll continued to rise, including John White, the acting governor and Reverend Heath's overly relaxed drinking companion, amongst its many victims:

We have had a very great Mortality since the great Earthquake (for we have little ones daily!) almost half the People that escap'd upon *Port-Royal* are since dead of a Malignant Fever, from Change of Air, want of dry Houses, warm Lodging, proper Medicines, and other Conveniencies.[11]

The richness of the documentation from those who witnessed the event, and the continuing preservation today of large parts of Port Royal on the seabed, are just some of the reasons that the earthquake is so memorable. But what continues to fascinate historians and general interest alike is that the earthquake freezes Port Royal's early history in a moment in time – a unique place, less than forty years old, that was already forty years ahead of its time. On the one hand Port Royal was 'the fairest Town of all the English Plantations, the best Emporium and Mart of this part of the World, exceeding in its Riches, plentiful of all good Things',[12] while on the other Jamaica and all within it was the 'Dunghill of the Universe, the Refuse of the whole Creation . . . The Receptacle of Vagabonds, the Sanctuary of Bankrupts, and a Close-stool for the Purges of our Prisons. As Sickly as an Hospital, as Dangerous as the Plague, as Hot as Hell, and as Wicked as the Devil.'[13]

The years after Jamaica's conquest by the English in 1655 never ran as smoothly as the initial, official surrender of the Spanish. Escaped slaves, or Maroons,[14] combined with the defeated Spanish to wage a guerrilla war on the new invaders from the mountainous interior. By 1657 most of the resistance had been arrested, but the former colonial power still threatened, unsuccessfully seeking to regain their territories at the Battle of Ocho Rios in 1657 and again during the Battle of Rio Nuevo in 1658. It soon became clear that England's new possession would require more troops to defend it than the powers back home were willing to send. Instead, in 1657, Governor Edward D'Oyley invited the Confederacy of the Brethren of the Coast to make Port Royal their base. The Brethren were a loose grouping of buccaneers mainly based on Tortuga off Hispaniola. Issued with Letters of Marque, they were given free licence to attack Spanish and other shipping that plied the fertile sea channels that criss-crossed the Caribbean around Jamaica. In return, they would be allowed to keep the booty, save for a substantial tax due to the governing powers, typically 25 per cent for the Crown, 10 per cent for the

Admiralty and 8 per cent for the governor. This strategy proved extremely successful, and was paralleled by a significant rise in contraband trade with nations and individuals using Port Royal as a base from which to avoid paying duties elsewhere. This was a consequence of Spain's consistent refusal to allow foreign merchants to trade directly with its vast American or Caribbean colonies, fiercely protecting its monopoly. By operating out of Jamaica, English merchants could ship European goods such as arms and ammunition, linen and silk, ale, wine and other luxury items quietly to the heart of the Caribbean and on to the Spanish Main, persistently undercutting the slower, official Spanish fleets. It is estimated that over half the goods arriving into Port Royal in 1687 were destined for Spanish colonial markets.[15] The ships would return either directly to Europe and the English North American colonies or via Jamaica, with gold bullion and other desirable goods, such

Fig. 19 A pewter trifid spoon depicting the two co-reigning monarchs at the time of the 1692 earthquake, King William and Queen Mary, on the handle.

as dyewood from the Yucatan peninsula, mahogany, sugar, cocoa, tobacco, cotton, indigo, spices and precious stones. Another highly profitable trade was in people, where again Port Royal was well placed to exploit Spain's disconnect from West Africa by operating as the sub-contractor to Genoese slavers who had been awarded the official *asiento* to supply labour to the Spanish colonies.[16]

The importance of both the buccaneer and tax evasion trade cannot be underestimated. In the eighteenth-century Jamaica was to become renowned for growing and processing sugar cane, all based on a slave economy. But during the second half of the seventeenth century that trade was in its infancy, with the island exporting only half the sugar of the leading English colony, Barbados, during the 1680s.[17] Nearly all the new colonies kept their accounts in sugar or other goods sold, but unusually in Port Royal there was '. . . more plenty of running Cash than is in London'.[18] Research by Nuala

Zahedieh notes that four years prior to the earthquake Port Royal was the destination for 213 ships, only slightly fewer than the 226 vessels arriving into all the other New England ports, including Boston and Plymouth. And after the earthquake, 50 per cent of the probate inventories of those who perished at Port Royal name the deceased as a 'merchant', compared to just 10 per cent recorded in Boston's shipping registers of the same period.[19] Port Royal was a trading centre like no other. The sheer scale of commerce brought significant wealth to the port's inhabitants, as evidenced by a visitor's description in 1683:

> The town of Port Royal, being as it were the Store House or Treasury of the West Indies, is always like a continual Mart or Fair, where all sorts of choice merchandises are daily imported, not only to furnish the island, but vast quantities are tense again transported to supply the Spaniards, Indians and other Nations, who in exchange return us bars and Cakes of Gold, wedges and pigs of silver, Pistoles, Pieces of Eight . . . Plate, Jewels, rich pearl necklaces . . .[20]

The operation of the port also brought with it an astonishing diversity of roles and characters. From the invitation to the Brethren to come to Port Royal in 1657 until the Treaty of Madrid in 1670, the town became home to an extraordinary who's who of the great and the grim of the Caribbean. Christopher Myngs is a good example: an English naval officer who arrived in 1656 shortly after the conquest of the island, he soon became commander of the naval station at Port Royal. From 1662 he was leading lucrative expeditions of privateers against Spanish interests in Cuba and Mexico. The fleet he gathered to attack San Francisco de Campeche in Mexico numbered fourteen ships and over 1,400 privateers and buccaneers, amongst them two Dutchmen, Edward Mansvelt and Abraham Blauvelt, and Welshman Henry Morgan. Wounded in 1663, Myngs returned to England and was made Vice-Admiral two years later.

Captain Henry Morgan's career had similar touch points. He probably arrived with Venables' invasion force but soon turned to a successful career as a privateer, launching an infamous attack in 1668 from Port Royal on Spanish Porto Bello, now in Panama. After more successful raids which, unfortunately for Morgan, coincided with the brokering of the English-Spanish truce, he was arrested and sent back to England. Here, rather than being tried, he was lionized, knighted by James II, and returned to Jamaica as Lieutenant Governor, where he was given the task of eradicating privateering. The latter task was rather half-heartedly executed, with Morgan receiving his share of illegal activity. He died in Port Royal in 1688 aged fifty-three, probably of disease related to alcoholism, and was buried in the cemetery destroyed four years later by the earthquake.

Decades after the catastrophe, when state sponsorship of privateers had come to an end, Port Royal still retained its strong connections with piracy. Edward 'Blackbeard' Teach and Henry Jennings used it as an occasional base. John 'Calico Jack' Rackham was executed on Gallows Point in 1718, while two of his crew – Anne Bonny and Mary Read – were spared because they were pregnant. Two years later Charles Vane, another infamous pirate of the Golden Age, suffered Rackham's fate. And for each of the captains in charge of a ship would be a crew ranging from masters and boatswains all the way through to gunners, riggers and powder monkeys.

To service this boisterous, burgeoning trade, the port required administrators – both official and unofficial – it needed traders and merchants, bankers and moneylenders; the wharfs would be filled with warehousemen, coopers and stockkeepers. The town had three markets, a bear garden, cock-fighting pits, and plenty of other places where customers could be parted from their money. A resident writing in 1664 complained that the town had a place licensed to sell alcohol for every ten men who lived there, while a visitor in 1690 estimated that 20 per cent of Port Royal's buildings were 'brothels, gaming houses, taverns and grog shops'. To address such sin and debauchery there was an Anglican church, Quaker and Presbyterian meeting houses, a Catholic chapel and a synagogue – albeit sometimes the task was hard, tending a flock of 'a most ungodly and debauched people'.[21]

After the 1692 earthquake many commentators, especially those back in Europe and the American colonies, were quick to label the catastrophe as an Act of God; righteous anger directed at the 'wickedness committed against his Divine Majesty'.[22] Some Jamaican colonists may have held the same view, but the frequency of earthquakes and hurricanes doubtless fostered an understanding of the natural phenomena. And, regardless, people soon returned to the ruins of Port Royal, partly rebuilding the city and returning it to its old ways as 'the very Sodom of the Universe'.[23] But Port Royal never again reached the heights of its heyday as a base for privateers and tax evasion. After 1692 the island authorities concentrated on building a new town at Kingston on the mainland end of the Palisadoes across the bay, a decision justified by the vulnerability of Port Royal to further hazards. A devastating fire in 1702, fanned by high winds, left few of the town's 500 newly rebuilt structures surviving, save Fort Charles and a new Fort William. Hurricanes in 1712 and 1722 caused significant destruction, and they were followed by a regular catalogue of over twenty major fires, earthquakes and further hurricanes – each knocking back any substantive revival. Part of the raison d'être for the continuing survival of the settlement was its retention as a naval station by the Royal Navy. Ironically, given the reason for Port Royal's pre-1692 earthquake boom, the purpose of the base was to police the waters of the Caribbean and to rid them of pirates – a case of the city turning from poacher to gamekeeper. During the following centuries, the station further served to protect British interests from its long-standing rivals, the French, Spanish and Americans, and was once home to the future Admiral Horatio Nelson on two occasions. The Station and dockyard were closed in 1905, and since then Port Royal's resident population has dropped dramatically. Today it has a population of 1,300, while Kingston's is just under 600,000.

Seventeenth-century Port Royal was an extraordinary place – one worthy of the World Heritage Status sought by the Jamaican National Heritage Trust (UNESCO 2009). The disaster of 1692 preserves a town that was unique in so many ways. It was a place of extreme wealth, with the population density, facilities and cash-based economy that would have looked more familiar in inner-city London than in the Caribbean. European-style buildings, everyday use of luxury goods and wearing of the latest fashions were part of a lifestyle that was adopted not just by the ruling classes, but by all those who made money through Port Royal's various trades. This was, as the tentative WHS nomination notes, one of the first places in the world to illustrate the very beginnings of a global consumer revolution and its links to the Industrial Revolution

(UNESCO 2009). Here was a place where the lower and middle classes were purchasing luxuries such as books, porcelain and fine cloth some twenty to forty years before their equivalents in Europe and America. It was also a contradictory place, both raucous and pious, a boomtown attracting adventurers and those after a quick profit alongside those who sought to save their souls. A place of trade that melded many different interests, which was both tolerant and, in the case of a large part of the population – the enslaved – the complete opposite.

Since Jamaican independence in 1962 there have been at least ten plans for Port Royal. The current Concept Plan (2020) focuses on both the protection of the town's heritage, above and below the water, and on the value of historic sites in attracting visitors. New facilities to dock cruise ships are planned, limited to one boat in port at any one time with a capacity for 2,500 people – more than

Fig. 20 Various items recovered from the sea: (a) a student diver admiring a corked wine 'onion' bottle, one of fifty excavated from a tavern floor; (b) the lead caming of a window originally in the ground floor wall of a two-storey brick building believed to be a victualler's establishment; (c) a French-made watch: X-rays showed the hands stopped at 11:40 a.m., the time of the earthquake.

the population of the town itself. Five miles further east from the town, halfway along the Palisadoes spit, lies Kingston's International Airport. The opportunity for heritage tourism is considerable.

Seventeenth-century Port Royal still exists. Under the water, the streets, buildings, artefacts and lives of those who once traded in its warehouses and marketplaces survive in the only truly sunken city in the Western Hemisphere. For those who live there, and those who may visit in the future, this relatively modern Atlantis is an important reminder of the vulnerability of human life on the fringes of nature.

Ani, Turkey

> *On (the feast of) the Purification (2nd February) I was in a city called Aini, belonging to Sahensa, the position of which is very strong; and there are in it a thousand churches of Hermenians [sic] and two synagogues of Saracens. The Tartars have placed a Bailiff in it.*[24]

Fig. 21 The church of St Gregory of the Abughamrents in Ani, Kars, Turkey. Founded in around 980 CE as a private chapel by the Pahlavuni family (a branch of the Kamsarakans), it was later rededicated in 1040 CE as their mausoleum.

Today no one lives in Ani. No one worships in the churches, shops in its streets or relaxes in its bathhouses. Located on the edge of two ravines, this once thriving medieval city on the modern-day border of Turkey and Armenia is completely abandoned. Tourists visit, approximately 42,000 in 2017,[25] but this is a difficult place to reach. Forty-five kilometres from the Turkish city of Kars, the road to Ani is an hour's journey through the rolling countryside of eastern Anatolia. Travel direct from Armenia, separated only by the width of the River Arpaçay/Akhuryan, is impossible, since poor diplomatic relations between the two neighbours from their modern inception has led to a closed border. Ani is layered with irony: a place that is currently hard to get to yet owes its growth as a key destination to the braided Silk Roads that once traversed the region; a place that was once the capital of Ancient Armenia, but is now firmly in Turkey, and largely inaccessible to Armenians; a World Heritage Site, but also a place where the stories of different nationalities play out in very different ways. How did this ancient city collapse so comprehensively as to become unmapped and unvisited, a memory to all but a few by the late eighteenth century?

At the outset of this book, I emphasize that there is rarely a single cause for the collapse of civilizations or communities – a theme which we will repeatedly return to. This is one such story, about a place abandoned according to many narrators because of the destructive impact of earthquakes, in particular that of 1319. The truth is not quite as simple.

Ani is an old place. It's protected location at the joining of two deep, twisting gorges made it an easily defended site, positioned to make the most of crossings of the Arpaçay/Akhuryan and Ani rivers. Consequently, it is no surprise that archaeologists have discovered early human activity in the area, stretching back to the Iron Age, possibly earlier. But it is in the medieval period that the vague evidence of a prehistoric past turned into the magnificence of an important city.

A probable Zoroastrian Fire Temple, dating sometime between the first and fourth centuries CE, was excavated at Ani in 1909 and is the earliest structure found so far on the site. It offers a hint of a pre-Christian past and firmly connects those living there with a Persian and Parthian heritage. Four massive (1.3-metre diameter) column bases once held up a roof to shelter an everlasting flame which is fundamental to the Zoroastrian faith. Later the temple was converted to a Christian place of worship, possibly as early as the fourth or fifth centuries.

Ani sits on the apex not just of two rivers, but of empires, both benefiting from and torn by a complex, changing choreography of Romans then Byzantines, Ottomans and Turks to the west, Parthians then Sassanians and Kurds to the east, Georgians then Russians and Soviet States to the north, and the great Islamic caliphates to the south. In amongst this dance of nations the early Armenian state grew from its Iron Age tribal origins, first as a satrapy of the Achaemenid Empire, then gaining independence as a separate kingdom in the late fourth century BCE. At one time part of Alexander the Great's empire, then that of the competing claims of Rome and Parthia, Armenian culture and identity variously survived or thrived as its rulers became client kings to the bigger powers surrounding it. Rome and Parthia were replaced by Byzantine and Persian overlords in the fifth century, and Arabic ones in the seventh.

Ancient Armenia's central location on the edge of great territories is one of its defining characteristics; it is a country that pulls in and out of focus, one that is melded to others or sub-divided, ruling or subservient, cut off, a place of majorities in a minority. And Ani, on the porous western fringe of a land of moving borders, sits in the middle of this world of geopolitics. The infrastructure of defence, trade and religion characterize the medieval city. A residence belonging to the ruling Kamsarakan family is mentioned in the fifth century CE, and the earliest known defences date to the seventh century, focused on the citadel and palace complex at the southern promontory of the site. But the real cue for Ani's growth was when the ruling Bagratuni family purchased Ani and its territory from the Kamsarakans in the ninth century CE. Ashot III, 'Shahanshah' of Greater Armenia, a kingdom that stretched from the Caspian to the Black Sea, moved his capital from Kars to Ani. The transfer, in 971 CE, brought with it the entire bureaucracy of the court and, twenty-one years later, the head of the Armenian Church moved his seat there. The role of the church in Armenia cannot be underplayed in a country which, on the conversion of King Tiridates III in the early fourth century, became the first state to officially adopt Christianity.

Fig. 22 A double line of walls with semi-circular towers protecting the northern approach to Ani. Originally constructed in the tenth century, they were added to and heightened over the following three centuries.

The impact of the court's move is still visible today, marked by a massive expansion of the town and creation of not one but two sets of city walls over a kilometre to the north of the citadel. By the early eleventh century those entering the city would do so having already walked through unprotected suburbs through the Lion's Gate, one of three double-drum towers that announced the capital. Having passed under the symbol of the Bagratuni lion and cross, they would have travelled down the main street, through earlier defensive walls, past churches, shops, bathhouses, mills, workshops, residencies and fine mansions until they reached the citadel. Throughout that 1.1-kilometre walk they would have been constantly reminded of the presence of God. Known during the medieval period as 'The City of 1001 Churches', Ani's skyline was punctuated in all directions by the towers and cross-topped roofs of places of worship. The most important of these was the cathedral. Constructed at the turn of the eleventh century, to a design by Trdat, the court architect who also rebuilt the dome of Hagia Sophia in Istanbul after an earthquake, the cathedral was a tall rectangular building with a large, drum-shaped central tower, capped by a domed ceiling under a conical roof. Inside, the cathedral's pointed arches and clustered columns are considered by some to be the forerunners of the Gothic style, seen here almost two centuries before its arrival in Europe. This was the mother church for Armenian Orthodoxy for over fifty years.

But the cathedral was by no means the only prominent church in the city. Ani's Christian architectural heritage includes an extraordinary range of plan forms and styles, from the twelve-sided Church of St Gregory (*c.* 1040 CE) and quatrefoil form of Church of the Apostles (*c.* 1031 CE) to the star-shaped Church of the Shepherd (possibly eleventh century or earlier) and the domed hall of St Gregory of Tigran Honents (*c.* 1215 CE; Gregory was the saint responsible for Armenia's conversion to Christianity).

One of the most recognizable of Ani's churches is that of the Redeemer. An inscription of 1035 records that it was built by Prince Ablgharib Pahlavid to house a fragment of the True Cross brought back from Constantinople. Externally, the church is nineteen-sided in plan, with eight apses built within the 2.5-metre-thick walls of the ground floor; one, larger than the rest and fringed by two tiny

Fig. 23 Frescoes on the interior of the church of St Gregory of Tigran Honents, Ani, showing the lives of Christ, St Gregory the Illuminator and St Nino. The two saints converted the Armenians and Georgians respectively to Christianity. The church was built by the merchant Tigran Honents in 1215 CE.

AMONGST THE RUINS

chapels, held the alter with a fresco of an enthroned Christ above. Forming a domed drum, the church narrows from 15 metres externally to 10 metres internally above the ground floor, the whole creating a tall, elegant structure, typical of Ani's skyline.

A consistent theme for most of Ani's churches and chapels was their central-plan form, characteristic of eastern Byzantine tradition, their verticality (often being higher than they are long), and their prominent positioning within the townscape. Today, the first and last thing that visitors to Ani see are the churches: replicating something of the awe that ancient travellers felt as they first approached the harbour of the city walls, seemingly filled with the serried masts of Christian towers, pointed domes and crosses.

Not all of Ani's churches were created around a central plan. The Georgian church was based on a simple three-bay nave with no dome. Dating to *c.* 1218 CE, the church introduces another of Ani's defining attributes, this being the marks of alternative rulership over the centuries. In 1045 CE Armenia once more lost its independence and came firstly under Byzantine, then variously Seljuk Turkish, Kurdish, Georgian and Mongol control during the twelfth and thirteenth centuries. And nor was the religious influence solely Christian. Since the seventh century Muslim overlords and worshippers have built and reshaped buildings in the city, from the eleventh- and twelfth-century Mosque of Minuchihr to the Mosque of Abu'l Muamran, dated from an inscription on its minaret to 1198–9 CE.

Ani's function as a capital and religious centre were two elements which led to its growth as a major city in the region. A third crucial stimulus was trade. The Silk Road, a name coined in the nineteenth century by the German explorer Baron von Richthofen, described a series of caravan and sea routes that linked China to eastern Europe between 130 BCE and 1453 CE. Through a combination of political leadership and geography Ani came to control a branch of the famous trading road, connecting routes from Iran in the southeast with Georgia, the Black Sea and on to Constantinople to the north and west. The importance of the Silk Road per se is probably overstated, but the impact of becoming a regional capital, and the subsequent repositioning of Ani at the centre of a kingdom, must have driven people and business to the city, which then itself became an engine in the economy. A major bridge, spanning the Arpaçay/Akhuryan River in a single 30-metre arch, symbolizes the importance of trade to Ani's lifeblood, controlling access to the city and the opportunities beyond it. A toll or customs house would have mirrored others at the city wall gates to tax incoming merchants, while the city's hostelries, stables, warehouses, bathhouses and various forms of entertainment would have served the passing trade. Pastoral farming in the surrounding valleys and industry in the city would have contributed further to Ani's success.

How did this great city with an estimated population in the eleventh century of over 100,000 people come to have none today?

When I started to research this book, I was looking for a place where natural hazards, specifically earthquakes, had a devastating and terminal impact upon a major city. Imagine if Lisbon had failed to rebuild after the 1755 quake, or San Francisco after 1906 – that kind of place. And the guidebooks for Ani seemed to offer such a site. According to these sources, the great earthquake had dealt Ani a mortal blow. The city's location did not help. It sits on the messy fringes of the Anatolian tectonic plate, and, as such, has always been prone to earthquakes. Recorded as early as the tenth century, major quakes hit the city in 1132 and 1605, as well as the 1319 disaster which led to the collapse of the cathedral's great dome, amongst many other buildings. More recently, earthquakes during the last hundred years have made conservation efforts more complicated, as conservators sought to deal with buildings already weakened by historical collapse.

The 1319 earthquake was considerable, but it is wrongly attributed as the single cause of Ani's abandonment. In truth the city was already in decline, changing shape for a variety of reasons and on a trajectory that was bookended by the 1605 earthquake that truly marked the moment of terminal viability of the city. Aside from the repeated disasters brought about by being in an earthquake zone, changes in leadership and to trade patterns each contributed towards Ani's demise.

When the Mongols captured Ani in 1236 they accelerated a draining confidence in the city. Uncertainty fills a vacuum, and whereas Ani had been successfully rebuilt and adapted as part of a vassal state after earlier Turkish, Kurdish and Georgian takeovers, the devastation and chaos brought about during the first half of the thirteenth century marked a long decline from which the city would not recover. A century later, war and further changes meant that Ani went from being at the centre of the regional landscape to a backwater, with trade routes realigning further south, and the city bypassed. On a global scale, the fall of the Yuan and Mongol empires in the mid-fourteenth century, coupled with the opening of new, faster sea routes to Europe, completely changed the volume and complexion of overland traffic using the Silk Road. Seen within this context, Ani's decline was as much political as it was the result of the shaking earth.

There is one final twist to Ani's history – one that is again political and deeply rooted in both the complexity of the region's past and its current leadership. Ani, once the capital of Ancient Armenia, is now firmly in Turkey. Physically inaccessible to the Armenians who live in sight of the city a river's span away across the old Silk Road bridge, it is also distanced in terms of interpretation and understanding. Ani's medieval heyday and its defining monumental heritage

Fig. 24 The slender thirteenth-century chapel of the monastery of the Hripsimian Virgins stands overlooking the Arpaçay/Akhuryan River on the eastern side of Ani, which separates modern Turkey from Armenia. The ruins of the medieval bridge can be seen in the background.

are overwhelmingly Armenian and Christian – and its role as an early Armenian capital has ensured it became caught in nationalist power-plays. In 1579, towards the end of its period of decline, Ani became part of the Ottoman Turkish Empire, and remained a backwater until it was 'discovered' during the early nineteenth century by European travellers. This renewed interest in the city grew with the annexation of the region by Imperial Russia in 1877–8, as Ani's earlier history became caught up with modern imperial ambitions, and eventually led to Russian-sponsored excavations by the Georgian orientalist Nikolai Marr. Ani thus became a symbol for Armenian nationalism and orthodox Christianity, placing it in direct opposition to Turkish nationalism during the chaotic period of the Russian Revolution, the First World War and the Armenian Genocide of 1915–22. Material found on the site during Marr's excavations, including a 2.26-metre-high statue of the church-builder King Gagik I, disappeared.[26] Now under Turkish control, some of Ani's narratives are enhanced while others are underplayed. The importance of the Mosque of Manuchihr as the first mosque in Anatolia is put to the fore, and its restoration was prioritized alongside other secular sites such as the palace and town walls. It was scheduled to reopen for worship on 26 August 2021.[27] Even in 2021, it is the monuments created under the Turko-Persian Seljuk Empire that are top of the list for conservation.[28] As Heghnar Watenpaugh observes, the adjective 'Armenian' was notable for its absence across the interpretation of the site.[29]

Today the primary emphasis on the site, and in the documentation underpinning Ani's successful 2016 World Heritage Site nomination, is of 'a meeting place for Armenian, Georgian and diverse Islamic cultural traditions', 'a center of multi national and multi religious population'.[30] Does this 'rhetoric of multiculturalism' serve to 'gloss over, erase or silence Ani's most crucial layers', as Watenpaugh questions?[31] Or have the attentions of international organizations, such as the World Monuments Fund, in the conservation of the city, helped to elevate the rich thread of Ani's alternative histories above the weaponization of cultural heritage by nationalist extremists? The jury is out on the answer. A 1974 report by UNESCO identified 913 Armenian monuments in Turkey in 1923, with 464 completely destroyed, 252 in ruins and 197 in need of repair.[32] Today, President

Erdoğan's populist and conservative approach has caused concern for various of Turkey's minorities, and the decision to convert Hagia Sophia from a secular museum back to a mosque in 2020 brought condemnation from UNESCO and others. It is also largely at odds with the professional view of the cultural authorities which have shown strong support for conservation. The abandoned city of Ani could be a model for heritage multiculturalism, but only if nationalistic agendas of politicians are also abandoned by those passing through its ancient and magnificent gateways.

Plymouth, Montserrat

Volcanoes feature in eighty World Heritage Sites across the globe.[33] Of these, fifty-three are on the UNESCO designated list because of natural criteria, with three – Mount Etna, the Aeolian Islands, Hawai'i Volcanoes – inscribed solely because they represent major stages in the earth's geomorphological story. Twenty-seven places are included because of cultural criteria, either because volcanic activity has shaped the art, agriculture and architecture of historic

Fig. 25 A church spire showing above the ash, Plymouth, Montserrat.

communities, such as at Rapa Nui (see Chapter 3), or because it has uniquely preserved it, as at Pompeii in Italy, Joya de Cerén in El Salvador or León Viejo in Nicaragua. But there are other, lesser-known examples of such instant catastrophe, one of which still has an impact on the living population to this day. This is a story from the Caribbean of the loss of heritage and historic communities, destroyed or made inaccessible by volcanic eruption, and the impact that catastrophe can play on more recent culture.

Montserrat owes its existence to volcanic and tectonic activity. Created on the eastern boundary of the Caribbean Plate, where it meets and subducts the South American Plate, the island is the product of five major and three parasitic volcanoes. Prior to 1995, the last major eruption on Montserrat took place in around 1630 CE and, aside from occasional seismic reminders in the intervening three centuries, the island was considered dormant. Several earthquake swarms recorded from 1992 signalled that not all remained quiet, and in July 1995 the Soufrière Hills volcano on the south side of the island began to erupt. The first activity brought steam and clouds of ash – enough to prompt evacuations – followed in 1996 by major explosions and fast-moving, super-heated pyroclastic flows. A year later and larger flows, again made of hot gasses, ash, rock and lava, erupted from the core of the Soufrière Hills dome, and combined with mudflows (lahars) to issue great swathes of destruction across most of the south of the island to the sea. Nineteen people died, despite the evacuations, and the island's capital, Plymouth, was destroyed along with many other settlements. Such was the devastating impact that over 8,000 people left the area, over two-thirds of the entire population, many of them emigrating to the United Kingdom. The southern half of the island was declared an exclusion area, as it remains today.

In amongst this unquestionable human tragedy there is also the story of the physical loss of cultural heritage. Montserrat is a long-lived place with an intriguing history that is reflected in the historic buildings of its people and the abandoned archaeological evidence of their forebears. The volcanic eruptions of the Soufrière Hills bludgeoned and burned, for the most part completely eradicating humankind's centuries-old intervention in the landscape. That this took place in the archaeologically richer and historically more densely populated southern part of the island meant that the quantity of heritage sites was disproportionate, and the loss greater.

Evidence of Montserrat's earliest past was already ephemeral. The island has been occupied since 3000 BCE, firstly by prehistoric peoples migrating from South America across the Caribbean, followed by successive waves of Saladoid and Troumassoid groups (Taino), each distinguished by their distinctive pottery traditions. These Taino-speaking peoples lived in villages practising a 'slash and burn' agriculture, hunting, fishing and gathering from the island and sea. Trants, an early site now destroyed by the volcano, covered 50,000 square metres close to the coast on the east. Excavations uncovered a long-lived settlement spanning 800 years of occupation, with waste middens, and evidence for the use of stone tools, decorative beads and new animal species introduced from the South American continent.[34] Unpicking such sites where structural remains are slight is difficult at the best of times – doing so when they are incinerated by pyroclastic surges, swept aside by mudflows or covered in a layer of ash, is nigh on impossible. And these are the places that we know about. Locating previously undiscovered evidence of Montserrat's

Fig. 26 Enhanced 'infra-red' satellite views showing (in grey) extent of lava flows.

prehistoric past is an additional challenge that may only come to light with future technological advances.

Montserrat's Saladoid population and their successors were replaced by the Lokono, but the island was considered deserted by the time of Christopher Columbus's second voyage in 1493. The explorer did not land here, yet still Montserrat's mountainous profile evoked memories of the monastery of Santa Maria de Montserrate outside Barcelona, giving it its European name – the Lokono knew it as *Alliougana*, Land of the Prickly Bush. Spain never laid specific claim to the island, considering it unlikely to yield any obvious profit, so it was not until the first half of the seventeenth century that settlers from the Old World began to make their mark.

The early European history of Montserrat is a fascinating example of the chaotic scrabble for power in the region: one which reflected political and religious animosity transported to the warm, blue waters of the Caribbean. Spain, Holland, France and England each vied for territory, and, particularly alongside the latter, came peoples from Ireland. Permanent English colonies were first established on the American continent at Jamestown, Virginia, in 1607, and on the West Indian islands of St Kitts (1623) and Barbados (1625). St Kitts became the base from which to colonize other islands, including Montserrat which was first settled from there in 1632 by Irish Catholics sent by the governor, Sir Thomas Warner. We cannot know the reasons for Warner's decision to push them on from St Kitts, but the arrival of the French captain Pierre Belain d'Esnambuc on the island, first in alliance with the English against the native Lokono, and later in competition with them, might have contributed. At the time the Kingdom of Ireland was a client state held by the English Crown. This fractious relationship was inevitably split along religious lines. Irish Catholic settlers on St Kitts were much more likely to align with French Catholics than their Protestant English neighbours, so best to move them on to a more distant colony. Once on Montserrat, the presence of Irish settlers attracted more of their countryfolk, as the island gained a reputation as a place that welcomed those of the Catholic faith. These included peoples displaced from Protestant colonies in Virginia as well as those recruited directly in Ireland, where ports such as Cork and Kinsale were busy with ships carrying emigrants bound for the Caribbean.

Numbers of Irish settlers increased significantly after the English Civil War and Oliver Cromwell's victories in Ireland. Thousands of Irish Catholics were transported to the Americas and the Caribbean. And the greatest numbers as a proportion of the population were to be found on Montserrat, where a census of 1678 recorded 52 Scots, 761 English and 1,869 Irish. English fears of a Franco-Hibernian alliance came true in 1689, when Irishmen joined the French in rising against the English on St Kitts, doubtlessly exacerbating tensions on other islands including Montserrat, where there were 'Irish Papists upwards of eight hundred, men who of late have been very turbulent and rebellious'.[35]

These first European settlers on Montserrat almost certainly comprised speculators – those who were to become landowning planters – their tenants and their indentured servants, effectively transporting Anglo-Irish social stratification to the island. Irish influence extended from the top of society – six of the island's seventeenth-century governors were Irish – to the indentured who were almost at the bottom. Indentured servants were effectively contracted to plantation owners for a period of years (typically three to five years for adults, five to seven for children), after which they would be released from service, sometimes with a plot of land or financial recompense. Some entered into the relationship voluntarily, whereas others, such as the those transported during the time of Cromwell, were forced. Life was hard, with many indentured servants living on the poverty line, and receiving none of the promised benefits after their legal term of service came to an end. Once freed from service, many found it impossible to make a living as smallholders growing tobacco, indigo, ginger and cotton, especially as the economy and administration on the island turned to favour sugar production on large estates. Further conflict with France disrupted what for many was already a risky venture in search of quick profits rather than permanent settlement, and there was a subsequent wave of emigration to better opportunities found in the American colonies.[36]

Hard though it was for the indentured and free white population, it was as nothing compared to what awaited the final group of enforced immigrants to Montserrat. Enslaved peoples are first recorded arriving from Africa in 1664 and number 992 by the time of the 1678 census.[37] By 1805 there were just under 10,000 slaves working on the island, ten times the white population. Their arrival marked the evolving shift from an economy based on the growing of tobacco, utilizing white indentured servants, to the mass production of sugar cane with slave labour.

In 1700 there were forty-eight estates producing sugar on Montserrat and the industry reached its peak in 1735, aided by improved technology and a burgeoning slave labour force. And, while the island was amongst the smallest producers in the Caribbean, largely due to size, topography and lack of harbours, the sugar industry was still by some margin the most important economic driver.[38] As the eighteenth century progressed, the sugar plantations consolidated and became larger, often passing into the hands of absentee owners, who enjoyed their profits elsewhere.

The industry brought with it a distinctive and dark architecture. At its simplest, the sugar manufacturing process required fields and fertilizer to grow the cane, mills to extract the juice, boiling houses to clarify and concentrate the sugar liquid, and curing houses in which the sugar and molasses were separated, with the former dried and the latter often used to produce rum. Warehouses, storage sheds,

Fig. 27 William Clark's picture titled *Holeing a Cane-Piece* shows enslaved peoples using long-handled hoes to dig cane holes on an Antiguan sugar plantation in 1823; others are marking the field for where the canes will be placed.

AMONGST THE RUINS

animal pens, water cisterns, blacksmiths' and coopers' workshops, and administrative blocks might complete the typical industrial ensemble. Montserrat's census of 1729 recorded twenty-three windmills, fifty-two cattle mills and three water-powered mills. Alongside this industrial legacy is of course the social fabric – the 'Great Houses' of the plantation owners and the slave quarters of those who generated the wealth. While the former buildings would often blend European classism with tropical pragmatism – verandas and shutters for cool and shade – the enslaved people's accommodation ranged from barrack-type houses through to very simple village structures. Slave villages, such as the one recorded on the Galways Plantation in the south of the island, were built close to the business-end of the sugar manufacturing process, and comprised small (the largest on Galways was 3 by 6 metres), rectangular buildings, made of wood and slightly raised above the ground. Roofs were likely thatched with cane leaves and each house surrounded by a vegetable plot and room to keep a few animals. On the steep slopes away from the village, the slaves, and later sharecroppers, had growing plots, or 'grounds', on which they could produce beans, cassava, cocoa, pineapple, peanuts, soursop, yams and American Taro for their own consumption or to sell on.

Plymouth with its harbour was the principal town on Montserrat, administering to the needs of the island and the plantation estates. Here and elsewhere on the coast, the military presence was most visible in the form of forts and batteries. And, to provide for matters of the soul, there were churches and burial grounds.

Montserrat's sugar industry had been in a long, slow decline well before the emancipation of slavery in 1834. Competition from Brazil and other parts of the world, combined with the island's difficult geography, rendered many estates uneconomic. The ongoing wars with France, drought, soil exhaustion, hurricanes, blight amongst crops and disease for both humans and animals, all added to Montserrat's 'Long Wind-Down'.[39] Those plantations that were not consolidated were abandoned and the machinery of its industry gradually subsumed back into the forest. For a while slaves became a more important export than sugar. After emancipation Montserrat's economy stagnated further, with estates becoming abandoned. Joseph Sturge, a grain-dealer and philanthropist from Birmingham, visited two years after emancipation on a six-day tour of the island to review the post-emancipation apprenticeship system. Sturge was a quaker and fierce anti-slavery campaigner and his visit sparked a long-held interest in Montserrat by his family. In 1837 he purchased an estate close to Plymouth to prove 'that by fair and just treatment of the native labourers, sugar could be profitably produced without the aid of the servile labour . . .'.[40] Later, in a mixture of philanthropy and business acumen, the family benefited from the introduction of commercial lime production, for which Montserrat would become famous. From the mid-eighteenth century Sturge and others sought to improve the lives of previously enslaved peoples by purchasing old plantation estates and selling plots off to individual smallholders. In 1857 his family set up The Montserrat Company which grew to become the island's largest landowner, growing limes and cotton on 4,000 acres across a dozen estates. Such a mix, a legacy of large plantations and many smallholdings, is characteristic of Montserrat.

The Soufrière Hills eruption brought devastation to this rich historic landscape in the south of Montserrat. Within this context it is, inevitably, the historic voices of the poor and the enslaved

Fig. 28 The devastating impact of the eruption on Plymouth, Montserrat's former capital.

AMONGST THE RUINS

that are quietest, or mostly silent. Aside from stark numbers on an accounts ledger or the court record of a misdemeanour, it is to the archaeological evidence that we turn to unpick the lives of the vast majority who lived on Montserrat. Unfortunately, as we have seen, this is where the damage has been greatest.

Researchers David Watters and Gill Norton identified three categories of heritage loss resulting from the volcanic disaster: destruction or total obliteration; 'entombing' in which the archaeological site or building is buried; and loss through becoming inaccessible.[41] The issue of accessibility may be resolved over time with the advent of resources and application of technologies such as LIDAR survey, but there are further concerns that evidence of the island's rich cultural heritage will fade and disappear.

Heritage is not simply about the bricks and mortar of old buildings, or the carefully trowelled surfaces of archaeological sites. It is also about documentation, intangible traditions and, ultimately, people. Montserrat's written record has always been plagued by forces intent on its destruction, either accidentally or deliberately. Burnt by the French in 1712, the island's archives have also had to withstand hurricane, earthquake, flood, extreme heat, fire, mould, rot and a host of animals seeking to eat it or make it into bedding. Archives are rarely at the top of government priorities, resulting in underinvestment and inadequate storage facilities. Public records from Plymouth that survived the eruptions of the 1990s were transferred to the new de facto capital at Brades but are 'housed in unsuitable facilities and are deteriorating'.[42] Layer these issues on top of the impact of the volcanic eruptions, and Montserrat's written, drawn and photographic record is dispersed, highly selective and extremely fragile.

For over half the island, then, that broad swathe of ancient archaeological sites – seventeenth-, eighteenth- and nineteenth-century buildings, relics of industry and commerce, documents and artefacts – is at best inaccessible or, in places, lost forever. Pushed aside by the pyroclastic flow, entombed in its grey embrace or incinerated in the heat of the moment, an intriguingly layered historic landscape has gone.

The final dimension to the loss of heritage on Montserrat is that which is vested with the living community – not simply the interruption of the ongoing occupation of places, but also the traditions, folk-lore and intangible heritage of communities. Transported to the north of the island or, in many cases far overseas, these aspects of culture thrive, transform or die. With a long history of a transient population Montserrat has witnessed waves of emigration, not least the Windrush generation who responded to the call to fill labour shortages in the United Kingdom following the Second World War. But the scale of change after the volcanic eruptions from 1995 was completely different, with almost two-thirds of the island off limits and with a similar proportion of its population choosing to relo-cate abroad. For Montserratians the attachment to land and spirit of place is strong, so to be physically removed from it and for it to have changed out of all recognition is a real severance. However, for the diaspora communities the maintenance of a Montserratian identity is important, particularly through song, calypso, food, dia-lect and the Church:

> . . . we have lost our homes but not our voices. While the moment of crisis has passed, there remains a more potent reason for con-tinued collaboration – the preservation of the unique and fragile Montserrat heritage.[43]

Montserrat comprises just under 104 square kilometres, of which 44 square kilometres will never be used again for human occupa-tion, according to scientific advice. The volcanic eruption changed the dynamic completely, diminishing the population, reducing the space on which to live, grow food or work, consuming the capital city and closing the main port. From 1994 to 2016 the GDP of the island shrank by 46 per cent. In comparison, that of nearby Antigua and Barbuda grew by 67 per cent.[44] Montserrat's smaller economy is now dominated by the public sector, which represented almost half of GDP in 2016, compared with under a fifth in 1994. Rebirth after the trauma has been a slow process, but the island's links to the past and intangible traditions are recognized as the kernels on which the future of Montserrat will be based. Two quotes sum up the importance of Montserratian identity and heritage. The first is from an expatriate London perspective, outlining the value of taking the island's culture with you:

AMONGST THE RUINS

Me nuh need fo homesick gel, because Montserrat right here
Me home life is quite happy here
De people treat me nice
An since dem is Montserratian, ah still get Me dumplin, dasheen
an rice.[45]

And on the island itself, cultural heritage is a distinctive driver for tourism and increased community cohesion. This is a place which still celebrates its Irish heritage, not least through the national holiday of St Patrick's Day, a historic connection that is marked by a large legacy of personal and place names. The annual festivals of Calabash, Cudjoe Head and Carnival each mark Montserrat's African heritage, while the tourism webpages include tours to newly discovered petroglyphs and the 'buried' city of Plymouth. Turning 'Ash to Cash' and talk of a World Heritage Site nomination are the headlines of the island's current tourism strategy.[46] Here then is a place where the lessons of much older volcanic disasters give hope of future advantage:

When we finally get the chance, when the volcano stops, to go into that buried city, it is the latter-day Pompeii. People are gonna come from all over the world to walk through the ruins of that city.[47]

CHAPTER 3

HUMAN DISASTER

Oftentimes there is no one left to blame but ourselves. Selfishness, greed, ignorance or short-termism have each had a role to play in the decline or failure of historic peoples, themes which are explored here through three stories that look at the impact of poor decision-making and human frailty, leading to abandonment.

We begin in Ancient Sumer, a region credited as being the first urban civilization in the world. In the late fourth millennium BCE a number of city states developed in the Gulf and across the lower reaches of the Tigris and Euphrates rivers in modern-day Iraq. Typically, places like Ur, Nippur, Eridu, Uruk and Lagash contained temples, usually associated with ziggurats and palaces, and were lain out on grid systems with artisanal and residential quarters. Girsu is one such place, a holy city entered by crossing a vast ceremonial bridge over one of the principal canals. Record-keeping and dedication, using cuneiform, one of the world's earliest forms of writing, have given us unique insight into the organization of these early societies, and those who ruled them. The raison d'être underpinning the rise of Sumer was the surplus provided by agriculture. In particular, it was the irrigation technologies, including the cutting of canals to harness the silt-laden waters of the two great rivers, which unlocked a large and consistently fertile hinterland. Critically, these systems relied upon careful management to ensure waterborne salt did not accumulate in the soil. But, as the city states grew so too did pressure on the system, and with new canals bringing endless supplies of water to the region, the water table rose and slowly 'the earth turned white'. Increasing soil salinity is estimated to have reduced the population of Sumer by over a half. Southern Mesopotamia's gradual loss of productivity hastened its decline and abandonment, as influence and power transferred north to Babylon.

In the second story under the theme of human disaster we move from the macro-scale of southern Mesopotamia to the microscale of a small Scottish archipelago to explore the unexpected consequences of disease on historic communities. The four islands that make up St Kilda lie 65 kilometres beyond the Outer Hebrides. Occupied for over 4,000 years, the cultural heritage of St Kilda is one that is uniquely adapted to the isolated nature of the islands. The landscape of stone-built thatched blackhouses, field systems and *cleitaen* – unique drystone storage structures – culminates in the extraordinary landscape of Village Bay. The economic life on St Kilda was rooted in the resources that surrounded the islands: fishing, grazing Soay sheep, weaving of tweed and the harvesting of seabirds and their eggs. 'No bird is of so much use to the islanders as this: the Fulmar supplies them with oil for their lamps, down for their beds, a delicacy for their tables, a balm for their wounds, and a medicine for their distempers' (1805). Tourism also featured. And with visitors to the island so too came diseases to which the population were particularly susceptible. In the late seventeenth century St Kilda supported 180 inhabitants. An outbreak of smallpox in 1727 reduced the population to just forty-two people. For the very young, the impact of neo-natal tetanus was the cause of death of two-thirds of newborn babies for at least 150 years prior to 1920. Topically, low herd immunity, limited genetic biodiversity and malnutrition are just some of the reasons for the phenomena. More deaths of four young men from influenza in 1926, and Mary Gillies who with her newly born daughter died of pneumonia in 1930, contributed towards the request of the thirty-six remaining islanders to be evacuated from St Kilda later that year.

Disease also features in another island story. Rapa Nui, or Easter Island, is a summary in microcosm of the impact of human-made disaster on cultural heritage. A thriving Polynesian culture was established on the Pacific island in around the thirteenth century CE. Famous for the construction of over 900 moai statues, the Rapa Nui population could have numbered up to 17,500 people at its peak in the sixteenth century. But when Dutch explorer Jacob Roggeveen visited the island in 1722, this stood at less than 3,000, and James Cook recorded in 1774 that 'the country appeared barren and without wood'. His diary note was perceptive, because the removal of trees and subsequent loss of soil fertility was one of the reasons for the cultural decline. Matters were made far worse by the introduction of non-native predatory species, such as the kiore, diseases (syphilis and smallpox) and, later, slavery. But the story of Rapa Nui is also a cautionary one for those seeking to disentangle the reasons for decline. What really was the primary reason for the island's loss of its indigenous population? Ecocide, disease or the physical removal of its people?

Human decision-making has impacted on the loss of all civilizations – including each of those grouped under the other organizing themes in this book – either as a root cause, or in response. The stories here reveal the unintended consequences of our own ambition.

Girsu, Iraq

A common thread that runs through the theme on human fallibility is that it is often a slow, blind walk in the wrong direction; one where, unthinkingly, we suddenly find ourselves at the tipping point into disaster without really realizing that it was approaching. Sometimes we have passed the point of no return. And it is often born of success.

The list of Sumerian 'firsts' is astonishing. It was here that Sumerian peoples 'first poked cuneiform into wet clay and called it stored grain' – thus inventing, as Noah Harari puts it, a 'data-processing system . . . called "writing"'.[1] It was here that the newly invented wheel allowed mass-produced pottery to be made, that great rivers were tamed to irrigate the land, that the plough was successfully modified to exploit the new fertility of the black soil, and that cloth and bricks were manufactured on an industrial scale. As a highly successful culture, the Sumerians' ability to capture, manage and record their increasingly complex world through cuneiform, the creation of laws and the early development of mathematics was an integral part of that achievement.

Fig. 29 Gudea holding a jar from which flow never-ending streams of water containing fish. It is dedicated to Geshtinanna, a goddess associated with farming, fertility and dream interpretation, *c.* 2120 BCE.

The emergence of Sumer as more than a collection of villages began shortly before 3000 BCE. The harnessing of water across Mesopotamia – the 'Land between rivers' – combined with improved means of agricultural production, *and* an increasingly sophisticated socio-religious structure created a cycle of growth from which the Early Dynastic (2900–2350 BCE) cities of Eridu, Uruk, Ur Lagaš, Girsu and many others would rise. The theoretical background is simple, albeit there is a perpetual element of 'which came first' in the explanation; an elite with the ability to control large numbers of people was able to engineer and manage irrigation solutions on a landscape scale. Those solutions allowed more food to be produced, which in turn created the larger surplus needed to sustain the elite and the non-productive services that they offered. The greater the surplus, the greater the number of people that the emerging city could sustain, and the greater the elite. Trade and specialization emerged, underpinned by the same surplus, and society became increasingly ordered. Given that the origins of these cities lie in early prehistory, there is copious debate on the shape of those early elites, but the governing power of the gods as the begetters of bounty and the religious rulers who led on their behalf are a constant theme.

Each city state became associated with one of the gods of the Sumerian pantheon, with their temple and sacred precinct sitting at the heart of the urban area. Priests would govern that space, led by a ruler or *ensi*. The whole power system of early city life would emanate from the god in their precinct, projecting outwards in concentric circles to a hierarchy of intra-mural and extra-mural neighbourhoods and beyond that to a connected landscape of irrigated fields, fortified storehouses, watchtowers and villages. The glue that helped maintain the relationship between town, village and countryside was a series of annual ceremonies – pilgrimages (the prehistoric equivalent of walking the parish boundary) reinforced by physical boundary stele, frontier shrines and cuneiform documentation – that protected the territory and bound its constituent parts to the centrifugal force of the god at its centre.[2]

Unlike later empires, such as the Babylonian and Assyrian that succeeded Sumer, there was no single overarching authority across the city states, instead more coalitions and alliances, based on trade and a common set of gods. There was conflict, particularly when the city populations grew to a size where they needed to compete for resources, especially water. One of the world's first recorded legal agreements – the Treaty of Mesilim – was concluded in the twenty-fifth century BCE between the city states of Girsu-Lagaš and its neighbour Umma-Zabalam, in an attempt to address competing claims over water, probably prompted by diminishing supplies and concerns over salinization.[3] Nowhere is the relationship between protective deity, powerful *ensi*, the city state and its precious resources better summarized than on the 'Stele of the Vultures'. This carved stone stele, now in the Louvre, celebrates the victory of Girsu-Lagaš over Umma-Zabalam, after the Treaty of Mesilim broke down. On one side is Eanatum E-anatu, the *ensi* of Girsu-Lagaš, depicted with vultures flying overhead holding the severed heads of his enemies in their beaks, while on the other there is Ningirsu the city deity, god of farming, hunting, storms and war. After defeat the *ensi* of Umma-Zabalam swore an oath:

> Forever and evermore, I shall not transgress the territory of the god Ningirsu! I shall not shift the course of its irrigation channels and canals! I shall not rip out its monuments![4]

The European rediscovery of ancient Mesopotamia was spearheaded by Paul-Émile Botta's exploration of King Sargon II's palace at Dur Sharrukin, followed by the work of Sir Henry Layard at Nimrud and Nineveh (see chapter 4), all Assyrian royal capitals in the north of modern-day Iraq. Sumer, in the harsher and unsettled south of the country, lagged by comparison until the arrival of Ernest de Sarzec.[5] De Sarzec, the French vice-consul to Basra, recognized the importance of a large sculpture of the *ensi* Gudea, reported from Girsu, modern-day Tello, a series of low-lying mounds 50 kilometres to the north of Nasiriyah. In 1877 he was granted sole permission by the Ottoman authorities to excavate and after eleven campaigns his findings revealed not only the 'Stele of the Vultures' but an extraordinary quantity of sculpture and approximately 30,000 clay tablets inscribed in cuneiform. De Sarzec died in 1901 and the baton of discovery on the site was handed on to a succession of Frenchmen, including Gaston Cros (four campaigns between 1901 and 1909), Henri de Genouillac (1929 to 1931) and André Parrot (1932 to 1933). Between them, and the research associated with their discoveries, they began to unravel one of the most rewarding archaeological sites in Sumer.

The early city of Girsu sat on top of a natural hill, a turtleback, accented by the platforms of its inner precincts and the early temples within them, and accentuated by defensive ditches that encircled it.

Fig. 30 Excavations at the site of Girsu, Iraq.

AMONGST THE RUINS

Inside the town walls were various neighbourhoods, doubtless for the city priests, administrators and noble families, while beyond the city were further temple precincts, industrial zones and various artisanal and residential quarters. Running north to south to the east of Girsu was a major canal, with a branch that led off to a harbour immediately to the north of the city.

At the city's highest point, overlooking the harbour and within an inner set of walls, was the *iri-ku*, or sacred precinct, inside of which stood various earlier temples and later palaces, and, critically, the temple of Ningirsu, *Eninnu*, the White Thunderbird. The thunderbird was a lion-headed eagle and the avatar of Ningirsu, while *Eninnu* refers to the divine powers given to Ningirsu by Enlil, leader of the Sumerian gods. The *Eninnu* temple was created by the *ensi* Gudea and we know its exact form and plan due to an extraordinary calibration of archaeological research, cuneiform inscription and contemporary sculpture. The French excavators of the past repeatedly came across a cuneiform inscription, which read:

> For Ningirsu, mighty hero of Enlil, Gudea, ruler of Lagaš, made everything function as it should, and built for him his Eninnu, the White Thunderbird, and restored it to its proper place[6]

The inscription, which continues to be found during excavations today, is pressed on cones deliberately placed into the walls of temple buildings, or on special tablets carefully placed under the gate entrances to the site. It marks Gudea's devotion to the god of the city state, and his obsession with creating the temple. That fixation is also detailed on various statues and in a poem written on two clay cylinders which describe the purification of the city prior to the temple's construction and the acquisition of building materials such as cedar, fir and bitumen, as well as luxury decorative goods imported from long distances to Girsu. The inscriptions describe the laying of the first brick, hand-made by Gudea himself – the 'most beautiful' of all, naturally – and the thunderous moment when Ningirsu entered the temple after it was complete to a soundtrack of kettledrums and prayer.

Eighteen sculptures of Gudea have been found in Girsu, including examples that are now in the British Museum and the Louvre. One,

Fig. 31 A foundation cone, inscribed with cuneiform. These were buried under the foundations, or built into the walls, of important public buildings and temples during construction to sanctify the site and commemorate the ruler and his achievements.

in the Louvre, depicts a seated version of Gudea, carved in hard black diorite, a picture of pious modesty. He has on his lap a tablet, measuring device and stylus which have been used to create a plan of the temple he has built to Ningirsu. The plan on the tablet shows buttressed walls, six gateways and towers that would have defined an inner temple complex – the holy of holies. The walls are overly thick because they were built to contain the magical powers of the god – this was a vibrant living deity, one who was woken with ceremony in the morning and worshipped until the *Eninnu* was closed at night. The temple's walls contained niches for statues, including the very one of Gudea with its plan on his lap. Remarkably, the recent excavations by the British Museum and Iraq's State Board of Antiquities and Heritage (SBAH) led by Sébastien Rey, have identified that exact temple.

Another statue which may have once celebrated Gudea's piety within the temple, now in the Louvre, shows the *ensi* holding a jar from which flow never-ending streams of water containing fish; once again the powerful triumvirate of priestly ruler, god and the life-giving bounty given by water is literally carved in stone. This connection with water was crucial for the lifeblood of the city, and was nowhere more apparent than in the *Construction énigmatique* discovered by de Genouillac and Parrot between 1929 and 1932. In reality, the construction is not enigmatic, but a massive bridge crossing the canal that ran to the east of the city, possibly combined with the function of a regulator. Made of fired brick bonded with a mixture of lime, sand and bitumen, the structure effectively narrowed the banks of the canal from 40 metres to under four to allow a bridge to span across it. The need to heavily reinforce the pinch point of the crossing with multiple buttresses buried in the earth either side of the bridge's 40-metre-long revetment walls gives a sense of the volume of water that might at times have passed along this super-artery. Once more the Sumerian penchant for dedication is helpful: fifteen bricks from the structure are inscribed to Ningirsu and are dated to the rule of Gudea's son, Ur-Ningirsu, who succeeded him as *ensi*. We don't know what the gateway on top of the bridge's foundations looked like, but their complexity suggests something elaborate and impressive. This was the point of approach to the holy city. For visitors and

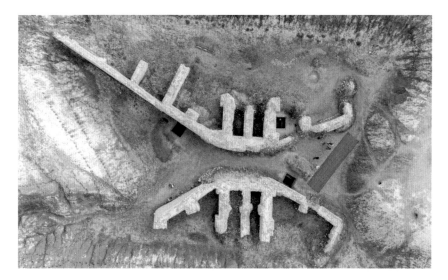

Fig. 32 The bridge or *Construction énigmatique* at Girsu. The canal ran from left to right, with its waters contained by revetment walls. It narrowed to allow a bridge crossing, identifiable by triple abutments mirrored either side. These would have been buried in earth and probably acted as foundations for an impressive gateway above. Other buried abutments strengthened the structure from the compressed force of water.

pilgrims who had spent days crossing Girsu's flat plains, the sight of a towering gateway and the sound of fast-flowing water under its bridge must have inspired a sense of awe, and the anticipation of further wonders beyond. The bridge would have also played a role in the ceremonial processions to and from Girsu's holy shrine, effectively parading Ningirsu out in a circuit of his villages and territory to mark his protection and benefice.

The link between Ningirsu, water and irrigation cannot be over-stated. In the epic Sumerian poem *Lugal-e* ('O Warrior King') the tale is told of Ningirsu's battle with Asag, a monstrous mountain demon whose presence was enough to make fish boil in rivers. In the story Asag is vanquished by Ningirsu (Ninurta in the poem) with the help of his speaking mace Sharur. After Ningirsu had 'smashed the heads of all the enemies', he set about rearranging the mountains so that the water trapped there flowed to fertilize the southern plains:

> At that time, the good water coming forth from the earth did not pour down over the fields. The cold water was piled up every-where . . . The Tigris did not bring up its flood in its fullness. Its mouth did not finish in the sea, it did not carry fresh water. No one brought offerings to the market. The famine was hard, as nothing had yet been born. No one yet cleaned the little canals, the mud was not dredged up. No one yet drew water for the fertile fields, ditch-making did not exist. People did not work in furrows, barley was sown broadcast.[7]

Afterwards 'He poured carp-floods of water over the fields . . . He provided water for the speckled barley in the cultivated fields, he piled up the harvest of fruits in garden and orchard. He heaped up the grain piles like mounds.'[8] Such a taming of the Tigris and Euphrates, and the irrigation systems that stemmed from them, was critical. In southern Iraq the modern annual precipitation rate is less than 100 millimetres. Rain-fed agriculture in this environment needs 300–350 millimetres of water per year.[9] While conditions before the second millennium BCE were slightly wetter than today, growing crops in the alluvial plain of the Tigris and Euphrates always required supplementary irrigation. The need to manage water resources was also linked to the two most commonly grown crops in antiquity, winter wheat and barley, which demand the most water when they are planted in September/October in the driest season of the year, and don't require it during harvest in April/May, when it is wettest.

Sumerian irrigation comprised a number of elements: the major rivers and their tributaries which carried water from the northern mountains and nutrient-rich silt. Natural and human-made levees raised and contained the river channels, protecting against spring flooding and containing the water when it was in destructive abundance. From these a hierarchy of canals, dams and ditches were cut to allow controlled flooding of the fields, managed by headgates, inlets, outlets, distributors and regulators.[10] The organization required to make these systems work was considerable, both in the original engineering of the major canals, and in their subsequent management, which demanded coordination in terms of tasks such as deciding when to release floodwaters or arranging to clear silt from the canal system. And that system was not static: during the earliest periods the first Sumerian settlements were perched along the natural levee of the major rivers. Channels would be cut in those banks to flood the surrounding fields, creating a narrow strip of towns and agriculture either side of the Tigris and Euphrates. Later, there was a complex interaction between the river and a much larger area, as the system grew and canals fed cities and villages that were distant from the source. Other changes of water management and engineering on a grand scale were in response to the movement of the rivers in the fourth and second millennia BCE, prompted by climatic, tectonic and fluvial fluctuations, requiring increased state intervention to keep their peoples and economies alive.[11] The greater the complexity of the system, the greater the resources required to maintain it, and the more vulnerable it becomes due to salt, silt or social breakdown.

The cuneiform records for Girsu's water management are astonishing, containing descriptions of four levels of irrigation from the primary canals, *i*, controlled by regulators, *geskesera*, to secondary canals, *pa*, and their dikes, or *eg*, and distributors, *kabtar*.[12] Excavation and maintenance of the canals was the responsibility of the temple and its dependants, including the *ensi*'s leading followers and the militia, and other ranks who received subsistence fields. They included carpenters, leather-workers, reed-workers, felters and foresters, potters and herdsmen, as well as scribes, cupbearers, cooks and brewers. Together these classes would be the ones called up for military service, temple construction or to work in the fields at sowing and harvest time. Those lower classes who were not allotted fields were not expected to maintain them.

The mid-third millennium BCE war between the Sumerian city states of Girsu-Lagaš and Umma-Zabalam, as illustrated on the 'Stele of the Vultures', arose because the latter, being further northwest and upstream, controlled a key watercourse which originated from the Euphrates. Part of Girsu-Lagaš' solution was to dig a new canal from the Tigris to the east, effectively bypassing Umma-Zabalam territory. This huge new waterway brought with it water in abundance. If the rise of Sumer and its city states, such as Girsu, can be linked to the technology and social organization that allowed irrigation to boom, then the same forces contributed to its slow demise. Increased demand, both to feed a growing population and to fuel the surplus that supported Ningirsu's priests and leaders, supplemented by a seeming profusion of water, led to more and more irrigation. At its height, the city state of Girsu-Lagaš was in control of approximately 3,000 square kilometres of irrigated territory.[13] But more irrigation also led to a raised water table and this is where the problems arose. The origins of the Tigris and Euphrates mean that those rivers carry salts from the sedimentary geology of the mountains in the far north, with more accumulating in the southern alluvial plain due to former sea incursions.[14] Too much salt in soil is disastrous for two reasons: firstly, sodium ions can be absorbed by clay particles deflocculating them to cause a hard, impermeable pan which then prevents water draining through it; secondly, salt impedes plant growth.

Overwatering brought more water closer to the surface of the agricultural fields, which combined with capillary action and evaporation also drew concentrations of salt into the root zone of the crop, greatly limiting growth and output.[15] Cuneiform records show that Girsu's fields were yielding an average of over three times as much grain per hectare in *c.* 2400 BCE than in nearby Larsa 700 years later.

Girsu's fertile soils slowly became less and less productive. There were ways of mitigating the problem, such as changing to more salt-tolerant crops by swapping wheat for barley, but the people of southern Sumer were already locked into a long-term decline. Solutions, such as leaving fields unwatered and fallow, hence allowing rain to wash out the salts and the water table to drop, meant less produce and the threat of starvation. Increasing soil salinity is estimated to have reduced the population of Sumer by over a half, hastening its decline and abandonment, as influence and power transferred north to Babylon.[16] And, while this was not the only reason for the slow decline of the Sumerian city states – climatic and fluvial changes, attack by foreign powers and internal rivalries each had a role – it is likely that salinization played a major part. Girsu continued to be occupied while under Babylonian control, and 2,000 years later the ruined city was chosen as the site of a late Seleucid palace by the Adad-nadin-ahhe. This Babylonian potentate was clearly obsessed by Girsu's ancient past, collecting Sumerian statues and copying their earlier rituals of burying foundation stones and stamping bricks with his name. Doubtless, the mimicry of such ancient traditions helped strengthen his connection to power.

Today, the great *tells* (artificial mounds) of the holy city of Girsu are abandoned, the surrounding landscape dry and barren. It seems that the ancient Sumerian and Akkadian curse of the god Enlil to 'let the black fields become white and the broad plains produce salt' came true.

However, over the past seven years there has been a renewed interest in this historic place. Iraq's State Board of Antiquities and Heritage, in partnership with the British Museum, has once more been exploring the city and its environs. As well as reopening the earlier French excavations and using them to navigate towards new discoveries, a key part of the future plans for Girsu is to conserve the site for the future, and, in time, to allow people to visit and enjoy this special place.

In a postscript to this story, when Genouillac and Parrot excavated Girsu's bridge in the early twentieth century, they not only removed a huge quantity of archaeological deposits from on top of the structure, but they also left it open to the elements after completing their work. Since then, the bridge's baked bricks have endured ninety hot, dry summers and cooler, wetter winters. The now-open site floods each year leaving the brickwork not only exposed to wind and rain, but also to the damaging crystallization of waterborne salts. The consequence is that there is a tidemark of erosion, like the action of the sea on the base of a cliff, which is slowly undermining the structure. This is amongst the earliest and largest civil engineering structures in the world, and has until now survived over 4,100 years. Its protection from the salt that contributed to the downfall of its makers is a significant challenge, but surely must be a priority for the conservation movement of the twenty-first century.

St Kilda, Scotland

> *If St Kilda is not the Eutopia so long sought, where will it be found? Where is the land which has neither arms, money, care, physic, politics, nor taxes? That land is St Kilda.*
>
> MACLEAN, *Sketches on the Island of St Kilda*, 1838

> *The St Kilda story is like a modern myth and, like a myth, I can't remember when I first heard it. Possibly in primary school. One afternoon we were shown a film. Barefoot, bearded men, and women cowled in shawls, and innumerable seabirds filled the screen. There were dreadful cliffs that the men lowered themselves down, to take birds' eggs and the birds themselves. We learned that the islands lay forty miles west of Lewis and Harris, out in the ocean, which was too far for much contact or communication, in those days. Nonetheless, people had lived out there for a thousand years or more . . . But their way of life broke on the wheel of the modern world.*
>
> JAMIE, *Sightlines*, 2012

We move from the macro-scale of southern Mesopotamia to the microscale of a small Scottish archipelago to explore the unexpected consequences of disease on historic communities.

The four small islands that make up St Kilda, MacLean's 'Eutopia' in the northern Atlantic, are Hirta, Soay, Boreray and Dun, which together are the most westerly occupied point of the British Isles. This jagged, treeless collection of volcanic rocks located in an inhospitable sea 64 kilometres beyond the Outer Hebrides and 160 kilometres from the mainland is the epitome of isolation. And yet, despite this, St Kilda has been occupied for up to 6,000 years, with evidence of

Fig. 33 Village Bay main street, Hirta, St Kilda. The thicker-walled ruinous blackhouses, now without their thatched roofs, are mixed with more recent cottages dating to 1861 and later. To the right of the street is a circular burial ground, while cleitean dot almost the entire landscape.

peoples visiting from the Neolithic period, followed by permanent settlement from at least as early as the Iron Age.[17] A stone circle, now lost, was recorded on Boreray in 1764, when a visitor described 'a Druidical place of worship, a large circle of huge stones fixed perpendicularly in the ground, at equal distances from one another, with one more remarkably regular in the centre, which is flat in the top'.[18] Other prehistoric evidence lies ephemeral and scattered across the islands: field systems, animal enclosures and possible settlement. Norse and later medieval activity present a marginally clearer picture – a fourteenth-century record mentions St Kilda as 'on the margins of the world'[19] – but it is only when we reach the early modern period that the solid foundations of life on the islands truly emerge from the North Atlantic sea-mist. Martin Martin, a Gaelic-speaking writer from Skye, visited in 1697 and recorded a way of life rooted in the limited natural bounty of the islands: sheep grazing, spinning and weaving of cloth, and the harvesting of seabirds and their produce.[20] The dramatic sea stacks of St Kilda are to this day the home to enormous quantities of gannets, fulmars, Atlantic puffins, guillemot, shags, cormorants, kittiwakes, Manx shearwater and razorbill. Unfortunately, the last great auk was killed by three St Kildans in 1844.[21]

These birds, alongside the native Soay sheep, formed a critical part of a largely subsistence economy, with feathers collected for export, to be used in stuffing bedding and cushions or for brushes, fishing lures and in the manufacture of golf balls. Oil from the stomachs of the fulmar was used for lighting and medicine, beaks for needles and quills, and of course the flesh and eggs were an essential part of the islanders' diet:

> The largest and the two lesser isles are good for pasturage, and abound with a prodigious number of sea-fowl from March till September; the solan geese [common gannet] are very numerous here, insomuch that the inhabitants commonly keep yearly above twenty thousand young and old in their little stone houses, of which there are some hundreds for preserving their fowls, eggs, etc. They use no salt for preserving their fowl; the eggs of the sea wild-fowl are preserved some months in the ashes of peats, and are astringent to such as be not accustomed to eat them.
>
> They have another bird here called fulmar . . . When any one approaches the fulmar it spouts out at its bill about a quart of pure oil. The natives surprise the fowl, and preserve the oil, and burn it in their lamps. It is good against rheumatic pains and aches in the bones; the inhabitants of the adjacent isles value it as a catholicon for diseases; some take it for a vomit, others for a purge . . .[22]

In spring and summer, during their seasonal migration to the islands, puffins were trapped using a snare on a long rod, while fulmars, guillemots and gannets, their young and their eggs, were gathered by abseiling down the vertiginous face of the sea stacks, barefoot, using ropes made from leather or pleated horsehair. The baby gannet, or *guga* (Gaelic for gannet), and other birds were feathered, singed, deboned, gutted and either salted and pickled, cooked or dried, in a tradition which still takes place today in the far Ness of Scotland. A census of 1764 notes that each islander ate an improbable thirty-six

Fig. 34 'Getting the fulmar' *c.* 1886. St Kildans climbed in bare feet or coarse socks, preferring to descend on a rope rather than climb from below. Climbing ropes were prized possessions, often handed down from father to son as heirlooms. The young birds were harvested over three weeks in August, to be eaten fresh or cured, with their oil used for fuel lamps and feathers exported for stuffing or manufacture.

eggs and eighteen birds daily;[23] whatever the number, the importance of the birds to the survival of the population was critical. Fish, surprisingly, were not nearly as valued, mainly because of the dangers of catching them in the great swells of the Atlantic.

The St Kildans' way of life was reflected in their architecture. The islanders' homes, 'Black Houses', were squat buildings, with thick, unmortared stone walls, and straw roofs held down by 'ropes made of twisted heath, the extremity of which is poised with stone to preserve the thatch from being blown away'.[24] Most had a byre area shared with animals and a central hearth, while some had bedchambers (*crùb*) contained in the thickness of the walls:

> Inside the door you had to climb over the manure . . . among the cattle, which, on account of the presence of a stranger, and the barking of dogs, and the shouting of your friends above, soon got very excited. Amidst great confusion and excitement you

got helped along and over the dividing fallan [partition]. Here you had to creep along on hands and feet, as it was only near the centre of the space that you could even sit upright. Carefully creeping along in the almost total darkness, you made your way to the top of the steep slope which led down to the bed opening. Down this you went head foremost, nothing visible above but your legs, while you spoke and prayed.[25]

There was only one permanent settlement in the early modern period, Village Bay, framed in a bowl by mountains in the southeast of Hirta with relatively easy access to the sea. Here an early township, clustered around a 'square', was overlain by the black houses of a linear village of a crofting community, which itself was improved and replaced in the 1860s by the construction of sixteen mainland-type cottages. An equally complex palimpsest of field systems extended beyond the houses of the St Kildans comprising drystone headwalls, kelp-yards, dykes and enclosures, each relating to the stewardship of animals or the growing of crops.

Fig. 35 A view of Village Bay, Hirta, St Kilda, from the north with a cleit in foreground. A complex field system frames the settlement, with land divided into long linear plots stretching from the head dyke high on the valley sites to the sea. More recent Ministry of Defence buildings can be seen close to the harbour.

AMONGST THE RUINS

Perhaps the most distinctive feature of the landscape seen throughout the archipelago were cleitaen. These small, drystone buildings were invariably constructed on a slope with an entrance to the uphill side, and a downward step inside to create a flat interior. With turf roofs and doors of wood, or a simple moveable stone slab, they served as fridges, larders and drying rooms. Locally gathered peat turves, hay and potatoes, bird carcases and their eggs, the latter preserved in ashes, even manure, would be stored inside each cleit, waiting to be used by the residents of Village Bay or for transport to the mainland. Occasionally, the cleitaen were used to overwinter sheep.[26] Surveys from the Royal Commission on the Ancient and Historical Monuments of Scotland (RCAHMS) between 2007 and 2011 identified 1,337 cleitaen on Hirta, with a further 173 on the other islands and stacks.[27]

Life was dictated by the rhythm of the seasons, with the short days of dark winters lived largely in the black houses, shared with cattle in the adjacent byre, warmed by a peat-fuelled central hearth and lit by fulmar oil – an olfactory feast! Cleaning, carding and spinning of the wool from the native Soay sheep, later knitted or woven into cloth, was a typical winter occupation, as was general maintenance and repair. In the warmer spring and summer months, where seventeen-hour daylight is recorded in June, focus returned to lambing, and the return of migrating seabirds. Animals would be taken to summer pastures, in particular at Glean Mòr, another more sheltered combe in the northeast of Hirta, where the villagers would live in temporary accommodation. Stone bothies serving a similar function are also dotted across the islands, often close to the cleiten where the fruits of their seasonal labour would be stored.

Contact with the mainland was limited. St Kilda was a minor part of the large island territory of the MacLeod clan from the sixteenth century, and was owned by different branches of the family until 1931.[28] As such, a steward, factor or tacksman would visit in the summer months to collect rents, largely in the form of produce. But the reality was that the forty-mile gap of the Atlantic and dangerously stormy seas limited visitors. Consequently, the St Kildans developed little 'herd immunity' that might limit the impact of disease on more genetically diverse, open communities on the other less isolated islands and the mainland. In 1697, Martin recorded:

The inhabitants are about two hundred in number, and are well-proportioned; they speak the Irish language only; their habit is much like that used in the adjacent isles, but coarser. They are not subject to many diseases; they contract a cough as often as any strangers land and stay for any time among them, and it continues for some eight or ten days; they say the very infants on the breast are infected by it.[29]

The impact of such vulnerability showed to devastating effect thirty years later when, in 1727, an outbreak of smallpox reduced the resident population to just over thirty people (there is some suggestion that it might have been chickenpox). The number of deaths would have been greater but for the fact that three men and eight boys were accidentally marooned on Stac an Armin, an almost 200-metre sea stack off Boreray, on a fowling mission at the time. They were eventually rescued in May 1728 having survived the winter, returning to Hirta to find only one adult and eighteen children remaining. The virus was thought to have been carried to the island on the clothes of a St Kildan who had succumbed to the disease when visiting Harris in 1726. Within two weeks of the return of his deadly effects, ninety-four people had died.

A population of thirty was clearly not sustainable, so, after the smallpox outbreak, the MacLeods began a programme of repopulation, settling families from Harris and Skye on Hirta and remodelling the settlement at Village Bay. By 1764 there were ninety islanders comprising nineteen families and nine individuals.

Increasing contact with the other Hebridean islands and the mainland during the late eighteenth and nineteenth centuries brought more external influence to bear. Missionaries sought to address the 'popish' practices and relaxed Christian worship that previously existed on the island, while boats brought tourists to marvel at demonstrations of the St Kildans' cliff-climbing skills, women spinning or to pose patronizingly alongside the curious natives. More visitors, combined with malnutrition and the weakening impact of an imbalanced diet which included no fruit – the first apple seen on the island in the late nineteenth century 'caused a great deal of astonishment'[30] – led to a vulnerability to disease and infection. Martin noted incidents of leprosy in the late eighteenth century, while in the mid-nineteenth century the Reverend Mackenzie, the islands' minister, recorded:

> The diseases to which they are most subject are spotted fever (!), dyspepsia and nervous disorders, with swelling and bowing of their limbs. There is also the mysterious boat cough. In their own opinion they get it by infection when a boat comes from Harris . . . When hooping [sic] cough, measles, or scarlet fever visit the island, there are more than the average number of deaths.[31]

For the very young of St Kilda the chances of survival were shocking, with neo-natal tetanus responsible for the death of two-thirds of newborn babies for at least 150 years prior to 1920, albeit the main cause was likely to have been poor hygiene.[32]

The vulnerability of the islanders to disease is sadly illustrated by the decision of thirty-six St Kildans to emigrate to Australia in 1852, a decision sorely felt by the seventy-six who remained behind. Funded by the Highlands and Islands Emigration Society, eight families travelled to Glasgow by way of Harris and Skye, and then on the *Princess Royal* to join the *Priscilla* at Birkenhead, Liverpool, for the three-month journey to Melbourne.[33] Measles broke out on board amongst the 300 passengers, followed by dysentery and diarrhoea, leaving half the St Kildans dead by the time they arrived in Australia. Further deaths on landing with the immigration authorities in the quarantine station left just seventeen of the original islanders, including many orphans.[34] The St Kildans represented 12 per cent of *Priscilla*'s passengers, but accounted for 45 per cent of the deaths. Understandably, the tragic news deterred further significant attempts to emigrate from St Kilda, and the islanders' numbers remained at around seventy until the 1920s.

A hard life for the reduced population was made harder still by declining soil fertility on the already limited arable land. Here centuries-old use of peat ash and bird carcases as fertilizer led to increased accumulations of lead and zinc minerals in the soil.[35] Greater exposure to the outside world also opened the islanders' experience to relative luxuries of life beyond their dramatic home and simple, but hard lifestyles.

Eventually it became too much, exacerbated by a particularly harsh winter in 1929–30. More deaths of four young men from influenza in 1926, followed by Mary Gillies who, with her newly born daughter, died of pneumonia in 1930, contributed towards the thirty-six remaining islanders' request to be evacuated from St Kilda later that year:

Sir,

We the undersigned the natives of St Kilda, hereby respectfully pray and petition H.M. Government to assist us all to leave the island this year and to find homes and occupation for us on the mainland. For some years the man power has been decreasing, now the total population of the island is reduced to thirty six. Several men out of this number have definitely made up our minds to go away this year to such employment on the mainland. This will really cause a crisis as the present number are hardly sufficient to carry on the necessary work of the place. These men are the mainstay of the island at present, as they tend the sheep, do the weaving and look after the general welfare of the widows. Should they leave the conditions of the rest of the community would be such that it would be impossible for us to remain on the island another winter.

The reason why assistance is necessary is, that for many years Saint Kilda has not been self supporting, and with no facilities to better our position, we are therefore without the means to pay for the costs of removing ourselves and furniture elsewhere.

We do not ask to be settled together as a separate community, but in the meantime we would collectively be very grateful of assistance, and transference elsewhere, where there would be a better opportunity of securing our livelihood.[36]

The islanders were evacuated on the sloop HMS *Harebell* on 29 August 1930, with most resettling at Lochaline on Argyll's Morven peninsula. The majority of their 1,500 sheep and cattle went too, transported to the mainland on SS *Dunara Castle*. The men were given work with the Forestry Commission – an irony for islanders used to a landscape devoid of trees.

Fig. 36 Leaving St Kilda. On 29 August 1930 the final thirty-six St Kildans left the island. The ship's log records the end of 2,000 years of permanent occupation: 'Embarked the inhabitants of St Kilda. 08.02hrs weighed. Proceeded 11.5 knots.'

For the first time in thousands of years, St Kilda was no longer permanently occupied. The MacLeod family sold the islands to the Earl of Dumfries in 1931, who preserved it as a bird sanctuary. On his death in 1956 he bequeathed it to the current owners, the National Trust for Scotland (NTS). A year later the British Army and Royal Air Force began to construct a radar station on Hirta, as part of a tracking facility for a missile range on South Uist and Benbecula in the Outer Hebrides.

St Kilda was declared a UNESCO World Heritage Site in 1986, for its natural *and* cultural richness – the only mixed site in the UK. A management plan is now in place to protect the natural terrestrial and marine heritage of the islands and their relict cultural landscapes.[37] The islands contain the most important seabird colony in Europe, but these are threatened by climate change, which is warming the sea temperatures and causing the sand eels and plankton to shift further north in search of cooler seas.

Today civilian operators of the small military base are the only year-round occupants of the islands, albeit they are joined by NTS staff and visitors during the summer months. Alas none can imbibe at The Puff Inn, a more recent addition to St Kilda's history and for over fifty years Britain's most remote pub. It closed in 2019.

St Kilda demonstrates the impact of disease on historic communities which possess little or no natural immunity due to their isolation, distance or lack of contact. It is a story repeated globally, whether on small island societies, such as Fiji, Samoa and Rapa Nui from the eighteenth century (see below), or to entire civilizations. The arrival of Europeans to the Americas during the sixteenth century brought influenza, smallpox, mumps and measles to a continent without any prior instances, and which subsequently had a devastating effect on the Inca, Aztec and indigenous North American populations.

The Covid-19 crisis of 2020–22 is a stark reminder of the impact of disease on today's society. Recognizing their special vulnerability, many small island and remote communities closed themselves to the outside world. This was prompted by ambitions to control the spread of disease and the limited facilities to tackle it should it arrive, more than by any lack of immunity. At the same time the crisis provoked a marked shift in where people wanted to live, prompted by the ease of working from home. The UK housing market was at a premium for those who wished to move to the countryside, with property prices increasing by up to 30 per cent in the popular rural locations easily accessed from London and other cities.[38] At its extreme, the attraction of remote mountain or island locations was revealed by the dearth of holiday accommodation availability while rules permitted people to travel.[39] The irony, of course, is that while sparsely occupied rural communities have a special appeal during times when a human-borne virus is rife, they often remain the places least able to cope with either outbreak or influx because of their very isolation.

Rapa Nui (Easter Island), Chile

There are few more popular places in the petri dish under the micro-scope of collapsology than Rapa Nui. And it is easy to see why.

Nine hundred gigantic staring heads on a remote, treeless pacific island with a small indigenous population were bound to raise questions from the moment of European discovery, and have done so ever since.

The critical statistics are that Rapa Nui, or Easter Island, 164 square kilometres of volcanic rock located 3,700 kilometres off the coast of Chile, may once have sustained a population of up to 17,500 people. By 1722, this had been reduced to 3,000 and in 1877 only 111 indigenous Rapa Nui were recorded. What brought about the collapse of a culture that created the extraordinary *moai* sculptures and remained isolated from other external influences for over a millennium?

Rapa Nui defines 'remote'. Not only is it nearly 4,000 kilometres from Chile, but its nearest neighbours are the forty-seven residents of Pitcairn Island 2,000 kilometres distant. Not an easy trip to borrow a cup of sugar. Santiago is closer to the borders of Colombia, Venezuela, Guyana and other countries on South America's northern Atlantic coast than it is to Chile's special territory. Which makes the feat of initial discovery and occupation by prehistoric Polynesian peoples even more impressive.

Fig. 37 *A View of the Monuments of Easter Island*, Rapa Nui, *c.* 1776. William Hodges was appointed by the Admiralty to record the places discovered on Cook's second voyage (1772–5); his paintings of the Pacific are vivid records of British exploration.

Where did it all start? The story of Rapa Nui is typically framed as 'mysterious'. The island's combination of isolation, astonishing heritage and other-worldliness has created a voyeuristic attention which is unique. The weight of scientific research into the island is matched by unscientific speculation, and there is as much disagreement within those communities as there is across them. 'I know of no other place which has been so battered by the lunatic fringe . . . Wild theories range from spacemen to elephant power [on moving the statues].'[40] Part of the challenge in unravelling Rapa Nuian history is that the indigenous peoples almost disappeared from the human record, so the oral traditions that persist have their origins in a tiny number of survivors. There is a script – *Rongorongo* – comprising a basic core corpus of 120 geometrical shapes, human, animal (such as frigate birds, turtles and squid) and plant glyphs, but it does not survive in significant quantities and remains undeciphered. In short, every twist and turn of Rapa Nui's story is up for debate, and this includes the date of the first settlement of the island, and by whom.

Carbon and obsidian hydration dating suggests that Rapa Nui was first settled sometime between 800 and 1000 CE, and by Polynesian peoples probably from the Mangareva Islands in what is now French Polynesia.[41] In 1947 the Norwegian explorer and ethnographer Thor Heyerdahl sought to prove a link that looked the other way. There was a connection, he argued, between South America and Polynesia and he sought to prove it by successfully sailing a balsa-wood raft, the *Kon-Tiki*, across the Pacific from Callao in Peru to Tuamotus. Heyerdahl's pseudo-scientific hypothesis was in part based on the similarities between pre-Columbian statuary and Rapa Nui's *moai*, and on the precise, mortar-free construction techniques that were favoured by the Incas and the Rapa Nui. Despite the eye-catching 6,900-kilometre journey, Heyerdahl's migration theory was disproved by the strong linguistic, DNA and archaeological evidence that linked Rapa Nui to a chain of island-hopping migrations that spread from Southeast Asia. Hitihiti, a Tahitian who travelled with Captain James Cook when he visited Rapa Nui in 1774 on his second voyage, sailing in the *Resolution*, was able to understand and translate for his distantly related fellow Polynesians without difficulty. Regardless of the *Kon-Tiki*'s failure to convince, it was a boat that launched a thousand other experimental ships. A reconstruction of a Polynesian vessel took just nineteen days to reach Rapa Nui from Mangareva, compared with *Kon-Tiki*'s 101 days, which further argued against the latter's efficacy. *Kon-Tiki2* set off from Lima in 2015 making Rapa Nui in forty-three days, but the two rafts of the expedition were both abandoned mid-ocean on the return leg.

Inevitably, the archaeological evidence from the earliest occupation of Rapa Nui is ephemeral and elusive. Excavations tell us that the initial settlers were proficient offshore fishers, using hooked lines to catch large pelagic fish such as jacks, wrasses, nibblers and tuna. Hens, petrels, terns and boobies were also on the menu, alongside sea urchins.[42] Polynesian rats were present, arriving as early stowaways and as food during the first migrations, much to the detriment of the bird population and, possibly, the native palm trees.

The early settlers brought with them an ancestor cult which developed as one of the world's most spectacular cultural landscapes. The *moai* statues, the icon of Rapa Nui, begin to appear across the

Fig. 38 Rano Raraku quarry as drawn by Katherine Routledge in 1914.

island from the 1100s CE. These giant torsos were shaped from volcanic tuff in the Rano Raraku quarry on the slopes of the volcano from which it took its name. Softened with water, the stone was chiselled by hand using *toki*, basalt picks, into statues that ranged from 2 to 20 metres tall. The quarry contains half of Rapa Nui's 887 *moai* sculptures in varying stages of completion. It resembles something of a factory, with examples of new *moai* shapes simply picked out in the rock or left almost complete only with a 'keel' of rock remaining, through to finished statues upright and buried in quarry waste at the entrance, presumably awaiting transportation. Some might never have been destined for travel and remain as guardians, while others were left in the coffin-shaped holes from which they were being crafted, possibly abandoned, as surmised by Katherine Routledge, because of faults or hard inclusions:

> In other instances the sculptors have been unlucky enough to come across at important points one or more of the hard nodules with which their tools could not deal, and as the work could not go down to posterity with a large wart on its nose or excrescence on its chin, it has had to be stopped.[43]

From the quarry, the statues were moved along specially constructed ceremonial roads to various destinations across the island. Some may have been abandoned along the way, or were deliberately left to mark the route. How they were moved is another debate that has split the academic community and fostered yet more reconstructions. Use of wooden rollers or rocking the statues side to side using teams with ropes are equally plausible, with the latter matching oral traditions recorded at the end of the nineteenth century that the *moai* 'walked'.[44] Rollers, however, might be less prone to accidental damage en route, an important consideration given the significant investment of time and resources. Other suggestions, such as of the use of sledges lubricated by crushed yams, are unnecessarily tortuous, while attribution to alien transportation descends into a realm of lunatic explanation which Rapa Nui frequently attracts.

There is an evolution in the completed *moai*, with the earlier examples being smaller, more rounded and with circular eyes, while the later 'classic' statues are large and angular, with long heads, eyes and noses, jutting chins and extended ears with stretched piercings. The common perception that the statues were simply heads can largely be attributed to the buried examples outside Rano Raraku quarry: excavations have since revealed that their torsos account for over half of most completed *moai*. Their arms are typically by their sides, clasped to bodies that usually end just above the thighs. Excavation has also shown that some *moai* are carved with petroglyphs on their backs, which may have eroded on those which are wholly exposed to the elements. Evidence of red pigments suggests that they were decorated, and their eye sockets once included obsidian or scoria pupils against a white coral background. Some of the statues are crowned by *pukao*, hats or topknots made from red scoria which came from a different volcanic quarry at Puna Pau in the southwest of the island.

Aside from the *moai* in Rano Raraku quarry, or those marking the route, the vast majority of remaining statues are located on Rapa Nui's coastline. Here they were placed looking inland on ceremonial platforms called *ahu*. There are over 300 *ahu* on the island, the largest at Ahu Tongariki which defines a complex of fifteen *moai*. These platforms typically include a central platform to hold the sculptures, with wings either side and a ramp to the front. Made of tuff or scoria, the walls were finely jointed and without mortar. Not every *ahu* was topped by statues, but all served as political, social and religious centres for the various clans and extended family groups of Rapa Nui. The platform was a place of gathering, of ceremony and celebration, and a place dedicated to ancestor worship, hence the presence of the *moai*. The *moai* are generally recognized to be the representation of deified ancestors and chiefs, able to protect the Rapa Nui clans, ensure fertility of people, land and sea, and guarantee a connection with the spiritual world. Their relationship with the sea is important, as it was to most Polynesian peoples, who saw their origins in the mythical island of Hiva far to the west. On death the spirits would return to the ocean and travel back to Hiva in a reverse of the great ancestral sea voyages with which so many Polynesian cultures identify.

Physically and spiritually linked to the sea was the village of Orongo, which is perched on the lip of the Ranu Kau caldera in

Fig. 39 The ceremonial village of Orongo perched on the lip of the Ranu Kau caldera. The grass-covered roofs of the settlement are in the left foreground, on the cliff edge where it narrows as the volcano meets the sea.

the far southwest corner of the island. Fifty-four stone-built houses, each up to 12 metres long and many distinctly boat-shaped in plan, make up a ceremonial complex which was only partially occupied during the year. Orongo was the centre of the bird-man cult, a religious introduction which emerged during the sixteenth century, and is depicted on some of the 1,700 petroglyphs and wall paintings recorded in the village. The *Hoa Hakanani'a Moai*, the sole ancestral sculpture from Orongo, was later carved with the *tangata manu* (bird man) on his back. He is now in the British Museum, having been transported to England on HMS *Topaze* in 1868–9. His name, appropriately, means 'lost, hidden, or stolen friend'.

Discussion of Rapa Nui's cultural traditions tends to concentrate on the *moai, ahu* and Orongo, but the island has a rich vernacular architecture which is often overlooked and under-researched. Basalt stone houses, either the elliptically shaped *paenga* similar to those found at Orongo but with thatched roofs that looked like upturned boats, or round *hare oka*, were the most commonplace, alongside *hare moa*, chicken houses.

The great 'mystery' of Rapa Nui is framed along the lines of 'Who made the *moai* heads?', 'What were they for?' and 'How were they moved?' In truth, these are relatively easily explained. The real debate focuses on when and why the population of indigenous islanders collapsed. For many decades the prevailing narrative has been one of ecocide which happened before first contact with Europeans in the eighteenth century, followed by successive waves of loss because of disease and slavery. In this model a growing Rapa Nui population, potentially as large as 17,500 people, cut down the palm trees that once cloaked the island, clearing the land to produce more food, but also utilizing the trees for their buildings, boats and to help transport the *moai*.[45] A disastrous consequence of the tree loss, which is recorded in the pollen record, was the exposure of the island's soils to wind and rain, leading to leaching, deterioration, and a significant reduction in fertility. No trees meant no boats, so the islanders' ability to supplement diminishing productivity on land was not balanced by traditional deep-sea fishing. Loss of boats also meant that they were effectively trapped, with emigration closed to them as a solution. Competition for food led to intra-tribal conflict, and increased cannibalism. The old gods of the ancestors were rejected, having failed to provide for their people in favour of the new cult of the bird man, and the *moai* were deliberately cast down in a great statue toppling. Rapa Nui society had effectively suffered a dramatic population loss through starvation and conflict before the Dutch Admiral Jacob Roggeveen arrived with a small flotilla of three ships on Easter Day in 1722.

There are variations to this theory, notably that the island's cover of *Jubaea* palm trees was not lost because they were solely cut down by the Rapa Nui, but also because its regeneration was prevented by rats. With few natural predators, save humans, the population of Polynesian rats introduced to the island by the settlers, grew unchecked on a diet that included the roots, seeds and nuts of the palms. Such was the appetite of the flourishing population that the seedbank available for trees dwindled, contributing significantly to deforestation. A similar theory has been used to explain the deforestation of the Ewa Plain in Oahu, Hawaii, which pre-dated the arrival of humans by over two centuries.

However, this collapse-by-ecocide theory is roundly rejected by others. An alternative argument for the disappearance of Rapa Nui's indigenous population is placed firmly at the door of the European settlers, who disrupted a way of life that was coping with a changing balance of resources. In this model its champions first dispute the more generous estimates of Rapa Nui's population, arguing that the island was never home to more than 3,000 to 5,000 people.[46] This makes sense given that there is little evidence to back up estimations of nearly 20,000 islanders, which by turn were perhaps put forward to justify the construction of an impressive array of *moai*, rather than explain the absence of hundreds of long-lived villages which might support it. If the population was in the low thousands, then there was no significant demographic crash. Next, the disappearance of Rapa Nui's tree cover is unravelled: today, the island's absence of woodland is hard to deny, but the date and extent of its loss is disputed. Roggeveen's men set foot on the island for a single day, 10 April, having anchored offshore since 5 April, hence *Paasch-Eyland* or Easter Island. It is described as 'sandy and barren' albeit the sandy nature was due to the fact that 'we mistook the parched-up grass, and hay or other scorched and charred brushwood for a soil of that arid nature, because from its outward appearance it suggested no other idea than that of an extraordinarily sparse and meagre vegetation'.[47] One day's observation of a small part of a mountainous island does not make a sound scientific evidence base that confirms early ecological disaster. Evidence for conflict and cannibalism is similarly challenged. In reality, there is clear evidence of a change to Rapa Nui's landscape, but this probably represents a gradual loss of tree-cover and human adaptation to it, rather than the apocalyptic disaster of those who favour ecocide.

What is less disputable is the impact of European settlers on the indigenous Rapa Nui. There was a gap of almost fifty years between Roggeveen's brief visit in 1722 and that of two Spanish ships commanded by Felipe Gonzales in 1770, during which the admiral took possession of the island of San Carlos (20 November 1770), with all the accustomed ceremonies in the name of the King of Spain – an annexation soon forgotten given the lack of obvious resources and difficulties of reaching the new colony. From then on other explorers arrived in quick succession including the English captain James Cook in 1774 and the French admiral La Pérouse in 1786. As Rapa Nui began to appear on the map, so it too saw the arrival of predatory vessels, including *Nancy*, a schooner from Connecticut which took 'twelve men and ten women [who] fell into his hands alive' after a bloody battle in around 1805.[48] This and the arrival of other slavers clearly accounted for the unwelcoming reception afforded the Russian Admiral Otto von Kotzebüe when he came across the island in 1816, departing after just one day.

Early encounters with European and American vessels, documented and otherwise, brought disease. Whalers, sealers and others introduced smallpox, tuberculosis and syphilis to a population without any build-up of natural immunity, a story which repeated itself throughout the remainder of the century.

The most catastrophic event took place in 1862, when slavers sought workers for Peru's guano islands and its mainland sugar plantations. For forty years from 1840, Peru's guano boom, a forerunner to Chile's nitrate story (see chapter 5), dominated the new country's emerging economy. Driven by the demand for fertilizer from Europe and North America, and supported by significant investment by British and other companies, the 'mining' of guano from the islands off the coast required mass labour. The new South American republics had for the most part banned the use of slaves from the Caribbean and West Africa, resulting in the immigration of large numbers of Chinese labourers as a cheap and plentiful source of workers. Chinese immigration was temporarily abolished in 1856, albeit ships continued to arrive, but the result was an insufficiency of workers to cope with a seemingly insatiable demand. The guano business community began to look elsewhere, and in 1862 Joseph Byrne was granted permission to import indigenous peoples from the Pacific; his first ship *Adelante* landed in Callao, Lima's seaport, with 266 islanders from the Cook Islands.

In late December 1862 eight ships approached Rapa Nui's western coast. There are varying accounts for how the islanders were enslaved, some as willing indentured servants (doubtless to be disappointed when faced with the reality of servitude on arrival in Peru), others were captured as they climbed aboard to trade, and yet more were enticed by 'mirrors, pipes, and other trinkets' on land, before being 'trussed up like sheep'.[49] A total of at least eighteen ships landed on

Fig. 40 Ships at the Chincha Islands during the height of Peru's guano boom, 1864. During this period over 12 million tons of guano were extracted for fertilizer, requiring the labour of enslaved peoples, prisoners and indentured Chinese miners.

Rapa Nui as part of the 1862–3 slaving mission, some to capture locals, while others had begun to use the island as a stop-off point on the long journey between the other Polynesian islands further west and mainland Peru to the east. Peruvian records show 2,069 Polynesians arriving in Callao, of which 1,353 were Rapa Nui and included the king, his son and priests. Others would have died en route or landed at different ports, so the number is likely higher. Once in Peru the Rapa Nui either worked in the guano industry or were drafted into domestic service and the fields. Many died, mostly of infectious diseases such as tuberculosis, dysentery or smallpox, not helped by both a lack of natural immunity and lack of vaccination which was available to the general population.

Reaction in Peru was mixed. Those who benefited from the raids sought to justify them as an introduction to civilized Christian society or as the recruitment of 'colonists', but public opinion moved swiftly against the slavers. The trade was banned in 1863, with many islanders held in a warehouse in Callao waiting transfer back to the Pacific. A particularly bad outbreak of smallpox hastened their departure and two of the ships involved in the first raid to the Cook Islands, the

AMONGST THE RUINS

Barbara Gomez and *Adelante*, set off to take 842 islanders home. Only 50 of the 360 Polynesians on the *Barbara Gomez* arrived on the Austral Islands, while none of *Adelante*'s human cargo of 482 survived disease and shipwreck on Cocos Island. The arrival of just 15 out of 100 Rapa Nui who set out from Peru as part of the wider programme of Peruvian repatriation was no less disastrous. The smallpox which killed their shipborne companions went on to ravage the island community, reducing Rapa Nui's already depleted, leaderless population to around 600 people.

There is more. After the cumulative disasters of the first seventy years of the nineteenth century, life for the small number of remaining Rapa Nui was to get no easier. With the hereditary leaders dead and the fabric of traditional Rapa Nui society completely disrupted by disease and emigration, forced and otherwise, the ability of the indigenous community to stand against further external changes was minimal. Jean-Baptiste Dutroux-Bornier, a French soldier, mariner and criminal, delivered two missionaries to the island in 1866. He returned over the following years seeking indentured labourers for the Maison Brander Company, a powerful Tahitian-based trading family, who married into the Tahitian royal family, and who required labourers for their coconut plantations. An opportunist, Dutroux-Bornier settled on Rapa Nui in 1868, purchasing land and inveigling his way into power by kidnap and violence. His aim to make the island a French protectorate, doubtless with himself as the governor, did not come about, but the wholesale conversion of the land to sheep ranching did, financed by Brander:

> After burning the natives' huts, Dutroux-Bornier had all their sweet potatoes pulled out of the ground three times, to facilitate the persuasion of the starving natives, who had thus little hope of surviving on their own island.[50]

The islanders' survival rates on Tahiti and Moorea were poor. At least a third of the 241 Rapa Nui transported in 1871 died within two years, either from malnourishment, disease or ill treatment.[51] Through such means of purchase, coercion, seizure and forced emigration, Dutroux-Bornier acquired nearly all the island, with the remaining Rapa Nui confined to the village of Hanga Roa. Dutroux-Bornier was murdered in 1876, but the damage was done. By 1877 we reach the shocking figure of just 111 indigenous Rapa Nui on the island, a people physically restricted to a small corner, disconnected from their cultural landscape to be replaced by sheep.

Alexandre Ari'ipaea Salmon, a relative of the Branders, became de facto ruler during the 1880s, acquiring further land, and introducing coconut plantations. He sold the Brander Easter Island estate to the Chilean government in 1888, which annexed the remainder of the island in the same year. The voice of the Rapa Nui in all negotiations appears to be completely forgotten, as the Chilean state leased most of the land to the *Compañía Explotadora de la Isla de Pascua*, a subsidiary of British-owned Williamson-Balfour, for sheep ranching until 1953. Some 700,000 sheep had the freedom of the island, while in contrast a detention centre was created in Hanga Roa:

> It was surrounded by a barbed-wire enclosure with two gates in it, and no one was allowed to pass through them without the permission of the Chilean military leader. At six in the afternoon these gates were locked . . .[52]

The Rapa Nui continued to be excluded from their ancestral lands after the Chilean Navy took over the island in 1953 up until 1966, when they were finally given Chilean citizenship. Some small balance was restored in the late 1960s when laws were passed authorizing the Chilean president to grant land titles to the Rapa Nui and restrict its transfer to non-indigenous peoples. However, General Pinochet's dictatorship brought more nepotism as land was illegally privatized and sold to outsiders. At the same time the island began to attract attention both as a tourist destination and as a focus for the conservation movement, aided by the ability to reach it by air via Mataveri Airport, which opened in 1967 and was lengthened with US support via NASA twenty years later. Today it's an aspirational bucket-list destination for millions, with tourism being a major driver for the economy.

In 2020 there were approximately 5,000 inhabitants living on Rapa Nui, 3,000 of whom were indigenous peoples.[53] By contrast, up until 2020, Rapa Nui was visited by between 80,000–100,000 tourists each year. In March 2020 the local government locked down

Rapa Nui in response to the Covid-19 pandemic, and the island remained closed to tourists until March 2022.

In terms of a case study into our human contribution towards the loss of civilizations, Rapa Nui has it all: humankind's relationship with a challenging and changing ecosystem, the impact of conflict and disease, people's inhumanity to our fellows, colonization and political alienation. Climate change and the future direction of the island's biggest industry – tourism – will be the next drivers for change. Perhaps Rapa Nui's greatest surprise is not the 'mysterious' culture of *moai* heads but that any small island nation could survive such successive waves of unexpected challenge. In this context it is perhaps time to stop framing Rapa Nui as an example of what can go wrong, but as a testament to the fragility *and* extraordinary resilience of indigenous peoples.

CHAPTER 4

WAR

Our diverse and unequal world is riven with political, ethical, economic and religious difference, which, at its extremes, has forever spilled out into military action. Lawrence Keeley estimated that 90–95 per cent of societies engage in war.[1] Cautious estimates suggest that almost 15,000 wars 'have taken place between 3500 BCE and the late 20th century, costing 3.5 billion lives, leaving only 300 years of peace'. This is borne out by the archaeological record, which is rich in the monumental structures and remains of conflict, from Iron Age hillforts, medieval castles and Cold War listening stations, to battlefields and cemeteries filled with those who have died a violent death. Conquest and subjugation are familiar partners in the fall and disappearance of culture.

For the first story we travel to Nimrud near Mosul. The area, at the source of the Tigris and Euphrates in northwest Iraq, was once the heartland of the Neo-Assyrian Empire (911–616 BCE), one of the world's most important early civilizations. Aššur, Nimrud, Nineveh and Dur-Sharrukin were each one-time capital cities in a territory that stretched from modern-day Turkey to Egypt and the Persian Gulf. The empire disintegrated after the death of Ashurbanipal, overrun by its former vassal states, the Medes and Babylonians, and the cities were largely abandoned. In that moment of transition from one power to another it was not only the rulers who were vanquished, but the buildings and temples that were their symbols of power. This deliberate breakage of the bonds with the past included smashing the decorative panels that lined the palace walls, looting the treasury and stores, and defacing sculpture that once celebrated Assyrian kingship.

Such events are repeated down the timeline of history, from Alexander's destruction of Persepolis in Iran and Cato's constantly repeated incitement to genocide (possibly the first recorded in history): *Delenda est Carthago* ('Carthage must be destroyed' – in 146 BCE) to the present day, as illustrated by a return to Nimrud in the twenty-first century.

In 2015 bulldozers flattened the 2,900-year-old ziggurat at Ancient Assyria's former capital, pushing it into the River Tigris. Nearby, the northwest palace was ransacked, and many of the lamassu, the characteristic half-man/half-bull statues which guarded the temple and palace entrances, were destroyed or removed. During the same campaign, ISIS terrorists rampaged through Mosul's Museum smashing statues recovered from nearby Nineveh, where they also demolished parts of the ancient city walls including the Mashki and Adad gates. A similar pattern of destruction took place at Dur-Sharrukin, compounded this time by further damage as Kurdish Peshmerga forces dug into the site to create an offensive position. ISIS's murderous rampage from 2014 to 2017 in and around Mosul, and their symbolic targeting of ancient sites will be used to tell a less well-known story of cultural destruction that is mirrored elsewhere in places such as Bamiyan in Afghanistan and Palmyra, Syria.

'Look what civilization has done to barbarism,' wrote Victor Hugo of the looting and subsequent destruction of the Chinese summer palace, Yuanmingyuan, by British and French forces in 1860, and the subject of our second story. Hugo's outrage was directed at an episode near the end of the Second Opium War during which European troops ran amok in the imperial palace of the Qianlong Emperor near Beijing. Officers stepped aside while frenzied looting took place, removing thousands of items of gold, jade, stone and marble carvings, porcelain and the clepsydra, a showpiece fountain that included twelve bronze animal heads from which water would spout to indicate the time. In a final official act, Lord Elgin, the British High Commissioner, ordered the burning of the early eighteenth-century palace. The site has been largely abandoned ever since. For the British and French foot soldiers pillage brought much-needed financial gain. Many items eventually found their way into the great

AMONGST THE RUINS

European museums, as well as into numerous private collections. The case remains live today, with China insistent on the repatriation of artefacts from the collection, and prepared to intervene at the highest political and economic levels to achieve that aim.

For the final story, we remain in China. On 1 June 1966 *The People's Daily*, the official mouthpiece of the Chinese Communist Party, published an editorial which entreated its readers to demolish 'all the old ideology and culture and all the old customs and habits, which, fostered by the exploiting classes, have poisoned the minds of the people for thousands of years'. The chapter will conclude with an exploration of the loss of heritage because of political, ideological and religious difference – a proxy war fought against cultural heritage. During China's Cultural Revolution, the Communist Party launched a campaign to destroy the *Four Olds* – old customs, old culture, old habits and old ideas. In 1966, the first year of the Cultural Revolution, the statues within the 2000-year-old temple of Confucius in Shandong were systematically destroyed. Over the course of twenty-nine days 100,000 classical texts were burned or pulped, over 6,000 cultural artefacts and 1,000 stelae were broken up, the interior of the temple was wrecked, and at least 2,000 graves were excavated in the cemetery. The true impact of Mao's programme of cultural destruction is difficult to assess, but the localized statistics are themselves compelling; for example 4,922 of 6,843 officially designated 'historical interest' sites in Beijing were destroyed.

These are just some of the ways in which civilizations and the cultural heritage connected to them are subjugated and lost.

Nimrud, Iraq

> *Out of that land he went forth into Assyria, and built Nineveh, Rehoboth Ir, Calah . . .*
>
> GENESIS 10.11

This is a story of the loss of a great city, not once, but three times. The first loss is a familiar tale of a once important place, conquered and rendered irrelevant by the new regime. The second is of the excavation and redistribution (or theft) of its sculpture, writing

Fig. 41 Nimrud from the air in the 1950s, showing the great ziggurat and citadel.

and architecture across the world. The third is of the destruction of heritage as an act of war. The great city? Nimrud in northern Iraq.

Nimrud is one of the most evocative places in Mesopotamian history. Identified by biblical scholars as *Calah* and known as *Kalhu* in Assyrian, it was a city said to have been established by Nimrod, 'the hunter' and the great grandson of Noah. No one knows when Calah turned into Nimrud or vice versa, except that the eponymous title was used by Arabic-speaking locals at least as early as the eighteenth century when the site was visited by Carsten Niebuhr, the Danish/German explorer, in 1766. Through that one connection, place and personality became linked in a melange of biblical narrative and ancient mythology.

Located just above the junction of the Tigris and the Greater Zab, Nimrud was already a 300-year-old city by the time the Assyrian king, Ashurnasirpal II (883–859 BCE), made it his capital at the expense of Assur 80 kilometres away. Assur, the place and god from which the Assyrians took their name, had been the principal religious city of the Assyrian Empire since its inception in 2025 BCE. But Ashurnasirpal wanted a statement of his authority, a place associated with his power and rise to kingship.

AMONGST THE RUINS

Ashurnasirpal succeeded his father Tukulti-Ninurta II in re-establishing the Assyrian Empire as an aggressive, expansive force after the Middle Assyrian Empire's quiet contraction from 1050 BCE. His rule saw Assyrian domination extend from the Mediterranean to Iran, and was contrarily characterized by the strong patronage of art and learning alongside the brutal repression of opponents.

The city is his biography. Most of what we know about Ashurnasirpal comes from Nimrud's remarkable collection of inscriptions and carved reliefs that recorded and amplified his achievements:

> In my wisdom, I came to Kalḫu and cleared away the old hill of debris. I dug down to the water level. I built up a terrace . . . and upon that erected my royal throne, and for my own enjoyment I built eight beautiful halls . . . I painted on the walls of palaces, in bright blue paint . . . I had lapis lazuli-coloured glazed bricks made and set them above the gates . . .

From these cuneiform and pictorial biographies we learn that Nimrud was built by the slaves of Ashurnasirpal's newly conquered domains; we hear about his temples, shrines and hanging gardens watered by a newly built canal from the Greater Zab where 'the pomegranates glow in the pleasure garden like the stars in the sky, they are entwined like grapes on the vine . . .'; and of an exotic zoo where the king kept animals or those given as gifts, such as elephants, bears, leashed monkeys and 'sea creatures', probably dolphins from the Mediterranean. Wild cats featured strongly too, including fifteen lions and fifty cubs that were captured, brought to Nimrud in cages, and bred in great numbers. They were slightly more fortunate than the '. . . 370 great lions I killed with my hunting spears . . .'

Aside from his brightly decorated palaces, Ashurnasirpal commissioned temples to Ninurta (the Assyrian name for Ningirsu; see chapter 3) and Enlil, guarding each with massive lamassu, protective winged deities with human heads and the bodies of lions or bulls.

The banquet celebrating the official inauguration of the city was appropriately hyperbolic. Nearly 70,000 attended, including delegates from across Ashurnasirpal's empire, as well as 16,000 inhabitants of Nimrud and 1,500 palace officials. Lasting ten days, they feasted on:

. . . 1,000 fattened head of cattle, 1,000 calves, 10,000 stable sheep, 15,000 lambs – for my lady Ishtar [alone] 200 head of cattle [and] 1,000 sihhu-sheep – 1,000 spring lambs, 500 stages, 500 gazelles, 1,000 ducks, 500 geese, 500 kurku-geese, 1,000 mesuku-birds, 1,000 qaribu-birds, 10,000 doves, 10,000 sukanunu-doves, 10,000 other [assorted] small birds, 10,000 [assorted] fish, 10,000 jerboa, 10,000 [assorted] eggs . . . 10,000 [jars of] beer, 10,000 skins with wine . . . 1,000 wood crates with vegetables, 300 [containers with] oil . . . 100 [containers with] fine mixed beer . . . 100 pistachio cones . . .

– before being sent back 'healthy and happy, to their own countries'.[2]

Ashurnasirpal's son, Shalmaneser III (858–823 BCE), consolidated his father's achievements at Nimrud, building an even larger palace and the Great Ziggurat that dominated the skyline in the northwest corner of the citadel. This massive, stepped pyramid, at least 50 square metres at the base, was made from unbaked clay bricks faced by baked versions of the same, some inscribed with Shalmaneser's name. Partly incorporated into the citadel's walls, the ziggurat stood up to 45 metres high and was physically as well as spiritually connected to the temple and shrine of Ninurta immediately to the south.[3] A home to the god, probably with a shrine on the uppermost platform, the ziggurat would have been accessible only by the priests of the temple. In the extensive town beyond the citadel, Shalmaneser's new palace combined a royal residence with an arsenal, complete with barracks, armoury magazines, tribute stores and workshops, from which large numbers of carved Phoenician ivories were discovered in the nineteenth century. These and others found in the citadel comprise one of the greatest collections of ivories in the world.

The new capital was enclosed by a fortified wall, 9 kilometres long, and in its heyday at the turn of the eighth century BCE it would have been home to 75,000 people. Nimrud continued to be an important capital throughout the following century, as illustrated by the extraordinary richness of several royal tombs found in the Northwest Palace. The burial chambers of Mullissu-Mu-kannishat-Ninua (consort of Ashurnasirpal II), Yaba, Banitu, Atalia and Hama, all Assyrian queens, revealed jewellery, much of it made of gold. Crowns and diadems, earrings and necklaces, bracelets, anklets and finger rings were complemented by clothing and grave goods that rivalled the more famous discoveries made in the great tombs of Egypt.

Nimrud was an important city: the urban centre of the world's most powerful and sophisticated empire of the period. But its precedence stemmed from its association with the king, both as his residence as a demigod and as his military and bureaucratic centre. And whereas Ashurnasirpal's immediate successors chose to build on his legacy, making it their own, others inevitably wanted a different capital to mark their ascendency. In 706 BCE King Sargon II declared Dur-Sharrukin (Khorsabad) the new centre of the Neo-Assyrian Empire. Already ten years in construction, Dur-Sharrukin remained the capital for just one year, when Sargon was killed in an ambush while on campaign in 705 BCE. Sennacherib, his son, regarded his father's death as an omen from unhappy gods who had not been given due prominence in the new city, and subsequently made the ancient town of Nineveh (modern-day Mosul) his capital in 701 BCE. While Nimrud lost its rank as the foremost city in the Neo-Assyrian Empire, it continued as a provincial centre and retained its leading role for scholarship, focused on the Temple of Nabu, god of wisdom and writing, and its extensive libraries.

The first true loss of Nimrud was as part of the tumultuous events that marked the end of empire. After the strong leadership of Sennacherib, his son Esarhaddon and grandson Ashurbanipal, the succession of Assyrian kingship descended into argument and then crisis, made worse by the rise of external powers. Nineveh fell in 612 BCE to an alliance of former Assyrian subjects – Babylonians from the south and west and Medes from the north and east – who '. . . carried off the city's vast booty, and the temple (and)[turned] the city into a ruin heap'.[4] With the collapse of the capital other cities were quick to follow. Nimrud was no exception and as a former royal centre it was subject to a purposeful act of humiliation by the new conquerors – a ritual smashing of the temples and symbols of the Neo-Assyrian regime. This 'ultra-violence' was not only an act of revenge, but a campaign to sever the power of Ashurnasirpal and his successors, rendering them blind, mute and broken.[5] Throughout the palaces and temples, the reliefs of the king, which had once so haughtily boasted his achievements, were:

. . . blinded, their lips and ears removed, their pointing fingers severed, bowstrings cut, the accompanying genies stabbed with a burning torch and their fingers holding the 'sacred cone' cut, and the all-seeing hovering figure of the god Ashur partially pounded away before the entire relief was split with wedges.[6]

The thoroughness of such decommissioning of the conquered is reinforced in another example from Nimrud. Here, not only are the king and his protective genie symbolically mutilated, but a sinister new head is carved into the relief which stares directly at the neutered ruler:

His personal legacy is transformed to that of an eternal helpless mute, devoid of his senses, manhood, worldly power and godly support, forever haunted and taunted by a ghostly Iranian nemesis in an endless nightmare of a total reversal of fortunes.[7]

Fig. 42 A defaced Assyrian relief from Nimrud (Kalhu) showing Ashurnasirpal II (centre) with damage to his hand, eyes, nose, beard, Achilles tendon and bow, and a crudely added genie, shown as a ghostly figure staring directly at the king on his right.

Some settlers returned to the city, squatting in the ruins of the demolished buildings, but Xenophon, the Greek soldier and historian, passing Nimrud over 200 years later, described it as deserted. Village life in and around the area certainly continued over the succeeding centuries, but the great city slowly crumbled into obscurity.

The second loss of Nimrud was directly linked to its rediscovery by Europeans during the mid-nineteenth century. Prior to this the city had been reduced to a quarry by men working for the provincial Ottoman governor. However, at a time of expanding rivalry between the empires of France, Great Britain and Russia, travellers to the region began to bring back tantalizing glimpses of the great Mesopotamian civilizations. Expeditions by antiquarian adventurers such as Claudius Rich and Paul-Émile Botta resulted in the export of the first carved reliefs and lamassu back to the British Museum in London and the Musée du Louvre in Paris, and a growing public appetite for more.

In 1845 a young British archaeologist, Henry Layard, with the backing and financial support of Sir Stratford Canning, the British ambassador to Istanbul (cousin of Prime Minister George Canning), and with permission from the Ottoman government, began to excavate Nimrud. Layard's motivation was largely one of romantic discovery at the cutting edge of the extended Grand Tour, while Canning's was personal glory and to 'beat the Louvre hollow'.[8] Through luck and enthusiasm Layard's first season brought immediate success. After just two days his team had uncovered alabaster-lined chambers and gilded ivories. Spurred on by these early discoveries he went on to find the palaces of Ashurnasirpal and Shalmaneser III, and within them miles of carved reliefs and thousands of artefacts. This was proto-archaeology – half scientific research, half treasure-hunting consisting of crude trenching and tunnelling along walls to find carved art that could be transported back to England, as much to reveal the buildings and fabric of ancient Mesopotamian life. Layard, like Botta, cut reliefs off the walls, often discarding or selling on duplicates, and arranged shipments to London and Paris. Most made it – some did not. One of Botta's transport crates broke on the way to Mosul and its magnificent lamassu abandoned to be burned later for lime by local farmers. Carefully boxed containers were lost to the water at docksides, and curious travellers could not resist removing trophies for their personal collections. Exposed to the air for the first time in centuries some of the reliefs, calcinated by fire during the earlier destruction of the palaces, crumbled to dust, a common problem across many Assyrian sites. The reaction back in Europe however was rapturous, encouraging the British Museum to offer greater financial resources and a variety of more [or less] suitable specialists to assist Layard and his deputy, Hormuzd Rassan. Layard's final season in Iraq was in 1851, during which time he had similar success at Nineveh, excavating over three kilometres of reliefs and seventy-one rooms and hallways.[9] Encouraged by a friend to 'Write a whopper with lots of plates . . . Fish up old legends and anecdotes, and if you can by any means humbug people into the belief that you have established any points in the Bible, you are a made man. . .',[10] Layard went on to publish his findings in *Nineveh and its Remains* (originally Nimrud had been mistakenly identified as Nineveh) and *Monuments of Nineveh*, which became best-sellers.

Further spectacular discoveries were made by others, notably British archaeologist Max Mallowan, assisted by his wife Agatha Christie (her time in the region inspired several novels, including *Murder on the Orient Express* and *Murder in Mesopotamia*) and, from 1956, by Iraq's Directorate of Antiquities. Layard's successors at Nimrud reflected the professionalization of the discipline of archaeology: the transport of artefacts away from the site and out of the country slowed, as interest turned to research, recording and, eventually, conservation in situ. That said, a significant proportion of Nimrud's treasures are not at Nimrud. Some are close to home in nearby Mosul or Baghdad, but the majority are spread across the world, spectacularly displayed at the British Museum, the Louvre, as well as in museums in the United States, and in countless private collections.

One of the issues faced by the nineteenth-century excavators of Assyrian sites was the reaction to their discoveries by the local governors and population. Sculptures discovered earlier at the royal palace at Nineveh by Claudius Rich were destroyed in the belief that they were blasphemous, and Layard faced similar concerns about the idolatrous nature of the great lion- and eagle-headed beasts he uncovered. History was to repeat itself 200 years later.

Fig. 43 A member of ISIS using a sledgehammer to destroy bas-relief sculptures from Nimrud displayed in Mosul Museum, 2015.

The fundamentalist group Islamic State of Iraq and Syria (ISIS) declared a new Islamic caliphate in northern Iraq and Syria in June 2014, and soon moved to take over territories surrounding Mosul. A brutal cleansing followed with the group's execution of people, and destruction of buildings and shrines that did not conform with their strict interpretation of Sunni Islam. Heritage came next. Videos circulated by ISIS showed their fighters destroying statuary in Mosul Museum labelled idolatrous, and in February 2015 they moved on to Nimrud. Their first target was the gates of Ashurnasirpal's Northwest Palace, where they used sledgehammers and electric drills to deface and remove the reliefs and lamassu, which they subsequently piled in fractured mounds outside the gate. A little later, in April, they returned and used barrels of ammonium nitrate to wreak further havoc on the palace structure. Wherever they were found carved reliefs were smashed and destroyed. The mermen guarding an arched gateway leading into the Temple of Nabu were also destroyed using explosives, a captured moment of billowing smoke that is now resonant of scenes which were to take place at Palmyra a few months later in the year.

Why? Beyond the official justification in the name of opposition to blasphemous worship, such staged moments were pure propaganda.

Fig. 44 ISIS using explosives to blow up the temple of Nabu, Nimrud, in 2015.

Supplemented by provocative claims that the Pyramids of Egypt and the Sphinx were next, these carefully choreographed scenes were guaranteed to provoke outrage and capture media attention, which they did. There are also echoes of the Babylonian response to the symbols of the Neo-Assyrian Empire here – the same desire to eradicate what had gone before, to remove relics of earlier authority and to impose a new uncontested will. And to humiliate the opposition, be it the long history of pre-Muslim achievement or the modern concept of conserving and celebrating the remains of the past.

There is one further reason, perhaps best illustrated in ISIS's final act of destruction at Nimrud. In 2016, over a year after ISIS released its propaganda videos, they returned to the ruined city. During the course of two separate campaigns, the 3,000-year-old ziggurat was bulldozed flat and pushed into the river course, and part of the nearby Temple of Ishtar was destroyed. No media announcement, no video. The most likely explanation is that this was part of a campaign to recover 'treasures' which might then be sold to further fund the group's terrorist activities. There is evidence to suggest that the sale of portable antiquities looted from archaeological sites, or specially commissioned fakes, were part of ISIS's monetary armoury. Unfortunately for ISIS the ziggurat contained no hidden chambers full of riches. Unfortunately for humanity, the world lost a symbol of one of the greatest ancient civilizations.

The Old Summer Palace, China

War erodes culture and destroys civilizations in many ways. We have already explored the physical redaction of peoples and their history through targeting the historic buildings and monuments that define them – erasing cultural memory as a weapon of mass destruction. But there are other mechanisms of war that assault cultural identity, including theft on a grand scale. Looting and the wholesale removal of the spoils of war is yet a further action that hastens decline and extenuates loss.

Fig. 45 'The Beautiful Scene of the Square Pot' was a whimsical title for Scene 29 of the *Forty Scenes of the Yuanmingyuan* set on the perimeter of the Sea of Blessing. In it a large complex of spacious two-storey halls and surrounding pavilions were decorated with gold glazed tile roofs, while the buildings were painted deep red with green, blue and white decoration, contrasting with the white marble balustrades of the terrace walls.[11]

The Imperial Gardens (also known as the Old Summer Palace, and collectively as Yuanmingyuan) was a complex of palaces and three adjacent gardens in northwest Beijing – not to be confused with the Summer Palace in the same Haidian district. The first garden, Changchunyuan (the Garden of Joyful Spring 暢春園), was built from around 1687 CE as a private pleasure garden for the Kangxi Emperor and his family on the site of an abandoned Ming Dynasty garden, Qinghuayuan. In 1709 Kangxi began constructing a second garden for his son, later the Yongzheng Emperor, a kilometre further to the north: Yuanmingyuan (the Garden of Perfect Brightness). Yongzheng expanded Yuanmingyuan, leaving Changchunyuan for his mother, and the complex became the main imperial residence, a place where official business was conducted, with the Forbidden City in central Beijing reserved for formal ceremonies. From 1747, Yongzheng's son, the Qianlong Emperor, added to his predecessors' work, and created two further gardens: Changchunyuan (the Garden of Eternal Spring 長春園), completed in 1752 and Qichunyuan (the Garden of Elegant Spring), completed in 1774.

In their heyday under Qianlong, the Imperial Gardens extended to over 350 hectares, and comprised over 3,000 buildings and structures. An army of gardeners, soldiers, eunuchs and workers were housed in the purpose-built villages that surrounded them, and annual maintenance costs would have totalled approximately $1.3 million today.[12] Described by Qianlong himself as 'a realm in which heavenly treasures and earthly wonders are gathered',[13] the gardens are the epitome of Chinese imperial culture, the universe in miniature laid out for the pleasure of the emperor, and an affirmation of his intellect, interest and spirituality. The designs reflected a precis of the wider natural world in which the elements of sky, mountains, water, rock, trees and plants were recreated in a series of carefully curated tableaus, designed for all the senses. Countless paths and bridges guided those fortunate enough to be permitted entrance through the intricate landscape, over streams and across water, to pavilions, halls or simple viewing seats, each constructed with a specific purpose in mind. Some would be positioned to catch the perfect reflection of the moon in a lake, others to listen to the thrum of bamboo groves in the wind, more still to make the most of the rising or setting sun, or the scarlet show of autumn leaves. Principles of harmony, contrast, calmness and respect for the natural world, and the spirits that were seen to share it, underpinned the gardens. Buildings were to be read as part of the whole, organic rather than highly planned, and complementary as opposed to the limelight-hogging star of the show. Symmetry was largely eschewed.

While there was a harmony across the gardens, each emperor brought something of their interests to the whole. Kangxi initiated the move away from the 'prison like' Forbidden City,[14] desiring the more open and natural space on the fringe of the city where he was able to create a residence more in keeping with the Manchu Dynasty's homeland of wide vistas and raw nature beyond the Great Wall. His favourite part of the garden was the Peony Terrace, a pavilion surrounded by the eponymous flowers which he used to hold court. Yongzheng completed the move from central Peking and with less interest in either hunting or travelling the kingdom, invested heavily in the Imperial Gardens. He brought elements of fantasy to them – inspired by poems and paintings or by real life – eunuchs dressed as farmers acted out scenes of rural perfection, and a make-believe township of squares, temples, halls and shops was built simply to create a 'condensed picture of the bustling life in a great city'.[15] The township, also known as Market or Suzhou Street, was once again populated by eunuchs playing the roles of shopkeepers, hawkers, porters, wedding guests, policemen, nobles and thieves, in a fanciful reconstruction of reality in which the real nobility could interact.

The Qianlong Emperor, like his grandfather Kangxi, travelled extensively across the empire, and sought to recreate some of the great gardens he visited in the south, particularly those of Jiangnan, at the Imperial Gardens in Peking. Many of these reconstructions were captured in a large album of silk paintings commissioned by the emperor in 1744 from court artists Shen Yuan and Tangdai and calligrapher Wang Youdun.[16] The *Forty Scenes of the Yuanminguan* illustrate everything from the Hall of Rectitude and Honour – the main audience hall and a copy of the equivalent in the Forbidden City – to the Island of Heavenly Light (copied from the Yueyang Tower on Dongting Lake, Hunan province), Yongzheng's Universal Peace Building (built in the shape of the Chinese character for Buddha's heart) and Kangxi's favourite Peony Terrace.

The illustrations are important, as we shall see, because of later events that befell the gardens, but we also have a contemporary description by Father Attiret, a French Jesuit missionary who painted for the imperial court, writing of a visit in 1753:

> In each of these Valleys, there are Houses about the Banks of the Water; very well disposed: with their different Courts, open and close Porticos, Parterres, Gardens, and Cascades: which, when view'd all together, have an admirable Effect upon the Eye. They go from one of the Valleys to another, not by formal strait Walks as in *Europe*; but by various Turnings and Windings, adorn'd on the Sides with little Pavilions and charming Grottos: and each of these Valleys is diversify'd from all rest, both by their manner of laying out the Ground, and in the Structure and Disposition of its Buildings.[17]

It was not just the landscape and exterior of the buildings that impressed, but the extensive collections of books, art and decorative furnishings that adorned their interiors:

> The Inside of the Apartments answers perfectly to their Magnificence without. Beside their being very well disposed, the Furniture and Ornaments are very rich, and of an exquisite Taste. In the Courts, and Passages, you see Vases of Brass, Porcelain, and Marble, fill'd with Flowers: and before some of these Houses, instead of naked Statues, they have several of their Hieroglyphical Figures of Animals, and Urns with Perfumes burning in them, placed upon Pedestals of Marble.[18]

Treasures within the palaces included the emperor's original version of the 'Forty Scenes'.

There is one further addition made by the Qianlong Emperor worthy of note. From 1747 he commissioned the construction of a series of European-style palace buildings (Xiyang Lou), designed by Giuseppe Castiglione, an Italian Jesuit artist in the Qing court and Michel Benoist, a French Jesuit missionary with a talent for hydraulics and fountain design. Under Castiglione's leadership and with the help of Chinese architects and engineers, three groups of

Fig. 46 Castiglione and Lantai's Hall of Calm Seas, one of the European buildings in the Old Summer Palace, Beijing, China, with Benoist's 'zodiac' fountain in front. Only turned on for special occasions, such as the emperor's visit, the fountain required fourteen workers to prepare it with water.

buildings were completed.[19] Predominantly Baroque in style, the halls and pavilions also blended French rococo and Renaissance influence, as well as adaptations to accommodate Chinese sensibilities – no nude statuary! Castiglione was talented, but he was an amateur, working off memories of Europe which he had left thirty-two years previously, and engravings or the experiences of other missionaries, the result being 'loaded with amateur imagination, but lacking in professional rigor'.[20]

Perhaps the most celebrated of the missionaries' designs was not the new palaces, but Benoist's 'zodiac' fountain that was positioned in front of the Hall of Calm Seas (Haiyantang). A water clock, the structure consisted of twelve bronze statues, each a seated human figure with an animal head representing the twelve Chinese hours. By turn, on the allotted hour, the individual creatures would shoot a spume of water into the central fountain bowl; 12 p.m. was marked by the thunderous sound of all the figures venting in concert.

But the European section – originally known in China as the Fountain Palaces – was only a small part of the entire palace complex, tucked away and screened by trees in the far northern boundary of the gardens. Comprising a mere 2 per cent of the whole, it often receives more attention from commentators than the sublime traditional Chinese composition that stood adjacent.

The emperor's successors continued to develop and expand the Imperial Gardens, stolidly rather than with the spectacular and innovative flourish of Kangxi, Yongzheng and Qianlong. Maintenance became an issue, particularly of the fountains in the European section, which fell into disrepair, the copper piping taken for reuse elsewhere. Suzhou Street and its eunuch cast of vendors and shoppers was removed in 1804. By the mid-nineteenth century the gardens, palaces and extraordinary collections still left visitors in awe, albeit there was a whiff of decay perhaps indicative of the Qing Dynasty's gradual decline:

> In one of these palaces, built in the Louis XV style, we saw a series of rooms covered in Gobelins tapestries with the French coat of arms and on whose walls were hung full-length portraits of beauties of the French court, with their names below. But tapestries and paintings alike were tattered and ripped, and smacked of long-term neglect.[21]

While the influence of Europe on the Imperial Garden complex was limited to the Haiyantang palaces and the decorative interiors in the eighteenth century, the true impact of Western imperialism was felt with far greater impact during the nineteenth century, to devastating effect.

The First Opium War (1839–42) was the result of commercial and cultural tensions between Britain and China, in which the latter traditionally sought to keep external influence at bay, tightly controlling foreign powers and restricting them to a limited number of port cities. A trade imbalance in which the European demand for Chinese imports of tea, silk, porcelain and cotton greatly surpassed the sale of any products made by the industrial nations, led to a largely one-way flow of silver required to purchase them. This was partially offset by the illicit trade in British opium from Bengal which found a growing market in China, much to the concern of the imperial powers. By 1838 the annual opium trade to China had grown from the sale of 200 chests in 1729 to 40,000, a quantity large enough to reverse the trade deficit, as well as resulting in soaring rates of addiction.[22] In response, the Chinese authorities destroyed 20,000 chests of opium held by the British in Canton, and the Daoguang Emperor ordered a blockade on the Pearl River at Hong Kong. In reply, Palmerston, the British Foreign Secretary, sent in the gunships and after a series of engagements where British military superiority heavily defeated larger numbers of imperial troops, the Chinese conceded. The subsequent treaty of Nanking gave the British free trade, financial compensation, access to five more Treaty Ports to complement Canton, and ceded the island of Hong Kong. Defeat significantly weakened the Qing Dynasty prompting insurrection and the Taiping Rebellion (1850–64).

The First Opium War ended favourably for the British, but trade conditions remained restrictive, with western powers ever on the look-out for opportunities to unlock the vast Chinese market. The confiscation of the *Arrow*, a British-flagged Chinese merchant ship on suspicion of piracy, and the murder of a French missionary in 1856 afforded just such an opportunity. Using the two incidents as an excuse, the British and the French, supported by Russia and America, sent expeditionary forces to China, sparking yet another unequal conflict where better western technology – particularly battleships – tactics and training outweighed Chinese numbers and tradition.

The Second Opium War (1856–60), or Arrow War, began with the quick concession of Canton to the expeditionary forces in 1857, with the Chinese forced to the negotiating table by the time warships reached the coastal city of Tianjin, around 100 kilometres from Beijing, in 1858. The subsequent Treaty of Tianjin and other negotiations legalized the opium trade and gave the western powers new trading ports and rights. The conflict reignited the following year when the Chinese refused to ratify the Treaty after the British-led forces failed to bludgeon their way to Beijing by way of Tianjin and the Hai River. More gunships finally forced the Chinese aside and a joint expeditionary force led by General Grant and General Cousin-Montauban marched on the Imperial City arriving in 1860. Ahead of them travelled a delegation comprising British and French negotiators, and journalists, who were to meet members of the Chinese Court. Early on the morning of 17 September, as they approached an agreed rendezvous to discuss peace, the delegation came across

40,000 Mongol troops and were subsequently arrested, held hostage in the Imperial Gardens and tortured.

News of the arrest reached Lord Elgin, the highest-ranking British diplomat, at his headquarters in the Western Yellow Temple to the north of Peking's walled city, while at the same time the French arrived at the Summer Palace on 7 October, followed later the same day by British troop divisions. And the looting began.

Faced by the token resistance of a handful of badly armed eunuchs, French troops entered the palace and the commanders set up guards. What happened next is open to conjecture, with the French and British placing the blame for beginning a frenzy of looting and destruction on each other and on the Chinese. Garnet Wolseley, Grant's deputy quartermaster-general, described the scene:

> Guards were placed about in various directions; but to no purpose. When looting is once commenced by an army it is no easy matter to stop it. At such times human nature breaks down the ordinary trammels which discipline imposes, and the consequences are most demoralizing to the very best constituted army. Soldiers are nothing more than grown-up schoolboys . . .
>
> The ground around the French camp was covered with silks and clothing of all kinds, whilst the men ran hither and thither in search of further plunder, most of them, according to the practice usual with soldiers upon such occasions, being decked out in the most ridiculous-looking costumes they could find, of which there was no lack as the well-stocked wardrobes of his Imperial Majesty abounded in curious raiment. Some had dressed themselves in the richly embroidered gowns of women, and almost all had substituted the turned-up Mandarin hat for their ordinary forage cap. Officers and men seemed to have been seized with a temporary insanity; in body and soul they were absorbed in one pursuit, which was plunder, plunder.[23]

The Comte Maurice d'Hérisson, General Montauban's aide, also records a similar scene of uncontrolled chaos and mayhem:

> There were soldiers with their heads in the red lacquer boxes from the Empress's chamber; others were wreathed in masses of

brocade and silk; others stuffed rubies, sapphires, pearls and bits of rock-crystal into their pockets, shirts and caps, and hung their necks with pearl necklaces. Others hugged clocks and clock-cases. Engineers had brought their axes to smash up the furniture and get at the precious stones inlaid in it. One man was savagely hacking at a Louis XV clock in the form of a Cupid: he took the crystal figures on the face for diamonds. Every now and again the cry of 'Fire' rang out. Dropping whatever they had hold of, they all ran to put out the flames, which were by that time licking the sumptuous walls padded with silks and damasks and furs. It was like a scene from an opium dream.[24]

Eventually the commanders regained control, and jointly agreed the subdivision of the remaining treasures. Since the fifteenth century the British had codified the principles of redistribution of plunder during warfare, first by acknowledging the sovereign's claim, and later through parliamentary laws which legalized looting and created processes to ensure the fair distribution of prizes. At Yuanmingyuan,

Fig. 47 Anglo-French forces dividing the spoils at the Old Summer Palace in 1860, illustration by Godefroy Durand.

General Grant appointed four officers as prize agents who would work with the French officers to agree an allocation of precious objects between the two armies, and then coordinate the British troops in the collection of loot. D'Hérrison commented on the organization and efficiency of the well-practised British, who 'arrived in squads, like gangs of workmen, with men carrying large sacks and commanded by non-commissioned officers'.[25]

After all the art, artefacts and curiosities had been gathered, the prize agents coordinated a grand auction. By all accounts it was a spectacular affair with great rolls of silk, collections of furs, gold and silver statuary, antique bronzes, imperial jewellery, carved green and white jade, enamelled porcelain, paintings and precious books. Those who could afford it bid on each item and the sum proceeds of the sale – £26,000 – were redistributed amongst officers and troops. First-class field officers received £60, while the lowest private was given £5.[26] For comparison, a private would usually earn £1 a month.[27] The Indian troops did not benefit from the auction, but were allowed to keep the items that they plundered from the palace.[28] The contents of Yuanmingyuan were thus stripped from the palaces, pavilions, storehouse and gardens, and either taken home as trophies, gifts and mementoes, or sold to other Europeans and Chinese merchants. Huge numbers of items found their way into collections across Britain, France and further afield, and were regular items in the sales of London and Parisian auction houses during the 1860s. Gifts to Napoleon III included weaponry and the emperor's war costume, while Queen Victoria was presented with the emperor's cap and a Pekingese, or lion-dog, renamed 'Looty', who had been found wandering one of the palace pavilions. Looty remained a royal favourite, living in an alternative royal luxury in England until his death in 1873.

The looting of the palace is not the end of the story. While the Yuanmingyuan was being ransacked, several hostages from the captured negotiation party were released or managed to escape, including the diplomat Harry Parkes and Henry Loch, Elgin's secretary. The bodies of the eighteen members of the delegation were returned, but 'even the liberal use of lime in their coffins could not conceal the fact that they had suffered horribly before expiring'.[29] British outrage at the treatment of the representatives and their

Fig. 48 'Looty', the Pekingese, or lion-dog, depicted sitting on a red cushion in front of a Japanese vase, was found by Captain John Hart Dunne and presented to Queen Victoria for 'the Royal Collection of dogs'. She was one of the first Pekingese dogs in Britain.

escort, who were supposedly under a flag of truce, led to Elgin's decision to order a 'solemn act of retribution'. Over two days the five regiments and over 5,000 men of the First Infantry Division razed the Summer Palace to the ground, burning pavilions and destroying temples, so that a great pall of smoke would have been clearly seen by the emperor's officials in the Imperial City. By the evening of 19 October Wolseley recorded:

> ... the summer palaces had ceased to exist, and in their immediate vicinity, the very face of nature seemed changed: some blackened gables and piles of burnt timbers alone indicating where the royal palaces had stood. In many places the inflammable pine trees near the buildings had been consumed with them, leaving nothing but their charred trunks to mark the site. When we first entered the gardens they reminded one of those magic grounds described in fairy tales; we marched from them upon the 19th October, leaving them a dreary waste of ruined nothings.[30]

Reactions against the destruction were strong: Montauban and the French argued vehemently against it, and many on the British side clearly felt uncomfortable with the decision, including Charles Gordon (later General Gordon of Khartoum), who spoke of the beauty of the buildings and the 'wretchedly demoralizing work for an army'.[31] 'This is what civilization has done to barbarism,' wrote Victor Hugo in 1861, also remarking, 'Mixed up in all this is the name of Elgin, which forever calls to mind the Parthenon'.[32] The leading British diplomat was the son of the seventh Earl of Elgin who infamously removed the marble frieze from the Temple of Parthenon on Athens' acropolis. The eighth earl justified his decision to desecrate the Summer Palace not merely as a symbol of retribution and a statement of British dominance, but also as a specific act carefully designed to humiliate the emperor as opposed to the Chinese people. The Yuanmingyuan was the private pleasure gardens of the Qing Dynasty, a place where very few ordinary mortals would enter, and a physical manifestation of the pride, taste and power of the imperial family. To destroy the palace and its gardens was to undermine its authority and bend the Chinese to Western will.

With the Yuanmingyuan in flames and the Imperial City surrendered, the Xianfeng Emperor, through his brother Prince Gong, sued for peace. A second treaty was signed, the Beijing Convention, ratifying earlier concessions and ceding the southern portion of the Kowloon Peninsula to the British, adding to the territories around Hong Kong.

As if the events of 1860 were not bad enough, the century following saw yet further decay – slowly the gardens disappeared. Attempts at reconstruction were made during the 1870s to create a retreat for the Regent Empress Cixi, but accusations of imperial extravagance led to the plans being abandoned, and Yuanmingyuan became a quarry for other buildings, plundered for materials and trophies. Thousands of trees which were once so important in framing the gardens were cut down, and countless wooden structures that survived were dismantled. After the Revolution of 1911, it was the stone that became the target of official and illegal interest, with cartloads being sold off for private homes or for the new public structures of the communist regime. Some of the grounds reverted to farmland, and during the Japanese occupation (1937–45) more of the gardens were turned over to food production, with lakes infilled and mountains levelled. During the Cultural Revolution the attitude towards the Imperial Gardens was ambivalent at best, and at worst was targeted by the Red Guards (see below) as a location for the re-education of the bourgeoisie, namely a venue for hard but pointless labour.[33] More recent threats include use of the site for development as the march of Chinese urbanization consumes ever more open space, and, conversely, piecemeal, ersatz reconstruction as the authorities sought to grab a piece of the tourist action.

Today the destruction of the Yuanmingyuan has taken on new meaning, serving as a lightning rod for the current communist regime's interpretation of nationalism and attitude to the past. Alongside China's economic growth from the beginning of the twenty-first century, there has also been a fundamental philosophical pivot away from the dogma of the Cultural Revolution, which considered everything prior to the Revolution to be dangerous baggage. In 1949 China had just 25 museums; by 2019 there were 5,500, excluding non-state-owned ones. These needed content with which to celebrate the new China through the old. Over a million objects were looted from the Summer Palace, with artefacts and artworks finding their way into some major museums across the world and many smaller ones, as well as into private collections.[34] China now wants them back.

Fig. 49 The horse, one of twelve bronze animal sculptures from the 'zodiac' fountain at the Old Summer Palace.

At the leading edge of the Chinese campaign are the twelve bronze zodiac sculptures from Benoist's fountain. In 2000 the Ox, Monkey and Tiger were purchased at auction for 33 million Hong Kong dollars. The pig was recovered in 2003 from a private collection, while in 2007 the horse was purchased from Sotheby's and donated back to China. The rabbit and rat, both part of a collection by Yves Saint Laurent, were put up for auction by Christie's in 2009, causing consternation with the Chinese authorities. The sale went ahead, but Cai Mingchao, the purchaser and advisor to China's National Treasures Fund, refused to pay the winning bid of 30 million Euros, while China immediately levelled stringent restrictions on the sale, import and export of art from the country. In the end, such was the value of the Chinese market to the auction house that its CEO purchased the two items and handed them to the National Museum of China.

The power of the Chinese market speaks volumes. In May 2006 Steve Wynn, casino owner and luxury hotelier, donated a $10 million fourteenth-century Ming vase back to China. Largesse? Maybe. Practical business? Almost certainly. Wynn went on to open the first Las Vegas-style resort in Macau in September of the same year. Its gilded cupola ceiling contains a rabbit and a rat.

The artist Ai Weiwei made two sets of copies of the zodiac, inspired by its story of ownership, migration and authenticity. Faithfully replicating the seven surviving heads, he had to reinterpret the missing five. His is also an interesting challenge on the theme of repatriation:

> It was designed by an Italian and made by a Frenchman for a Qing Dynasty emperor, which actually is somebody who invaded China. So if we talk about 'national treasure', which nation do we talk about?[35]

The whereabouts of the dog, dragon, goat, rooster and snake remain a mystery. If these priceless items of loot ever see the light of day, it will be difficult for their current owner to resist the weight of China's restored passion for the past.

The Temple of Confucius, China

A clean sheet of paper has no blotches, and so the newest and most beautiful pictures can be painted on it.

MAO ZEDONG, 1958

The destruction of the Old Summer Palace in 1860 remains a highly resonant moment in Chinese history – an event which marked the long decline of the last imperial dynasty and a national humiliation at the hands of western powers and all that they represented. The deliberate dismantling of cultural property as an act of retribution and a warning for the future, organized *and* opportunist looting, and heritage caught between opposing ideologies are all themes that re-emerge during another defining moment in the country's

Fig. 50 A Red Guard rally in Tiananmen Square, Beijing, with guards holding copies of *Quotations from Chairman Mao Tse-tung* during the Cultural Revolution in China, 1967.

more recent past. In the summer of 1966 Red Guards targeted the 2,000-year-old home, temple and grave of one of the world's greatest philosophers, Confucius (551–479 BCE), in an attempt to redact the past, clearing the slate of what had gone before. Here is the loss of heritage at the hands of ideology: a proxy war in which historic buildings and ancient monuments are swept away to establish that 'clean sheet of paper' for the creation of a new history.

The root of the story lies in the wider narrative of Mao Zedong's rise to power and the Cultural Revolution. After the fall of the Qing Dynasty in 1911–12 during the Chinese Revolution, the chaos of the Republic during the first half of the twentieth century gave way to the bitter civil war between Nationalists under Chiang Kai-shek and the Communists under Mao. That conflict continued throughout the Japanese invasion and occupation (1931–45), and afterwards, only concluding with the retreat of the nationalists to Taiwan in 1949, leaving Mao to proclaim the People's Republic of China in October of the same year. Under Mao, China's ruling Communist Party initiated a series of state-run social, agricultural and industrial reforms or five-year plans. While the first plan (1953–7) resulted in economic growth, the second, the Great Leap Forward (1958–62), led to upwards of 45 million deaths. Mao's response was to blame the disaster on the failure of the revolution to completely purge middle class materialism and influence, and on the revisionism that he perceived was diluting the communist ideal in the USSR after Lenin's death. Effectively old elites had been replaced by new elites who had vested personal interests which trumped those of the state and the people. His solution, after a number of modest reforms failed to move fast enough, was to launch the Great Proletariat Cultural Revolution.

The principles behind the Cultural Revolution were simple, summarized in the Notification (Zhongfa [66] 267) of 16 May, released by the Politburo Standing Committee and sanctioned by Mao:

Chairman Mao often says that there is no construction without destruction. Destruction means criticism and repudiation; it means revolution. It involves reasoning things out, which is construction. Put destruction first, and in the process you have construction. Marxism-Leninism, Mao Tse-tung's thought, was founded and

AMONGST THE RUINS

has constantly developed in the course of the struggle to destroy bourgeois ideology. (para. 6)

In practical terms, the Cultural Revolution took the form of mobilizing students to form paramilitary units, the Red Guards, who would champion the cause, overriding and taking power from party revisionists who Mao felt threatened the revolution and his personal legacy. Eight enormous rallies held in Beijing during 1966 in Mao's presence inspired fanatical loyalty and fostered his cult of personality. Frenzied propaganda, typified by the rallies and 'big-character' posters (*dazibao*), and formal 'struggle sessions' in which victims were forced to confess their 'crimes' while being publicly abused, sometimes by thousands, were all a part of the armoury. And it was not simply about verbal abuse: physical attacks on teachers, intellectuals and moderate party administrators often led to torture, imprisonment and death.

An important part of such destruction was a call to do away with the Four Olds, these being old customs, old culture, old habits and old ideas. On 1 June 1966, *The People's Daily,* the official mouthpiece of the Chinese Communist Party, published an editorial by Lin Biao, the CCP Vice-Chairman, which entreated its readers to demolish 'all the old ideology and culture and all the old customs and habits, which, fostered by the exploiting classes, have poisoned the minds of the people for thousands of years'. The 'monsters' of bourgeois scholars, authorities and 'venerable masters' would be swept 'into the dust'.

While Mao and Lin Biao's appeals to 'sweep away the monsters' were clear, quite how it would be implemented was not, with multiple Red Guard units competing with one another in their unquestioning zeal. The results were random, vicious and chaotic, with traditional ordered society turned upside down in a mob-led frenzy of political posturing and real bloodletting. From the summer of 1966 Red Guard units broke into thousands of middle-class homes, looting and destroying property, and humiliating their owners, or far worse. Books and paintings were burnt, alongside family histories. By October official documents praised the Red Guards for the confiscation of some 65 tons of gold.[36] In the wider arena, the campaign led to the renaming of streets and important public spaces:

in Beijing, Stability Gate Inner Street became Great Leap Forward Road, Táijī Factory Street became Perpetually Ousting Road and Yangwei Street became Anti-Revisionism Street. Traditional family names too were changed with the Red Guards favouring those that explicitly illustrated their support for the cause, such as 'Protect Biao' or 'Defend Qing'.[37] The Red Guards rampaged through the Summer Palace and attacked the Ming-period Great Wall, with its wall tiles reused to build roads, pigsties and toilets.[38] Protection for historic monuments and cultural sites was withdrawn: key sites such as the Hall of Scriptures Right Monastery and Emperor Guan's Shrine on the Water in Guangdong province 'no longer enjoy protection as municipal key cultural relics'.[39] But by far the most significant attack on ancient cultural heritage was that which took place at the Temple of Confucius, Shandon Province, in November 1966.

The Temple of Confucius in the town of Qufu is a complex of temples consecrated in 478 BCE soon after the death of the philosopher. Extended, restored and modified on numerous occasions over the centuries, the site includes a range of buildings contained

Fig. 51 Main building at the Temple of Confucius, Qufu, China, 1904.

within a later enclosure dating to 1331 CE, and arranged around nine courtyards on a linear north-south axis. Today as in the past, visitors make their way through a series of gateways and courtyards before reaching the focus of the complex, the Dacheng Hall (the Hall of Great Perfection) with the Apricot Platform, an open space, immediately in front. The hall serves as the main temple where offerings in memory of Confucius are made, while the platform is where an apricot tree offered shade for the great man to teach his students. At over 1.3 kilometres long and at one time comprising over 460 rooms, it is one of the largest temples in China, befitting a place of veneration and pilgrimage regularly visited by emperors and their delegates. More than a thousand stelae and precious objects adorned the courtyard and interior spaces, dating from the Han Dynasty (202 BCE–220 CE) onwards, some commemorating Confucius, others marking the various campaigns of construction and reconstruction.

To the east of the temple is the Kong Mansion, home to Confucius's male direct-line descendants (Confucius is also referred to as 'Old Kong') and the administrative centre from which the aristocratic Kong family governed one of the largest private estates in the country. Located just over a kilometre to the north is the Kong family cemetery, also known as the Cemetery of Confucius, where he, his followers and around 100,000 members of the Kong clan were buried.

Given Confucius's family background, the reverence paid him by numerous emperors and his pre-eminence as an educator and leader of Chinese thought, it is no surprise that the temple dedicated to him would soon be fixed in the crosshairs of the Red Guard.

To be 'nurtured' on the thoughts of Confucius never did anyone any good and only produced cowardly bastards who exploit, oppress, cruelly injure, and bully other people. What those in favour of 'educating' people with the thoughts of Confucius want is to foster landlords, rich peasants, counterrevolutionaries, bad elements, rightists, monsters and freaks, foster counterrevolutionary revisionist elements, and hire men and buy horses for a capitalist restoration on behalf of the capitalists.[40]

As they witnessed what was happening elsewhere across the country, local Red Guards in Qufu and the nearby city of Tai'an sought to take up the mantle of destruction, marching on the Confucius Temple. However, Qufu party officials backed by the local peasantry blocked access to the site, arguing that it was state property (as opposed to a feudal symbol), protected by the official State Council protection stele, and was to be used as a place of education. However, even those defending the site insisted that they were not opposed to destroying the legitimate Four Olds and, to prove their Maoist credentials, they turned their attention to the rich cultural heritage that made Qufu the 'holy land' to the Chinese people.

> . . . countless other cultural and historical relics in Qufu were methodically identified and physically destroyed. The Qufu government even created a special incentive whereby whoever pulled down any historical or cultural relics got to keep any reusable materials from them, such as stones and bricks. Soon, house by house, village by village, and community by community, a significant part of what made the millenniums-old Qufu one of the preeminent world culture centers was systematically dismantled for the first time in history – not by any wartime intruders or natural disasters, but by its own people in peacetime. Qufu was in mourning . . .[41]

A further local ploy to protect the Confucius Temple included covering the complex's statues with revolutionary posters and images of Mao, papering over the ancient with new 'red' credentials. Such misuse of a wider Red Guard initiative to turn China into a 'Red Sea' was soon banned by the Beijing leadership. Local protection was not to last.

In November 1966, 200 Red Guards of the Jinggangshan Regiment from Beijing Normal University gathered under student leader Tan Houlan and swore to 'thoroughly demolish the Confucius Family Shop',[42] the root of the Four Olds.[43] On 9 November, Houlan and her corps of student volunteers followed an advance party and made their way by overnight train and then by truck the 300 miles to Qufu. Here they joined with students from Qufu Normal College, and other Red Guard units, and set up the 'Revolutionary Rebel Liaison Station to Annihilate the Kong Family Business and Establish the Absolute Authority of Mao Zedong Thought'.[44]

AMONGST THE RUINS

Fig. 52 'Scatter the old world, build a new world': a Red Guard destroying religious artefacts, books and other things considered old, bourgeois or decadent, 1967.

The following days saw successive stand-offs between Houlan and local party members, with the latter increasingly alarmed about threats to 'Set the Confucius Family Shop on Fire'. Directives from the CCRG in Beijing added fuel to the flames in favour of the Red Guards:

> Han Dynasty steles should be preserved, as should be steles from before the Ming Dynasty. Qing Dynasty steles may be smashed. The Confucius Temple can be repurposed, like the Rent Collection Courtyard. Confucius's grave may be dug up.[45]

On 13 November the local party officially conceded defeat, stepping aside and allowing access to all three Kong sites for the first time since 1948. Locals as well as Red Guards wandered through the gates.

The last line of resistance occurred on 15 November when Red Guards destroyed the State Council protection stele, the final safeguard of the Temple, mansion and cemetery. Such was the symbolism of the moment that the physical toppling and shattering of the large 450-kilogram granite slabs was re-enacted for the cameras.

Almost immediately Red Guards entered the temple, mansion and cemetery. At the latter they broke through the memorial archway, while in the temple they set about destroying the shrines and statues of Confucius's disciples by knocking off their heads and breaking them apart. The statue of Confucius himself was removed, saved for the culminating moments of the first phase of destruction: a two-day rally in Qufu Teachers' College (28–29 November) attended by over 100,000 people including Red Guard units, local party officials and peasants. After more struggle sessions several famous Confucian scholars who had been specially brought to Qufu were paraded around the town on a truck alongside the reserved statue adorned by a dunce's cap inscribed 'Down with No. 1 Scoundrel Confucius'. Stopping outside the cemetery, the scholars were once more abused, and the statue was thrown onto a bonfire along with other cultural items. Once inside, a team of 300 gravediggers began the task of digging up the first and last of the Kongs – the first being Confucius, his son and grandson, and the last being Kong Lingyi, Confucius's seventy-sixth direct descendent, and his two predecessors. Once again symbolism prevailed: by removing the first and last of Confucius's line, one of the defining motifs of the Four Olds was expunged, leaving nothing to poison the fresh start of Mao's Revolutionary Thought. And once again the moments were caught on cameras sent from Beijing to specially record the occasion. It took several days to uncover Confucius's tomb, with initial patience eventually giving way to frustration and the use of dynamite, which revealed very little, the body long since rotted. The corpses in the tombs of Kong Lingyi and the last Kongs, having been buried for only forty-six years, were in better condition, good enough for two to be strung up together from a nearby tree.

Tan Houlan and the Liaison Station's immediate objective had been achieved. The first and last of the Kong Family Shop had been destroyed and Confucius's tomb razed. She and her Beijing corps of Red Guards were called back to the capital in early December to help confront other revisionists threatening the latest phase of Mao's new order. Wang Zhengxin took her place as leader of the

Liaison Station and anti-Confucian movement in the town, with responsibility for levelling the entire Kong Cemetery, turning it into an orchard, and continuing to convert the other two Kong sites into places of re-education. Faced with the chaos of partially ransacked and defiled buildings, and an enormous collection of surviving cultural artefacts across the Kong sites, Wang created a Cultural Relics Trial Committee. This comprised experts and Red Guards who determined which were legitimate artefacts commensurate with the beliefs of the party, and which should either be repurposed as 'dirty linen' for educational purposes or destroyed. Far more was destroyed than preserved, for example 32,232 volumes of priceless Confucian family genealogies were shipped in eight horse carriages to a paper mill to be sold as wastepaper.[46]

The unearthing of the graves of the last three Kong descendants, which contained jewellery, precious memorabilia and grave goods as well as bodies, ironically brought to life to the Qufu peasantry the contrasting richness of their landlord's lifestyle compared with their own poverty. The same peasants who had at first protected the Kong sites turned into looters. First to turn up at the cemetery was a Red Guard corps made up of local peasants called the Southgate Brigade Breakthrough Team. Excavation and desecration of the wealthier tombs began, fulfilling a dual purpose of being seen to further the Maoist cause in taking action against the Four Olds, and lining individual pockets. Bricks and stones were pillaged from the site to be reused by the brigade to create their own Mao Zedong Thought School. Seven other local brigades quickly followed, then all fifty villages in Qufu province, and before long peasants joined from across the region, turning the cemetery into a feverish hunting ground. For ten days several thousand people lived, ate and slept on the site, ransacking tombs to extract whatever riches they could find. The powers that be, such as they were, were fearful of trying to stop the looters, because their overt purpose was a noble one – to smash the accoutrements of the bourgeoisie – and because of their unimpeachable credentials as members of the peasant classes, the very people Mao's revolution sought to help.

It was an extraordinary event, especially when set against a treasured place where very little looting had previously taken place. Now, under the banner of a new patriotism and in the absence of

Fig. 53 Destroying statues at the Temple of Confucius, including pulling down the marker stele and destruction of the tombs. In another image, Confucius's statue is covered in big character posters denouncing the philosopher.

authority, the world had turned upside down. The Kong sites had become a place where Kong family members robbed the graves of their own relatives (one-fifth of the local population shared the Kong surname), where the work of 'one night' would be enough to acquire 'one tractor' and where Qufu's small bank was so overrun by the huge volume of peasants wishing to cash in on their treasures that it set up a special fifteen-member purchasing team to deal with the demand.[47] The chaos came to an end in spring 1967, prompted by violent clashes resulting from the unearthing of recently buried local peasants by outside peasant groups. In truth it is likely that there was little left to steal, and the peasant groups returned to their homes.

By April 1967 Qufu and the three Kong sites had changed from one of China's richest cultural heartlands to a place of devastation. Confucius's grave had been levelled, alongside 2,000 graves of his extended ancestral Kong family; statues were smashed and stelae from the Ming Dynasty onwards broken up; precious archives and paintings had been burned or pulped; over 5,000 ancient pine trees had been cut down, and the stone, brick, tile and timber of the Kong buildings robbed for reuse elsewhere. Across Qufu there had once been 338 official cultural relic protection units; now only 87 remained.[48]

The true impact of Mao's programme of cultural destruction is difficult to assess, but Qufu aside the localized statistics are themselves compelling: for example, 4,922 of 6,843 officially designated 'historical interest' sites in Beijing were destroyed.[49] And it was not simply about buildings and monuments, but intangible heritage – everything from traditional festivals to costume and names was purged from everyday life.

The call to destroy the Four Olds belonged with the early years of the Cultural Revolution, but the anti-traditional policies only truly came to an end on Mao's death in 1976. Under the reforms of Deng Xiaoping, Mao's eventual successor, a man who had been purged during the Cultural Revolution for his reformist views, Mao's policies were slowly dismantled. Ironically, Deng Xiaoping's liberalization of the Chinese economy brought a new threat of relentless development to the heritage sites of China, but Confucius's reputation was restored, and key heritage sites picked out for preservation, reconstruction and presentation.

All three Kong sites were made a World Heritage Site in 1994. Remarkably, no mention is made within any of the WHS documentation about the damage wrought across all the Kong sites in 1966–7 – nor can the events be traced from the offers of countless tour operators for those visiting today. It is as if the formal destruction of Confucius's temple by the Liaison Station in the autumn of 1966 and the chaotic turmoil of looting by peasants in early 1967 had never happened. Mao's objective through the Four Olds campaign was to erase the collective memory of a feudal past by destroying its legacy of buildings, burials and artefacts – from a twenty-first-century perspective, it is Mao's legacy of destruction that has been purged. Neither is right.

One of the many burials ransacked during January 1967 in the Confucius Cemetery was the grave of Madame Yu. Yu was the wife of Kong Xianpei, seventy-second Yansheng Duke (the leaders of the Kong clan), and daughter of the Qianlong Emperor. Qianlong, as we have seen, was a major patron of the Old Summer Palace, destroyed and looted by European troops and local peasants at the culmination of the Second Opium War (see above). The parallels between Mao's destruction of the Confucian sites and Elgin's of the Old Summer Palace just over a hundred years earlier are fascinating. Both were punitive reactions against an enemy seen as decadent, backward and morally corrupt; both involved the deliberate demolition of the symbols of former power and authority; both campaigns sought to target the elite, not the common people; and both descended into an anarchy of looting, in which the poorest in society made the most of doors left open by others.

The change in attitude towards heritage by the Chinese authorities since the end of the Cultural Revolution has been marked. The benefits of associating with China's long history are now in favour, as illustrated by the enthusiasm with which the political administration has championed the designation of over fifty World Heritage Sites since 1987 (including the new Summer Palace and Kong sites). There is also great interest not just in ancient Chinese heritage, but in sites which tell the story of the Cultural Revolution, good and bad. As elsewhere in the world, the value of heritage can often be seen through a more commercial lens, and ancient sites are threatened by the priority given to development over conservation, but there is a significant change in perception which is led from the top. President Xi Jinping referred to the 'great rejuvenation of the Chinese nation' on becoming Secretary General of the Communist Party in 2012, and set out The Chinese Dream. Echoing a complete reversal of Mao's 'Four Olds', the Dream contains four parts: Strong China, Harmonious China, Beautiful China and Civilized China, with the latter listing 'rich culture' as one of its values. Indeed, the turnaround could not be more complete – or more ironic – with the latest ambition to declare a memorial hall on one side of Tiananmen Square in central Beijing as part of a World Heritage Site by 2035. The hall is, of course, the mausoleum of the Great Helmsman himself, Mao Zedong. This, in the context of Mao's contribution to historic preservation, is akin to giving the seventh and eighth Earls of Elgin a global conservation award for 'Best International Redistribution of Cultural Heritage'.

CHAPTER 5

ECONOMY

Money, trade or wider economic change is often at the root of failing civilizations, particularly when it is combined with growing populations and the overexploitation of finite resources. The final four stories focus on historic communities which disappear because they cannot compete, because newer, more efficient technologies make them redundant or because they simply get in the way.

Abandoned industrial communities are commonplace. Towns set up to service the extraction of minerals have an inbuilt shelf life determined by the quantity of resources, and unless the basis of industry diversifies, they lose purpose once the supply runs dry. They are also highly susceptible to technological advances leaving either the raw material or the processes redundant. Humberstone Mine in Chile's Atacama Desert was founded by the Englishman James Humberstone in 1872. The nitrate-rich resources of the desert were excavated, refined and exported to Europe as fertilizer. Humberstone was one of several mining towns in this deeply inhospitable region which was responsible for producing nearly all the world's salt-petre during the late nineteenth and early twentieth centuries and accounted for 60–80 per cent of Chilean exports. Workers from Chile, Peru and Bolivia lived in the town and forged a distinctive communal *pampinos* culture. However, it was not to last. During the First World War, the British blockade on Germany led to the development of synthetic fertilizers and Chile's saltpetre mining industry collapsed, leading to abandonment. Today Humberstone is a World Heritage Site and a stark reminder of the fickle quality of international trade.

The story of shifting trade patterns is updated to the more recent past using a twentieth-century example from the United States. Route 66 was formally established in 1926 as the major federal highway connecting Chicago with the coastal cities of California. It followed the course of earlier government-funded wagon roads. The route grew in popularity as the 'road of flight' during the Dust Bowl era, and again in the Second World War as people sought work in the munitions industry or military bases of the West coast, and once more in the 1950s, when it became a popular tourist route. Consequently, the road brought with it trade and economic opportunity: service villages sprang up to make the most of passing trade, villages became towns and new industries relocated to benefit from improved transport links. In 1956 President Eisenhower established the Interstate Highways Act which became the largest public engineering project in US history at the time, creating 66,000 kilometres of new roads. Over time more of Route 66 was bypassed to be replaced by larger, direct routes, and the road was officially declassified in 1984. As people abandoned the old route, so too was there a population decline in the rural towns and villages along its course, including places such as Afton, Oklahoma; Oatman, Arizona; and Newkirk, New Mexico.

Our third story explores the loss of country houses across Britain during the twentieth century and illustrates the devastating impact of changing economic circumstances on traditional ways of life. At its peak in 1955 an important mansion was lost in the UK every five days; 1,000 have gone since the Second World War. Eaton Hall in Cheshire, Trentham in Staffordshire and Hamilton Palace in Lanarkshire are just a few of many architecturally and historically significant buildings lost, primarily due to the cost of upkeep and the burden of taxation. Ways of life which had been sustainable for centuries were no longer so in the changing world of the twentieth century. Using the example of Beaudesert Hall in Staffordshire, this story concentrates on the reasons why such historic places became economic casualties.

We have already explored one aspect of the loss of heritage to water under the theme climate change (see chapter 1, Dunwich), but the economic demands to build substantial reservoirs account for some of the most spectacular examples of disappearance and conservation. This final case-study looks at how the need for water has led both to the abandonment of historic buildings in extant, living communities and to the submergence of already ruinous evidence of the past.

Abu Simbel in Egypt represents probably the greatest archaeological rescue mission of all time. The story begins in 1264–1244 BCE when Pharaoh Ramses II constructed two magnificent temples in the territories of Nubia. Cut into the red sandstone on the west bank of the Nile, the temples were lost to the outside world until their rediscovery by the Swiss antiquarian Johan Burckhardt in 1813. In the 1950s flooding through the construction of the High Aswan dam threatened the site and from 1963 to 1968 a UNESCO-led project moved both temples, stone by stone, and relocated them 60 metres above their original position in a new cliff setting. Astonishing though the mission was, it is only part of the story of heritage relocation which took place during the construction of the lake and dam. The sanctuary of Isis at Philae and three other groups of ancient sites at Amada, Wadi Sebua and Kalabsha were similarly reassembled, and a further four temples were donated to countries that supported the project. While the campaign was successful in saving the great Egyptian monuments, these were only a fraction of the cemeteries, settlements, churches, mosques or fortresses which, at best, could only be documented. Wadi Halfa in northern Sudan, a nineteenth-century town overlying settlement dating back to the earliest Nubian peoples (8000 BCE), was completely destroyed by Lake Nasser, alongside twenty-seven nearby villages, displacing 52,000 people. The worst affected were the Nubian population, leading to protest and campaigns. A third dam on the Nile, at Kajbar, is being proposed by the Sudanese government. It would displace 10,000 people, submerge 90 villages and destroy about 500 archaeological sites.

Local, regional and national economies are reliant on resources, either natural or human, neither of which are infinite. Within this context historic communities – sometimes empires too – are born, thrive and disappear.

Humberstone Mine, Chile

Industrialization, manufacturing and production are some of the hallmarks of civilization, but they come with an inbuilt vulnerability to change. Abandoned industrial communities are commonplace. Towns set up to serve the extraction of minerals have a shelf life determined by the quantity of resource, and, unless the basis of industry diversifies, they lose purpose once the supply or demand runs dry. They are also highly susceptible to technological advances which can leave either the need for the raw material or the processes redundant. And if the product is destined for an international market, then the industry is exposed to a whole world of political and economic decision-making which is completely outside its control, and both potentially lucrative or disastrous.

The Atacama Desert is one of the driest and least hospitable places on earth. With rainfall that is effectively zero, an average temperature of 30 degrees Celsius during the day, dropping to 2 degrees at night, and a vast interior that can only sustain microbial life, this is not a landscape conducive to permanent human occupation.

But, as when a butterfly flaps its wings, the exploitation of this unpromising area has repercussions that extend well beyond the sight of the Andes. This is a story that begins and ends in the dry, salt-laden desert, but it travels from Chile across the world and is catalytic in the history of three nations, prompting war, inspiring social change and leaving an extraordinary physical legacy. At the root of the transformation is a simple, naturally-occurring chemical compound: sodium nitrate ($NaNO_3$), or saltpetre.

The story starts in Chile's Tarapacá region at the northern end of the Atacama Desert, close to the modern borders of Bolivia and Peru. Here the Cordillera de la Costa, a coastal mountain range, slides into the Pacific Ocean, with no more than occasional alluvial river fans affording foothold for the coastal city of Iquique and the port of Pisaqua. Behind this narrow coastal strip there is a high plateau, or pampa, resting between the Andes and the Cordilleras, which is the key to its mineral wealth. Runoff from the Andes to the east was met by the impermeable granite dam of the coastal range to the west, creating an upland plateau dissected by valleys, or Pampa de Tamarugo (named after the salt-tolerant Tamarugo tree that characterizes the area). Salt pans formed on the surface of the desert and saltpetre beds were created by filtration in the fissures of the plateau's valleys. Such geological conditions created the richest source of saltpetre on earth.

The presence of saltpetre in the Atacama Desert has been known to the outside world since French scientist Joseph Dombey brought back samples of sodium nitrate to Europe after a scientific expedition in 1778. At the time the area was split between the Spanish colonies of the Viceroyalty of Peru, which administered Tarapacá, and the Viceroyalty of the Rio de la Plata, which covered Antofagasta, another saltpetre-rich province some 400 kilometres further south. The long reach of the Napoleonic Wars and subsequent demand for gunpowder accelerated interest in the area. Britain's failed attempts to invade Montevideo in 1806 and Buenos Aires in 1807, both major cities in the Viceroyalty of Rio de la Plata, prompted Spanish investment across its South American colonies. By 1812 several companies had been established inland from Iquique to mine saltpetre and convert it from sodium nitrate to the potassium nitrate required for manufacturing gunpowder.

The technology of the early industry was crude, and limited in efficiency, requiring concentrated ores of over 60 per cent nitrate content, large quantities of fuel and transport reliant on mule trains. Using the *Paradas* system, individual miners would extract the ore, crush it and sell it on to manufacturers. These, by turn, would dissolve the ore in *fondos*, cone-shaped iron tanks, over direct heat, with fuel provided by the once ubiquitous Tamarugo tree or fossil wood excavated from the pampa.[1] Once dissolved, the 'mother liquor' was tapped off using a gravity-based system to drain into *bateas*, wooden or iron tanks, where the more soluble sodium nitrate would crystallize out, leaving the less soluble impurities behind.

Historically, saltpetre has been used for curing food and as an essential ingredient in the manufacture of gunpowder. However, the compound commonly used to create 'black powder', as gunpowder was known, is ordinary saltpetre, or potassium nitrate. It burns fiercer, at a lower temperature and is less absorbent (and therefore less prone to dampness) than the sodium nitrate of the Chilean version. And, while it was possible to convert Chilean saltpetre to ordinary saltpetre, the limitations of transport, expense and the relative ease of manufacture of potassium nitrate using manure or urine, limited the early growth of the pampa industry.

A number of events during the nineteenth century dramatically changed the situation. In an acceleration of the scientific and agricultural revolutions begun in the eighteenth century, the industrial nations of Europe and North America demanded greater agricultural productivity to feed their increasingly urban populations. Scientific advances in England, France and Germany during the first half of the century demonstrated the usefulness of sodium nitrate as a fertilizer.

In South America, the value of saltpetre as a fertilizer was already known among the native Atacameños and Inca population of the region, who would add crushed nitrate ore to their fields of corn, wheat and potatoes.[2] But it was people like Alexander von Humboldt, the German scientist, who drew global attention to the effect of nitrogenous fertilizers such as guano and saltpetre on plant growth, observed during his three-month stay in Peru in 1802. Research by German botanist Justus von Liebig and the French chemist Jean-Baptiste Boussinghault a prodigy of Humboldt and another traveller to Peru, later explained the science behind the nitrogen cycle.

The British naturalist Charles Darwin, arriving in Iquique in 1835 on HMS *Beagle*, described, not altogether flatteringly, the saltpetre industry in its infancy:

> July 12th We anchored in the port of Iquique. The town contains about a thousand inhabitants, and stands on a little plain of sand as the floor of a great wall of rock, 2000 feet in height, which here forms the coast . . . The aspect of the place was most gloomy: the little port, with its few vessels, and small group of wretched houses, seemed overwhelmed and out of all proportion with the rest of the scene.
>
> . . . I hired, with difficulty at the price of four pounds sterling, two mules and a guide to take me to the saltpetre works. These are the present support of Iquique. During one year the value of one hundred thousand pounds sterling was exported to France and England. This saltpetre does not properly deserve to be so called; for it consists of nitrate of soda, and not of potash, and

Fig. 54 Painting of the port of Iquique, a saltpetre boom-town, 1789.

is therefore of much less value. It is said to be principally used in the manufacture of nitric acid. Owing to its deliquescent property it will not serve for gunpowder.[3]

Darwin's description was of an industry on the cusp of massive expansion. In 1840, five years after the famous naturalist's visit, the Tarapacá area was producing 73,000 tons of saltpetre, which had increased to 500,000 by 1870.[4]

Ironically, at the time the fledgling saltpetre industry took off, prompted by the demands of the Napoleonic Wars, the same conflict served to light the touchpaper for Chilean independence from Spain, which was officially declared in 1818. Further north, Peru followed in 1821, with Bolivia proclaiming independence in 1825. The creation of new nation states gave opportunities to foreign adventurers and entrepreneurs. Land was given freely in return for a share of the profits and European investment in saltpetre industry grew substantially, led by characters such as the Englishmen James Thomas North, the 'Nitrate King', and James 'Santiago' Humberstone.

New technologies improved the efficiency of mining. In 1853 Pedro Gamboni introduced a system of steam heating into the extraction process, allowing the removal of nitrate from lower-grade ores. He also patented techniques for iodine extraction from the sodium nitrate leaching process, which unlocked an extremely lucrative by-product of the saltpetre industry. So much so that by 1904 Chile was producing over 70 per cent of the world's iodine.[5] From 1863 the introduction of the Shanks technique transformed the cottage-industry of the *paradas* tradition into a fully fledged industrial process, with a gravity-based system based on vast hoppers, conveyor belts, mechanical crushers, leaching tanks, crystallization troughs and huge drying yards.

The growing importance of the saltpetre industry to the national economies of Chile, Bolivia and Peru was to result in war. After independence from Spain, a disputed border between Chile and Bolivia was finally agreed, in 1866, to be the 24th parallel. Recognizing the complexity of interests in the region, the treaty also made provision for both countries to share the tax revenue of mineral exports from between the 23rd and 25th parallels on either side of the new border – the Zona de Beneficious Mutuos. A further treaty in 1874 handed Bolivia all the tax revenue from the area, but gave Chilean companies fixed rates for a period of twenty-five years. This worked in Chile's favour, particularly with significant outside investment in those companies from Britain, which saw massive expansion of Chilean interests in Bolivia, alongside a growing Chilean population who served as railway builders and labourers to the industry. In 1878 the Bolivian government imposed a backdated increase on the Chilean companies, who refused to pay and were subsequently threated with confiscation. Bolivia's seizure of the Antofagasta Nitrate & Railway Company in 1879 led to the arrival of 2,000 Chilean troops in the Bolivian city of Antofagasta and the start of La Guerra del Pacifico, also known as the Saltpeter Wars. Peru found itself drawn into the conflict, when Bolivia called on a secret treaty agreed just six years earlier. The war lasted until 1883, beginning as a conflict fought at sea and culminating in a series of land battles with the Chilean army moving ever further north, through Bolivia's coastal territories and on to Peru's capital, Lima, which fell in January 1881. Peruvian resistance continued until the Treaty of Ancón. Signed on 20 October 1883, the treaty handed Tarapacá and Antofagasta to

Chile, and marked a dramatic rewriting of national boundaries that still has repercussions today. Bolivia's loss of its coast, leaving it a land-locked nation, still plays heavily in the country's psyche, and diplomatic relations have been cut off with Chile since 1978. Peru and Chile only agreed to implement the final parts of a later related treaty (Treaty of Lima) in 1999. Chile too, in 1881, had to concede large parts of Patagonia to guarantee Argentina's neutrality, another source of modern discontent and political grandstanding.[6]

After the war, the saltpetre industry in Chile reached its zenith. Railways and foreign investment flooded into Tarapacá and Antofagasta, significantly reducing transport expenses that had previously relied on mules. The first railway in the region was constructed in 1871 connecting La Noria Works with Iquique, from where boats could transport the saltpetre to a hungry world, and the network had expanded to almost 1,800 kilometres by 1905. British investment also increased – before the war British investors had interests in 13 per cent of Tarapacá's saltpetre industry, rising to 34 per cent after the war, and 70 per cent by 1890.[7]

In 1888 the modernizing Chilean president José Manuel Balmaceda sought to nationalize the saltpetre industry, blocking the sales of state-owned concerns to foreigners. This, combined with Balmaceda's aspirations for a presidential system, led to the Civil War of 1891, where the British commercial interests of people such as James North and the Chilean political class united in rebellion against the president. A rebel junta formed in Iquique, and its army, equipped by the saltpetre businesses, overthrew Balmaceda's forces to form a new government. Unsurprisingly, the incoming government supported an outward-looking economic policy which encouraged both further foreign investment and export. In return, taxes were levied which brought enormous financial gain to the Chilean state, so much so that by 1890 50 per cent of the country's *total* revenue came from the duty on saltpetre, a percentage which would remain at that level for almost three decades.

The impact of saltpetre wealth on Chile was profound and far-reaching, extending to every area of life. Firstly, it was the state that grew: administrators, defence, education and transport infrastructure (government funding of the railways increased the network to 5,000 kilometres by 1917). The wealth coming into the country was evident in the growth of ports such as Iquique's, which was home to eleven different shipping companies transporting saltpetre across the globe, and returning laden with British coal and textiles. The other ports of Antofagasta, Mejillones, Taital and Pisagua saw a similar expansion, as did the capital Santiago. Chile could afford to embrace the architectural styles emanating from Europe; in Santiago government wealth paid for new law courts, the Central Post Office, the National Library, the Museo de Bellas Artes and the remodelling of important churches. The Central Railway Station belongs to this period, designed by Gustave Eiffel in 1897. Valparaiso, Chile's principal port city, was home to affluent alcoves of British and French ex-patriots who lived in neighbourhoods that had more in common with European homes than local ones. It is little surprise that Valparaiso Wanderers, founded in 1892, is the oldest football club in Latin America – and that their fierce rivals are Everton de Viña del Mar, located just across the bay – each founded by expatriate Britons.

Let's now turn to the industry itself, to understand something of the process, product and people that was the source of such extravagant wealth and global connections. The Humberstone Saltpeter Works and those of nearby Santa Laura are located in the Tarapacá region and together represent the best-preserved survival of the extractive industry, so much so that they were made a World Heritage Site in 2005 (UNESCO). Humberstone was founded initially in 1862 as La Palma by the Peruvian Nitrate Company, while Santa Laura, less than two kilometres away, was constructed ten years later. The two operations were to become one of the largest works in the Tarapacá, and home to nearly 3,500 residents.

The industrial operation at Humberstone and Santa Laura was initially based on the paradas system, but both were early adopters of the more-efficient Shanks process. Consequently, the sites are characterized by silos (*buzón*), conveyor belts, crushers (*chancadoras*), storage tanks (*chulladores*) and leaching plants, chimneys and drying yards. Vast tailings mounds of waste stone, gravel and sand dominate the landscape, while railways, storage yards and offices served an industry that sought to extract the sodium nitrate from the desert and transport it to the coast as efficiently as possible.

While the process of saltpetre harvesting is itself fascinating, it is the human story that truly captivates. In a desert landscape

Fig. 55 Humberstone's industrial buildings, including a 40-metre-high chimney and the *torta de ripio*, a tailings mound which covers at least four times the area of the living accommodation.

previously devoid of all but the occasional passing human, new towns sprang up, with all the accoutrements of modest civilization. Humberstone's grid plan, focused on a central square, echoes a Roman military camp and an urban plan uniformity commonplace among hastily formed towns across history and the world. The town's grid of ten-by-six blocks – big, but still a quarter of the size of the tailings mound – was largely made up of accommodation for workers and their families. Constructed in Douglas fir, with stuccoed walls and corrugated zinc roofs, there was a strict hierarchy of buildings reminiscent of Victorian town planning in places such as Saltaire in the UK, or many of the East Lancashire mill towns. Single workers, or 'bachelors', lived in their own 4-by-3.5-metre rooms in barrack blocks with shared bathrooms, while families had small five-room terraced houses that included a front garden and a back yard. Semi-detached accommodation marked a step up the hierarchy for married employees, while the managers had a block of grander houses in one of the smaller of the public squares, each entered by an arcaded porch and finished with decorative flourishes.

Fig. 56 Family accommodation at Humberstone in the Tarapacá Region, Chile, with timber frames and a corrugated iron roof that extended over the front of the property, offering some shade from the strong Atacama sun.

A town needs services, particularly when the nearest alternatives would require an arid 72-kilometre trip to the coast. Physical sustenance could be found in the canteen, central market and general store (*pulperiá*), while the spiritual equivalent was served by a chapel, cinema and theatre. Those seeking more exercise could enjoy basketball, tennis, swimming, pitch-and-toss or football, and the town's children had a school, nursery and scout centre. A hotel and social club looked after guests and locals respectively. Public squares, a bandstand and administrative buildings, including a bookkeeper's building and yard that connected the plant with the town where workers would clock in and out at the beginning and end of each working day, completed the ensemble. Santa Laura had a similar but far smaller arrangement of buildings to accommodate the 500 or so workers that called it home.

Given the available materials and desert location, the architecture of all the desert settlements was simple and functional: most materials, such as the wood that framed most buildings, had to be imported from abroad and brought from the coast. But there were architectural touches illustrating an adaptation to the harsh environment, in

AMONGST THE RUINS

particular verandas and covered walkways to afford protection from the sun. And the towns were characterized by distinctive building materials, such as calamine zinc and a 'Pampa cement', the latter made from the saltpetre tailings, alongside extreme examples of upcycling – the swimming pool was the recycled iron hull of a boat shipwrecked off Iquique.

At a glance the facilities appear impressive, but the reality of life in a company town varied depending upon status and wealth. The owners, for the large part British, visited from their luxurious homes in the coastal cities. Managers enjoyed relatively spacious housing and the range of facilities on offer, while the 'Pampinos' workers at the lower end of the hierarchy, predominantly men, led hard, dangerous lives. The workers would arrive either from the coast or from the Andes, tempted by the promise of riches, to be equipped, clothed and accommodated by the mining company. Payment was by token, only spendable in the Company shop, which made a healthy profit, leaving most workers tied to the place and without the support of a distant family. Corporal punishment by the company administrators,

Fig. 57 An aerial view of the central square of Humberstone, with its surrounding shops, public buildings and residential accommodation.

combined with a lack of regulations to protect workers, often led to unrest and brutal repression. It is out of these conditions that the Chilean labour movement grew, firstly through Mutual Societies and later as Unions. A pivotal moment took place in 1907 when 5,000 pampinos marched to Iquique to demand an end to the token system, fixed pay (the strike became known as the 'Eighteen Pence Strike' – the minimum wage demand), severance pay and other basic rights. Panic among the ruling authorities led to the massacre of over 2,000 people, mainly saltpetre miners and their families, who had taken refuge in Santa Maria school. This and other bloodshed during the 1920s led to reform, albeit government recognition of the scale of the Santa Maria killings was not acknowledged for decades.

It is rare to be able to pinpoint the collapse of a society to a specific moment in time, and for the repercussions to be so all-enveloping – an unseen cliff edge. Aside from Chile, the major investors in the South American saltpetre industry were the United Kingdom and Germany, who together accounted for two-thirds of nitrate exports during the first decade of the twentieth century. The outbreak of the First World War served to boost the industry and demonstrate its vulnerability: never was saltpetre in more demand for gunpowder and fertilizer, but Allied naval blockades in the South Atlantic significantly reduced Germany's access to the source product, despite studied Chilean neutrality throughout the conflict. The threat of nitrate demand outstripping supply and the need for new sources had been identified in 1898 when Sir William Crookes spoke of 'the fixation of atmospheric nitrogen is one of the greatest discoveries awaiting the ingenuity of the chemist'.[8] Such ingenuity was to be found in the work of two German chemists, Fritz Haber (also known as 'the Father of Chemical Warfare' for his oversight of the first use of poison gas during the First World War) and Carl Bosch in 1913, who developed a commercially viable means of synthesizing nitrate from ammonia. With no access to Chile's saltpetre fields, German production increased significantly, overtaking that of Chile by the early 1930s. The impact in Chile was dramatic, and, despite the development of the new, more efficient Guggenheim system brought in by American companies taking the place of the German ones, and failed attempts to nationalize the industry, the desert economy collapsed over the course of two decades. By 1950 Chilean nitrate accounted for just

15 per cent of global nitrate production, compared to about 80 per cent during the 1890s. In the 1990s, 100 years after its peak, the country accounted for just 0.1 per cent of the world's market share.

The impact locally in the Atacama was of civilization's return to the desert. Thousands of workers moved to Santiago and southern Chile to find employment, and the mining towns were abandoned, their structures sold, leaving only the vast tailings mounds as evidence of a once global industry. Humberstone and Santa Clara closed in 1958 and 1960 respectively.

For Chile, the loss of such a crucial part of the national economy was devastating. The League of Nations declared it to be the country most affected by the Great Depression (1929–32) and it took a long time to wean the economy off the easy tax receipts from saltpetre, which distracted from alternative industrial and economic strategies for growth.

Globally, there is a further negative outcome caught up in the story of saltpetre mining in Chile's northern desert. While there is no doubting the benefits of increased crop yield brought about by the application of nitrate fertilizers, the carbon emissions resulting from the manufacture process and impact of run-off on groundwater, lakes and rivers is a growing twenty-first-century problem. Excessive use of nitrate fertilizers can lead to oxidization and loss to the atmosphere as nitrous oxide, which is 300 times more potent than carbon dioxide and contributes to global warming.[9] It can also impact upon human health and the state of the environment, leading to unbalanced ecosystems and a deterioration in biodiversity. There is, for example, a summer 'dead zone' in the Gulf of Mexico that averages 14,000 square kilometres and is in large part caused by nitrous-rich run-off, which devastates fish stocks and alters migration patterns.

This all seems a long way from the bleak natural beauty of Tarapacá and the Instagrammable ruins of Humberstone, but it neatly illustrates the interconnectedness of industrial communities to the market. Here success and failure are far fickler than with long-lived places that have diverse raison d'êtres. And it is a global phenomenon as old as history: Cornish tin mining collapsed in the nineteenth century after 4,000 years of production when cheaper tin could be obtained beyond England's shores; the hunt for gold, silver, diamonds or other metals led to the short-lived explosion of mining towns in America, Australia and Namibia, each abandoned once supplies were depleted and newer, more profitable sources discovered. Nor is it a phenomenon limited to remote locations: the demise of the UK coal-mining industry because of domestic policy and overseas competition, brought massive structural change prompted by unemployment which has taken several decades to start to address. The speed and surprise of enforced change does not necessarily match the time and resources required to tackle it.

And what of the future? What of the paradox of plenty, the Midas touch, in which geographical locations are blessed with geological abundance which brings disaster after short-term gain? Some of the petrostates of West Asia have seen the writing on the wall and are seeking to diversify their economies, from Saudi exploration of alternative energy technologies to the UAE's aspirations to become a global trade hub alongside growing commercial ship-repair and tourism industries. But oil dependence, like that of saltpetre, is a difficult habit to kick. With a tiny public sector, political rigidity and a reluctance to embrace social and economic change, one wonders whether the oil towns of Ahmadi, Awali and Dhahran will one day mirror those of Humberstone and Santa Clara?

Route 66, US

A place to 'get your kicks', 'America's Main Street', Steinbeck's 'Mother Road' or the 'road to opportunity' – is there a better-known twentieth-century road than Route 66? This American highway starts in Chicago on the shores of Lake Michigan, traverses the plains of the Midwest, the deserts of the south and the mountains of the west, before ending its 2,400-mile journey in the heat and smog of Los Angeles at Santa Monica.

This is a story rooted in American culture, about a road as a symbol of hope, escape and a new life, about freedom, vacations and entertainment. But most of all it is a story about the rise and rise of the car.

The history of the United States of America is often presented as one of arrival and migration, be it the waves of early European settlers to the country, ships carrying enslaved peoples from Africa

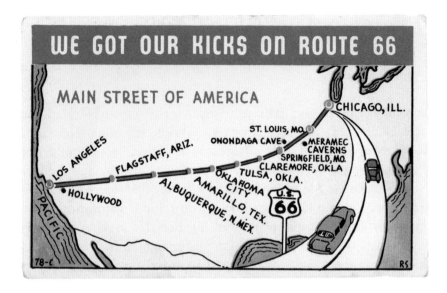

Fig. 58 Route 66 to the sun: a vintage postcard showing the route and major towns it passed through.

or more recent immigrants seeking refuge or economic opportunity. The welcome torch of the Statue of Liberty or the razor-wire on the wall that border's Mexico present two symbolic extremes of that narrative, while the displacement of Native American populations nods to the fact that this was by no means an empty place. Given the size of the country, and the early historic predominance of the eastern seaboard cities, much of this story is framed as pulses of migrants heading west. Tempted by furs, gold or land, or pushed out in search of employment, the 'west was won' via wagon trails, military roads and rail tracks that grew like tendrils opening up opportunities in one new territory beyond the other.

Roads, such as they were before the arrival of the car, varied hugely from metalled commercial turnpikes built in the 1700s to the unsurfaced horse and mule tracks that threaded across much of the populated countryside. Bridges, trading posts and accommodation for people and animals were the priority, especially in more rural lands away from the towns and cities – more so than the costly preparation and maintenance of roads. Guidance offered to travellers setting out from Independence, Missouri, to San Francisco in 1849 warned:

The journey is not entirely a pleasure trip. It is attended with some hardships and privation. The road is a simple wagon trail – part good, and part very bad. Large parties are annoyed by a fine white dust.[10]

Ironically, one of the earliest advocates for improved road surfaces came from enthusiasts of two wheels, not four. The Good Roads Movement of 1880s began as a cyclists' lobbying group when the League of American Wheelmen was formed, later publishing *Good Roads Magazine* in 1882. The league, which still exists today, became the largest cycling membership organization in the US, governing the sport of bike racing but also seeking to ensure that cyclists were heard by the state, campaigning for better roads. At the time the League also sought to stand up for its members by addressing 'antagonism from horsemen, wagon drivers, and pedestrians'.[11] Soon, however, the League would be joined in their crusade by a new road-user, 'the automobilist'. Outside the town, these adventurers were initially few and far between: 'Automobiling,' said the *Brooklyn Eagle* newspaper in 1910 with little foresight, was 'the last call of the wild.' Cars were expensive and required an infrastructure rarely seen beyond the town, so by the end of the nineteenth century there was only one motorized vehicle for every 18,000 people in America.

During the first decades of the twentieth century Good Roads organizations grew throughout the country, extolling the virtues of improved roads for trade and speed as well as safety, leading to state contributions to their construction. But, without federal support, the task was piecemeal and overwhelming.

Henry Ford's introduction of the Model T in 1908 was to change everything. The 'Tin Lizzie' was the first car to be successfully designed and marketed to 'the great multitude'.[12] With cheap production costs aided by significant improvements to the assembly line system, and a design that was so adaptable the car could be used as a tractor as well as a delivery wagon or passenger vehicle, sales grew exponentially during the first three decades of the century. The Model T was also extremely robust, able to cope with the rutted roads and rough farm tracks of the time. By 1923 production peaked at just over two million Model Ts rolling off the automated lines in

Detroit, and by 1925 the car, which originally cost $825 in 1909 (the equivalent of about $23,500 today), could be purchased for just $260 (around $3,800 today). Other manufacturers responded to Ford's drive to get the middle classes on the road, reducing prices so that by 1928 American factories, including those belonging to Ford, were producing 4,359,000 cars a year.[13]

While car ownership expanded massively, the infrastructure was soon revealed to be woefully inadequate – no matter the Model T's off-road capability. Eventually, the national government stepped in. Woodrow Wilson's Federal Aid Road Act built the legislation for national support for public highways in 1916, and was followed by the Federal Highway Act of 1921, amended in 1925 and 1926, which effectively placed real levels of federal funding on the table for road construction and improvement. Under these conditions the US Highway system was born. As a general rule, each road was given a unique number, with odd numbers for north–south routes, starting with US 1 on the east coast to US 91 on the west coast, and even numbers on the east–west routes, starting with US 2 on the Canadian border and US 90 deep in the south.

Cyrus Avery, an oilman, farmer and entrepreneur from Tulsa, Oklahoma, was an advocate of the Good Roads movement, later becoming involved as the president of the Associated Highways Associations of America. He joined with John Woodruff of Springfield, Missouri to plan a new federal highway connecting Chicago to Los Angeles. They successfully lobbied for the route that was to become US Route 66 by promoting the road's advantage in not having to cross the high passes of the Rocky Mountains and the economic benefit it would accrue for all the places it would pass through en route. Most of the route was not new, instead it effectively adopted the high streets of hundreds of towns, small and large, justifying Avery's title of the 'Main Street of America'. Unlike other highways of the time, it did not follow an arrow-straight course, instead traversing across Missouri, Kansas, Oklahoma, Texas, New Mexico, Arizona and California, improving the roads that connected America's rural hinterland to the market.

Route 66 was officially designated in the summer of 1926, but the task of surfacing, resurfacing and maintenance was a long one, only completed by 1938. For many, it was the significantly enhanced local access for transporting grain, goods and gravel, rather than the opportunity for long-distance travel, that was critical to its early success. For example, trucks, the mainstay of the road, increased from 1,500 per day to 7,500 on the Chicago to St Louis segment in the decade from 1931. But, for the impatient, Route 66 could be driven in its entirety from Lake Michigan to the Pacific coast in just under five days.

During the 1930s Route 66 took on a new role as a migrant highway, a conduit for thousands escaping the economic consequences of the Dustbowl era. Steinbeck evocatively captured the desperation and hope of those people in *The Grapes of Wrath*:

> 66 is the path of a people in flight, refugees from dust and shrinking land, from the thunder of tractors and shrinking ownership, from the desert's slow northward invasion, from the twisting winds that howl up out of Texas, from the floods that bring no richness to the land and steal what little richness is there. From all of these the people are in flight, and they come into 66 from the tributary side roads, from the wagon tracks and the rutted country roads. 66 is the mother road, the road of flight.[14]

Fig. 59 Escaping the Dust Bowl Midcontinent, 10 August 1938.

AMONGST THE RUINS

And, from 1933 the road itself became part of an employment programme as Roosevelt's response to the Great Depression extended
to include infrastructure such as the national highways network.
Through the Second New Deal's Civilian Conservation Corps and
the Works Progress Administration, thousands of unemployed people
from across the country – mainly men – not only surfaced and
resurfaced the road, but built bridges, culverts, underpasses and
even parks for travellers to stop and take a break.

If the birth of Route 66 was to foster access and economic activity
along the highway, and its first decades were characterized by its role
during the Great Depression, the 1940s were to witness the impact
of war. The growth of the US military machine in response to the
conflict with the Axis Powers during the Second World War was felt
disproportionately strongly in the western states. Californian companies won 12 per cent of all US war contracts and were responsible
for supplying 17 per cent of war materials. 'Between 1941 to 45 the
government invested approximately $70 billion in capital projects
throughout California, a large proportion of which were in the
Los Angeles–San Diego area.'[15] Munitions factories, training bases,
dockyards and aircraft manufacturers across the region ensured a
steady stream of military personnel and equipment into and out of
the west, alongside a growing army of civilians in the industries
required for the war effort. By turn, Route 66 and other all-weather
roads serviced that demand.

The golden years of Route 66 were to follow. Rising car ownership, combined with post-war prosperity, a booming population
and cheap fuel, meant that the road offered the middle and working
classes realistic prospects of a holiday away from their hometown. For
many vacationing Americans the highway became a road to the sun,
entertainment and adventure. Route 66 would take them to sandy
Pacific beaches, Santa Monica pier and Disneyland by way of the
Grand Canyon, 'cowboy' country and the Petrified Forest National
Park, to name but a few attractions. Entrepreneurs along the road
recognized and responded to this, giving their new customers what
they needed and what they never knew they wanted. Motels with
swimming pools, gas stations and garages, roadside diners and sou-
venir stores, frozen custard stands and steakhouses cashed in on the
burgeoning holiday trade. The architecture was distinctive, designed

Fig. 60 Wigwam Village Motel No. 6, Holbrook, Arizona, one in a series of seven chain motels on Route 66 built between 1936 and 1950. The tepees (rather than wigwams) were built in steel and concrete.

to catch the passing eye, but also taking inspiration from each region the road passed through. Route 66 served as an ever-changing shop window on the local vernacular, albeit one that could descend into exaggeration and pastiche: 'Sometimes,' comedian Billy Connolly observed, 'there's a tackiness about Route 66 that out-tacks any tackiness I've ever seen anywhere else.'[16]

Accommodation in tepees, colonial bungalows and log cabins was complemented by a proliferation of competitive neon and the siren cry of advertising billboards. The futuristic Googie style of the 1950s, itself inspired by technological optimism and the space race, was a commonly recurring motif along the route, spreading east from its California origins at Googie's coffee shop in West Hollywood. Here a new roadside architecture of plastic, steel and yet more neon combined with sharp edges and oversized signage in a style perfectly matching the exaggerated tailfins, sweeping lines and chrome of the cars of the era. Route 66 offered everything. Travellers could see dinosaurs, visit caves, meteor craters or Cadillac graveyards, pan for gold or stop for a burger in the original McDonald's restaurant. That Nat King Cole exhorted people to 'get their kicks' was rooted in the highway's appeal as a road of entertainment, free from the nine-to-five routine of a working week. Route 66 then and now came to represent certain American values: the freedom of the open road, perseverance in the face of adversity and a pioneering spirit.

One net result of Route 66's ever-growing procession of farm vehicles, military convoys, delivery trucks, Greyhound buses and holiday-bound cars was the blossoming of places along the highway that serviced them. Over a period of forty years the road acted as a fuse to population growth, turning single farmsteads into stop-over villages and villages into service towns.

But popularity was to be the highway's undoing. Route 66's meandering course, frequent stops for traffic lights and narrow twin carriageways simply could not cope with the increased volume of vehicles. The tread of heavy military traffic and the huge numbers of trucks using the road during the war years had also taken their toll, leaving a legacy of poor surfaces. This by turn was exacerbated by cars that could go faster – but effectively couldn't – and 'are we nearly there yet' expectations of lifestyles lived at a faster pace. The road developed a reputation as 'Bloody 66' because of the increasing number of accidents. Meanwhile, soldiers returning from Europe, including Eisenhower, the new president, saw what the future could look like in the autobahns of Germany. Split multi-lane carriageways, limited access points and sweeping engineering which ignored the twists and turns of nature's topography by creating bridges, cuttings and tunnels, 'offering the possibility often lacking in the United States, to drive with speed and efficiency at the same time'.[17] Eisenhower has history here. As a young lieutenant he took part in the US Army's first motor convoy across the United States, a journey which in 1919 took two months and resulted in broken bridges, truck axles and copious quantities of mud, and was significantly memorable to feature in his later writing.[18]

The Federal Aid Highways Act of 1956 was not the first piece of legislation to herald the arrival of the US Interstate Network, but it was the most important. The Act led to the construction of 66,000 kilometres of new roads at a cost of $26 billion, largely funded through an increase in the tax on fuel. From the late 1950s through to 1970, Route 66 was slowly replaced along its entire length by five new Interstates, each one bypassing the former course of the road and many of the communities that had grown up along its length. In some places the new roads would take traffic and trade many kilometres away, such as a stretch of the I-40 in Arizona between

Seligman and Kingman which cut a new path 32 kilometres south of the old highway. In others the interstate would run immediately alongside Route 66, but a lack of access ramps would render communities that were once a casual pull-in away from trade, bereft of wheel-fall. For many of the smaller places, the substitution of one highway by another and relocation of passing business was the final straw; motels were sold, gas forecourts abandoned and residents moved on for new opportunities elsewhere. Route 66 begat a series of ghost towns and shrunken settlements, such as Arlington (Missouri), Texola (Oklahoma), Glenrio (straddling New Mexico and Texas) and Two Guns (Arizona). In other places it was a slow atrophy.

The bypassed communities campaigned first against the interstates, and then when the writing was on the wall, for the least-worst option of ensuring that business loops were constructed through the bypassed towns. 'Look at Route 66 quickly, for tomorrow it will be gone; in no time it will be all streamlined super-highway straight and impersonal as the New Jersey turnpike,' wrote Richard Strout in 1956.[19] Route 66's individuality, its quirky idiosyncratic attractions and mom and pop stores were slowly to be replaced by the uniformity of national franchises on the interstates where the product would be the same whether in Missouri or New Mexico. Leon and Ann Little's story in Oklahoma was repeated elsewhere along the route:

> They didn't move the traffic till 1962, but we knew this was coming, of course, and so I came down to Hinton and took the postmaster job, and Ann managed the business out there until the traffic moved in 1962. And, of course, the day the traffic moved, well that was it.[20]

The replacement of Route 66 took three decades, and those who could not move, or did not wish to, 'watched construction of the interstates often with the same apprehension as a sick person watching the construction of a coffin'.[21]

Route 66 was officially decommissioned in 1985. Thereafter, the future of the road was left to a jabberwocky of interests and, consequently, the physical fabric of the route fragmented into a mixture of state, local government and private control, with some stretches abandoned entirely.

Fig. 61 The former general store in the Route 66 ghost town of Goffs, California, stands abandoned. Goffs was an early casualty of a 1931 realignment of Route 66 itself which bypassed the village 6 miles to the south. It also had a bar, restaurant and dance floor.

The postscript to this story is a happy one. While the infra-structure of Route 66 may have crumbled, the romantic idea of the Mother Road persisted. During and after decommissioning, a growing number of Route 66 businesses and enthusiasts refused to let the road disappear. Primarily motivated by the loss of trade, this was not a case of rose-tinted nostalgia, but a very real threat to people's livelihoods. Over the years a groundswell of public opinion built up which recognized that the loss of the road would constitute a loss of a piece of classic Americana. The moteliers, gift shop and attraction owners lining the road were joined by those who remembered the route on vacation, or were simply inspired by its architecture and the highway's legacy as captured in book, film or TV. 'Historic Route 66' came to the fore as an American icon, melding the concepts of the 'open road' with 'freedom'. This cultural road trip began with the adventurous spirit of the early pioneers, took new form in the writing of Steinbeck and Jack Kerouac (*On the Road*), before arriving by way of *Easy Rider* (1969) and Pixar's *Cars* (2006) to appear in countless posts, tweets and travel blogs of the digital era. By 1990 Congress authorized the US National Park Service to research ways to commemorate the route which had played such 'a significant role in the 20th-century history of our Nation' (Law 101-400). The result was put into action nine years later, when the Route 66 Corridor Preservation Program was created to preserve the highway's cultural resources (Law 106-45, 1999), alongside federal appropriations which authorized up to $10 million. Grants, technical assistance and research combined with private and state initiatives to preserve the historic character of the route, its stories and to encourage visits. Research published in 2011 highlighted the significant economic impact to the communities straddling Route 66 brought by heritage tourism – conservatively estimated to be worth $132 million annually in direct benefits, rising to $425 million when all indirect, tax and wealth creation benefits are accounted for.[22]

The highway and communities that lie alongside it are unlikely to see a return to the visitor numbers of Route 66's heyday, but such aspiration is to miss the point. 'We can't have 2,400 miles of Williamsburg,' remarked David Knudson of the Historic Route 66 Federation;[23] instead, the road has a future in which it continues to harness the power of the past for future economic benefit. Uniquely, at the same time, it can help revitalize some of the poorest areas of the States and, because it passes through areas rich in Native American and Hispanic influence, it offers an opportunity to rebalance the narratives of those with underrepresented histories. Like any slice of twentieth-century America, Route 66 was a reflection of the values of its time, which unfortunately included discrimination and racism. Certain sectors of society were not always welcome on this most liberating of US highways: 'It's important to elevate this understanding not to diminish Route 66 in any way [but to] to uplift and promote a more inclusive and accurate understanding of the road and our history.'[24]

Transport corridors constantly evolve, waxing and waning because of political decisions, economic change or advancing technology, and with that evolution comes change to the communities that service them. Route 66 has survived, despite being largely surpassed in its original purpose to get people and goods from A to B. The reason? Because it has such a distinctive cultural legacy – one that is representative of *the* dominant nation of the twentieth century. Route 66 is America's Via Appia, its Camino de Santiago, its Silk Road. It is the yellow brick road brought to life.

Beaudesert Hall, England

A 'squint test' is a useful way to filter out the detail. Looking at the world through almost-closed eyes forces the viewer to concentrate on the largest, brightest things in front of them. If such a test were to be applied to a nation's heritage, then the UK might be defined by Stonehenge, Hadrian's Wall and an impressive legacy of industrial heritage. The country house and landscape garden would also be on such a list, particularly those dating to the long eighteenth century (1688–1815). The fine Georgian mansion and its associated estate runs as a thick storyline through English literature, from Jane Austen to Evelyn Waugh, and is conserved and gently reinvented by organizations such as the National Trust and English Heritage. Privately owned palaces, such as Blenheim, Castle Howard and Chatsworth, are powerhouse icons, not only visited by millions but also directly and indirectly employing thousands in their catchments. They play a mute but starring role in upstairs–downstairs stories on the small and big screen, such as the fictional Downton Abbey, Bridgerton or Brideshead. Dame Maggie Smith's perpetually raised eyebrow is often well matched by Highclere Castle's gothic arches, each a national treasure.

But this love story with the country mansion went through a very difficult period during the twentieth century, so difficult it is estimated that over 1,200 houses in England alone have been demolished since 1900.[25] A similar tale of asset stripping and wrecking balls took place in Scotland, Wales and Ireland. At its peak in 1955, Britain lost an important mansion every five days. The homes of the British nobility and minor gentry alike have always been built, adapted, knocked down and rebuilt – this after all was where the wealth of the nation was vested. The buildings and their estates reflected the tastes and aspirations of their owners, and as fortunes waxed and waned over generations, so the art and architecture changed too. But for centuries the balance sheet had remained for the most part static, leaving the country with a rich and diverse stylistic heritage. The twentieth century changed all that. A perfect storm of conditions combined to create an era of the lost country house, as lifestyles sustainable in the past were no longer tenable.

Fig. 62 William Paget, 1st Baron Paget of Beaudesert Hall, Staffordshire. He is painted wearing a jewel showing St George, the symbol of the Order of the Garter.

With nearly 2,000 lost historic houses across the United Kingdom, there are an overwhelming number of ruined places which tell the sad story of destruction and the reasons behind their demise. Some are well known, such as the enormous Hamilton Palace in Larnarkshire, Scotland, which was demolished between 1921 and 1926, or the gothic extravagance of Eaton Hall in Cheshire, owned by the Dukes of Westminster, which was replaced by a contentious, scaled-down modern hall in the 1970s. But it is often the smaller, (relatively) less grand examples that reveal the pressures faced by the majority of historic country-house owners.

Beaudesert Hall was originally constructed as a small Cistercian monastery in the mid-twelfth century on the heathy hills of Cannock Chase in Staffordshire. Its remote location, on the fringes of a royal hunting forest, and French name, meaning 'beautiful wilderness' (like Strata Florida in mid-Wales, another secluded Cistercian house, this time with a Latin name, 'Valley of Flowers'), were typical of a religious order that sought to be apart from the distractions of humanity and closer to the grace of God. Its remoteness, elevation and the availability of good hunting led to its selection by the Bishop of Lichfield as a summer palace or hunting lodge, complete with a large private park or chase. The same characteristics probably appealed to William Paget, who was given the property by Henry VIII after the king forced Bishop Sampson to surrender the estate during the Reformation in 1546. Originally from Staffordshire, Paget was a man of considerable influence in Henry's court, being at one time Chancellor of the Duchy of Lancaster and one of those responsible for Prince Edward, the heir to the throne. Paget was created Baron Paget de Beaudesert in 1549 and the house was to remain in the family for almost 400 years.

By the time the Pagets acquired the estate the main hall had already seen a variety of improvements, particularly during the fifteenth century, but new wealth, new responsibility and a new principal family seat demanded more than alteration to an already old building. In 1573 Paget's younger son, Thomas, Third Baron, began the construction of a fine Elizabethan mansion. Incorporating the earlier stone-built medieval fabric, Thomas created an impressive new east front in brick, with a central entrance tower and balancing wings in a style mirroring other mansions of the period such as Hatfield,

Montacute and Shaw House. Before it was a great courtyard, entered through a gatehouse. It was remarkable that the hall was completed: Thomas, a devout Catholic and supporter of Mary Queen of Scots, fled to Paris in 1583 to join his brother on the uncovering of the Throckmorton Plot. The plot was one of many which sought to replace Elizabeth with Mary, and the Pagets' association with the Catholic cause led to the loss of titles and estates in 1587. Thomas died in exile in Brussels in 1590, and it wasn't until Elizabeth I's death and succession of James I, Mary's son, to the English crown, that the baronetcy and properties were restored to the family.

The Pagets' wealth derived from their estates, their offices and a degree of commercial entrepreneurship. The First Baron made the most of the natural resources of Cannock – iron ore, water to power mills and wood to turn into charcoal – to establish ironworks that would slowly change the wooded landscape of the area to grazing heath. William, the Fourth Baron, invested in the Virginia Company, which founded the Jamestown settlement in the Virginia colonies in 1607, and which was instrumental in the English claim to the Caribbean island of Bermuda. One of Bermuda's parishes still bears William's name. And while Beaudesert was the chief seat of the family, it was by no means their only estate. Gifts, acquisition and marriage brought the Pagets land and property across Staffordshire, in London, at Drayton in Buckinghamshire and, in the late eighteenth century, Plas Newydd overlooking the Menai Strait on the island of Anglesey, Wales.

The connection with Plas Newydd is important. By the eighteenth century the male line of the Paget family died out and the title was passed through marriage to Henry Bayly of Plas Newydd, who took his mother's name to become Tenth Baron Paget in 1769. The Anglesey estates brought wealth through copper mining, which supplemented the growing value of coal extracted from the Pagets' Staffordshire properties. Consequently, Henry was able to commission the architect James Wyatt and his assistant Joseph Potter to update the Elizabethan mansion at Beaudesert. From 1771 they removed the courtyard and lodge in front of the Elizabethan house, redesigned the interiors and created a new crescent-shaped stable block and coachhouse. Later in the 1790s, the pair worked on Plas Newydd, building a completely new entrance front to the Welsh mansion.

Fig. 63 Humphry Repton's proposals for opening up the landscape at Beaudesert as illustrated in one of his Red Books, 1816.

The same appetite for renewal and redesign was reflected in the landscape, where Henry Paget first commissioned William Emes, a follower of Lancelot Capability Brown (who was prolific on neighbouring estates elsewhere in the county), to create a new walled garden and to naturalize the wider estate landscape. Later, over the winter of 1813/14, Henry's son, another Henry, invited the great landscape architect Humphry Repton to Beaudesert. Repton had also worked at Plas Newydd in 1799 for the Tenth Baron. Here in Staffordshire, over a period of ten days, he compiled and sketched his recommendations in one of his famous Red Books. His plans for Beaudesert were to revive the historic spirit of its past:

> . . . a desert beautified – *un beau-desert* [in French]; rendered habitable, with all the elegance, magnificence, and comfort, of which it was capable. We must therefore look back to the reign of Henry VIII, when this mansion was presented to the family.[26]

To this end he suggested the removal of trees to restore the long views of the house and the balance between 'Ground, Rocks, Water, and

Wood' because 'at Beaudesert it is only the latter which abounds'.[27] Interestingly, he also began to push back on some of the overly designed naturalism of Capability Brown, his self-proclaimed predecessor, at the expense of formality:

> . . . *be-belted* and *be-clumped* in the newest style of the modern taste of Landscape Gardening – No – rather let us go back to former times, when the lofty terraces of the *privy garden* gave protection and seclusion to the noble persons . . .[28]

In response, Repton recommended exactly that, the recreation of geometrical gardens close to the southern side of the house. In such designs we see the start of a national transition between eighteenth-century landscape gardens which took nature up to the door of the grand house, and busier Victorian styles which offered something formal in between.

Repton's Red Book for Beaudesert was a consultant's report for a client. We don't know how many recommendations within it were implemented by Henry Paget, although an Elizabethan-style garden is hinted at in *The Journal of Horticulture, Cottage Gardener and Country Gentleman* in 1872.[29] Henry, now the Second Earl of Uxbridge, was busily occupied in the wars with France. He was a highly successful soldier, rising to the rank of Lieutenant General, who went on to command the allied cavalry at Waterloo. His share in that success brought him the title of Marquess of Anglesey, while the loss of his leg in the battle brought retirement from the military and a successful political career. The Waterloo Staircase was constructed at this time at Beaudesert, supposedly with wide treads and short risers to accommodate the Marquess's wooden leg.

Little alteration took place to the hall or its gardens for nearly 100 years until a fire in 1909 prompted the Sixth Marquess to restore the house, reversing much of Wyatt's work, to return some of Beaudesert's interiors to its Elizabethan heyday. The cost was over £30,000, and included a new lime avenue, rockery and kitchen garden as well as the works to the house.[30]

So far, so typical of many country mansions across Britain – an evolving story of construction and reconstruction for both house and gardens, interrupted by fire and interspersed with periods when

Fig. 64 The Great Hall at Beaudesert in 1919.

nothing much happened architecturally. Spendthrift heirs, scandal and enlightened patrons are equally part of the same narrative. The events of the twentieth century changed all that for the Pagets and Beaudesert, and for the nation. The Great War of 1914–18 not only led to the death of many of the would-be inheritors of these mansions, but it fundamentally altered the fabric of society. Labour become more expensive, and aspirations changed – opportunities for a life in service both diminished and were less desirable. Trends seen earlier in the previous century continued to apply pressure on country-house owners, including reducing profits from the large agricultural estates that funded an often extravagant aristocratic lifestyle. The agricultural depression of the 1870s was mirrored by Britain's loss of industrial advantage to other parts of the world, leaving families such as the Pagets, who relied on the income from both, with significantly fewer resources. The days of employing hundreds of staff – cooks, maids and butlers in the grand house, with gardeners, stablehands and gamekeepers beyond – were over.

Taxation too was increasing. Income tax, introduced in 1799 to fund the Napoleonic Wars, was raised for the same reasons during the Great War. In 1909 further proposals for an increased tax on the wealthy were unsurprisingly rejected by the wealthy sitting in the House of Lords – namely those with large houses. The move backfired, as the right for the Lords to veto Parliamentary decisions was removed in 1911, marking yet another loss of power by the aristocratic elite; the champions of grand country mansions found themselves denuded of political influence to help their own cause. During the Great Depression, and the run-up to the Second World War, there were few others who felt preserving the lifestyles and fabric of the privileged of previous centuries was a priority. A brave new world shaped by war, depression and the rise of socialism, had little sympathy for the preservation of monuments from an unequal past. Local people watched the 'wonderful sight' of Nuthall Temple going up in flames as it was demolished in 1929.[31] And not every owner of a historic mansion looked back on their disappearance with regret, albeit crocodile tears might be judiciously applied as a burdensome family heirloom recouped some financial benefit.

A final fillip for the auctioneer's gavel and wreckers-yard contract was the increased burden of death duties. In England, a tax on the dead has steadily increased since probate duty was introduced in 1694. Modern death duties can be traced to the Liberal government's announcement of estate duty in 1894, which sought to plug a £4 million deficit in government spending – a taxation response to the same depression that was already reducing estate income. William Harcourt, the chancellor at the time, was accused of 'carrying not only sack and pillage into the houses of England but also the demon of discord and treachery'.[32] In the early years estate duty stood at 8 per cent on taxable amounts over £1,000,000, but it was raised to 40 per cent after the Great War on estates over £2,000,000, reaching an enormous 75 per cent in 1945 at the conclusion of the Second World War. Throughout this period there were additional duties for legacy and succession. The impact of an enormous tax bill on cash-poor inheritors led to either the sale of historic houses and their contents, or demolition to remove the liability of upkeep.

And what of Beaudesert? Many of the pressures described above were felt by the Pagets. Beaudesert may have been the chief seat of the family for centuries, but in 1919 Plas Newydd became their principal home.

Sales in 1921, 1932 and 1935 resulted in the estate losing much of the surrounding land and all nine gate lodges. The great Waterloo Staircase along with panelling and fireplaces were sold in the 1935 sale, shipped to Australia and incorporated into the newly constructed Carrick Hill House in Adelaide. It is now a public museum and art gallery. A little closer to home, bricks from the demolition were repurposed at St James's Palace in London, where they were clearly the right age and quality to replace smoke-blackened facias. A 6.5-metre-long painted oak screen that once divided Beaudesert's Great Hall from its buttery and pantry can still be seen in Glasgow's Burrell Art Gallery and Museum, albeit there remains uncertainty as to whether it is the fifteenth-century original or a post-fire copy.

The Sixth Marquess wrote in the *Lichfield Mercury*:

. . . Unfortunately I have not been able to occupy Beaudesert since 1920. The very heavy burden of taxation, since the war, has made it impossible for owners all over the country to maintain everything as in pre-war days, and many heartbreak decisions have had to be taken . . . In this case Beaudesert has been offered again

Fig. 65 The remains of Beaudesert today.

and again to every possible public body . . . In 1932 Beaudesert was offered for sale by public auction, but not a single bid was made . . .[33]

The hall was purchased by demolition contractors for £800, who had all but completed the task before going bankrupt. The marquess stepped back in and the family continued to sell the now ruinous hall for building material. Today all that remains are elements of the medieval Great Hall, ironically reflecting one of the earlier periods of Beaudesert's history, and cellars. These ruins and park were gifted by the family to the current owners, the Beaudesert Trust, in 1937 for the benefit of Scouts, Guides and young people in Staffordshire. The tenacious remains of the hall are protected as a listed building under the Planning (Listed Buildings and Conservation Areas) Act 1990.

The period from 1870 to 1970 was disastrous for Britain's historic mansions, with hundreds following a similar path to destruction as at Beaudesert. But the fact that Beaudesert's ruins are now protected, and that the conscious demolition of important historic buildings is far rarer, is the final piece of this narrative . . . to date. The same post-war Labour government that increased and then reformed death duties also commissioned the Gowers Report. This investigation was 'to consider and report what arrangements might be made by the Government for the preservation, maintenance and use of houses of outstanding historic or architectural interest which might otherwise not be preserved, including, where desirable, the preservation of a house and its contents as a unity'.[34] The Gowers Report recommendations, adopted slowly over decades, led as the tendrils of good ideas to greater protection of the historic environment through planning legislation (the introduction of Listed Building Consent in 1969 was another factor in stemming the tide of demolition), to the exempting of historic houses from death duties providing they are looked after and open to the general public, to the establishment of what is now English Heritage and Historic England; and to the creation of the National Heritage Memorial Fund, which supports the acquisition, restoration and understanding of historic buildings.

Today, the general mood in the UK is that historic houses are an important part of our heritage, as evidenced by the growing membership of organizations such as the National Trust or Historic Houses. Country-house owners are now caterers, retailers, accommodation providers, festival organizers, as well as farm managers, custodians of nature and entrepreneurs of the imagination. Well-placed teazels permitting, visitors can sit themselves at a banquet in the dining room, or imagine the drudgery of the scullery maid, and exit via the obligatory gift shop with things they never knew they needed. That's not to say that there are no challenges, not least in the need to acknowledge where the wealth came from to construct and decorate some of these magnificent places – slave labour, industry, war, the profits of colonialism. Owners with public-facing aspirations must continue to reinvent their homes to remain relevant or face cancelling by demand or disinterest.

History does not stand still. There is a large gap in the number of historic houses of Britain and Ireland resulting from the events of the late nineteenth and twentieth centuries. Demolition of important historic buildings, whether planned or due to accident of fire or flood, will always occur, as it has in the past, and Beaudesert will not rise from the ashes. But an equilibrium has been restored . . . for the time being.

Abu Simbel and the Nubian Monuments, Egypt and Sudan

> My name is Ozymandias, king of kings:
> Look on my works, ye Mighty, and despair!'
> Nothing beside remains. Round the decay
> Of that colossal wreck, boundless and bare
> The lone and level sands stretch far away.[35]

We have already explored one aspect of the loss of heritage to water in the discussion on climate change (see chapter 1), but the economic demands to build substantial reservoirs account for some of the most spectacular examples of disappearance – and of rescue conservation. The final case-study in this chapter looks at how the need for water has led both to the abandonment of historic buildings in extant, living communities and to the submergence of already ruinous evidence of the past.

Fig. 66 The temples to Amon-Re and Re-Horakhte at Abu Simbel, *c.* 1845, by David Roberts.

The rescue of the pharaonic temples of Abu Simbel from the rising waters of the High Aswan dam is a well-known story, a pivotal and heroic moment in the history of the conservation movement. But it is also the poster child – the high (formerly low) point – of an ongoing battle between present-day demands for water and the conservation of the past, both ancient and more recent, which included thousands of other important sites across what is now southern Egypt and northern Sudan. This is a story of extraordinary innovation, particularly around the physical relocation of important monuments and a wide-ranging campaign of archaeological recording, but it is also about loss, with ancient Nubia and the very definition of history at its heart.

Upper Nubia, or Wawat, extended between the first and second cataracts of the Nile. Identifiable since 8000 BCE, the Nubians were at one time conquerors and conquered in a region which was subject to waves of ancient Egyptian, Hyksos (Hebrew), Assyrian, Greek, Roman and other desert kingdom influences. Consequently, it is a landscape rich in diverse temples (pharaonic, classical, Christian and Muslim), funerary monuments, palaces, forts and settlements. Inevitably, the life-providing qualities of the Nile – food, irrigation, transport – and the barriers of the cataracts, have meant that humans have long clustered close to the river edge, leaving a concentrated ribbon of historic settlements and archaeological sites within sight of its waters.

From empire to backwater, Nubian culture was never lost but rather receded into the background, split by new political borders, diluted by conflict and melded with a succession of alternative influences. The heritage of the region too was well known to those who lived in its shadow, albeit sand, erosion and the disconnect of understanding amplified by the march of time rendered many ancient sites as either a curious backdrop or part of a mythical ancestry.

The rediscovery of the region by and for Europeans in the early nineteenth century is an epic tale, involving English aristocrats, an Italian circus strongman and a Swiss explorer. The story of Lausanne-born antiquarian Johann Burckhardt's discovery of the temples of Abu Simbel could be the inspiration for an *Indiana Jones* movie. Travelling dressed in local costume, Burckhardt, who was also known by his adopted Muslim name Ibrāhīm Ibn 'abd Allāh, was commissioned by the Royal Society in London to explore the upper reaches of the Nile. His diaries make compelling reading, where discovery is laced with encounters of wild animals, robbery, disease, international rivalry and political obfuscation. Little wonder that six of Burckhardt's predecessors sent on the same mission by the Society failed to return. On 23 March 1813, aged twenty-eight, he was heading along the west bank of the river past the village of Ballyane:

I left my guide, with the camels, and descended an almost perpendicular cleft, choked with sand, to view the temple of Ebsambal [Abu Simbel], of which I had heard many magnificent descriptions . . . In front of the entrance are six erect colossal figures, representing juvenile persons, three on each side, placed in narrow recesses, and looking towards the river . . .[36]

Having, as I supposed, seen all the antiquities of Ebsambal, I was about to ascend the sandy side of the mountain by the same way I had descended; when having luckily turned more to the southward, I fell in with what is yet visible of four immense colossal statues cut out of rock, at a distance of about two hundred yards from the temple; they stand in a deep recess, excavated in the mountain; but it is greatly to be regretted, that they are now almost entirely buried beneath the sands, which are blown here in torrents. The entire head, and part of the breast and arms of one of the statues are yet above the surface; of the one next to it scarcely any part is visible, the head being broken off, and the body covered with sand to above the shoulders; of the other two, the bonnets only appear. It is difficult to determine, whether the statues are in a sitting or standing position . . .[37]

The two rediscovered temples were originally constructed on the orders of Pharaoh Ramses II around 1264–1244 BCE, with the larger dedicated to the sun gods Amon-Re and Re-Horakhte, the other for his favourite principal wife Nefertari for the worship of the goddess Hathor. Built to underpin his credentials as a god-king and great pharaonic empire-builder, it is one of several scattered across the New Kingdom's colony of Nubia, a reminder of Egyptian dominance.

Burckhardt's diaries of the trips he made throughout the region between 1813 and 1814 record many antiquities dating to the same period as the Abu Simbel temples and other eras. Some were already known to Europeans, such as the temple on Philae Island, while many were not. Where the Swiss antiquarian led, others were to follow, including the Italian Giovanni Belzoni, 'the Great Belzoni', one-time circus strongman, barber and inventor, and his English wife, Sarah. At Burkhardt's recommendation, Belzoni eventually cleared the mounded sand that prevented access to the temples at Abu Simbel.

This is a story about the disappearance and removal of heritage, and while both issues are illustrated at a grand scale prompted by a twentieth-century dam, they are presaged by events of the early nineteenth century as European nations and individual collectors sought to acquire a piece of Egypt to bring home. William Bankes, an English politician and passionate Egyptologist who visited Abu Simbel in 1815, commissioned Belzoni to remove the great obelisk on Philae Island and ship it back to England. Belzoni's diary records the moment when the mission nearly ended in disaster:

On my return, the pier appeared quite strong enough to bear at least forty times the weight it had to support; but, alas! when

AMONGST THE RUINS

the obelisk came gradually on from the sloping bank, and all the weight rested on it, the pier, with the obelisk, and some of the men, took a slow movement, and majestically descended into the river, wishing us better success. I was not three yards off when this happened, and for some minutes, I must confess, I remained as stiff as a post. The first thing that came into my head, was the loss of such a piece of antiquity; the second was, the exultation of our opponents, after so much questioning to what party it belonged; and, lastly, the blame of all the antiquarian republic in the world.[38]

The obelisk was recovered and was eventually re-erected at Bankes's mansion of Kingston Lacy in Dorset, with the foundation stone dedicated by the Duke of Wellington in April 1827, and the needle three years later. Interestingly, Kingston Lacy was redesigned by Sir Charles Barry, architect of the Houses of Parliament, who first met Bankes at Abu Simbel in 1819. A further Burckhardt recommendation led to the removal of the colossal statue of Ramses II from the Theban Necropolis (*c.* 1250 BCE), again by Belzoni, commissioned this time by the British Consul General in Egypt, Henry Salt. Belzoni successfully loaded the seven-ton head onto a boat in Cairo in 1816, from which it would eventually end up in the British Museum. In anticipation of its arrival and riding on the public interest in all things Egyptian, the English Romantic poet Percy Bysshe Shelley wrote 'Ozymandias' (Greek for 'Ramses'), a poem about hubris at a time when the frailty of emperors past and present – Napoleon, George III – was all too apparent.

The theme of empire brings us to the twentieth century. In 1952 Mohammed Naquib and Gamal Abdel Nasser overthrew King Farouk of Egypt, effectively ending nearly 150 years of the Alawiyya Dynasty. Frustrated by corruption and the continuing influence of Britain despite Egyptian independence in 1922, the new leadership consolidated under Nasser who became prime minister and then president in 1954. Two events underpinned Nasser's rise to power and popularity: firstly, the nationalization of the Suez Canal, previously owned by the British and the French, which culminated in the Suez Crisis in October 1956. And second, the construction of the Aswan Dam, designed to create a vast new 500-kilometre-long body of water, the eponymous Lake

Nasser. These are linked: America and Britain originally committed to fund the Aswan Dam in an attempt to curtail Nasser's pro-Soviet leanings, but later withdrew when it became clear that the Egyptian leader sought to play both sides. Consequently, Nasser accepted an offer of Russian assistance, and on 26 July 1956, merely a week after the American withdrawal, he also announced the nationalization of the Suez Canal, the proceeds from which would contribute towards the construction of the Aswan Dam.

Born out of such political chaos, construction of the Aswan High Dam began in January 1960. It was not the first such structure on the Nile: an earlier dam had been built by the British in 1898–1902, designed to capture and control the annual floodwaters to supplement dry-season irrigation. The earlier dam was successful, but continuing overlapping and increasing demands from agriculture required a new solution, despite the dam height being raised twice, in 1907–12 and 1929–33. The earlier dam also visibly illustrated the impact of the reservoir on the region's cultural heritage: as the water level rose, the temples on the island of Philae began to disappear, raising fears for its future conservation. Concern at the time led to archaeological survey and the creation of 1:25,000 scale maps showing heritage sites threatened by the first dam's floodwaters published in 1910 by the Cairo Survey Department.[39]

The new dam endangered a far greater area than the first, which led to UNESCO sponsoring a study of the area during the 1950s, but it wasn't until 1959, a year before construction started, that Egypt and Sudan requested international assistance to save the monuments. For the first time UNESCO found itself leading a major campaign, officially launched in 1960, to raise funds and coordinate rescue and research. With fifty countries taking part, the campaign focused on four different conservation approaches: preservation of monuments in situ; the relocation of monuments deemed to be the most important; excavation of archaeological sites that would then be submerged and lost ('preservation by record'); and recording of other archaeological sites which would remain, submerged by the rising waters of Lake Nasser.

It is the spectacular relocation projects that have received most attention, and with good reason. Twenty temple, fortress or secular complexes, dating from the New Kingdom (1539–1075 BCE) through to the Roman period, were physically cut up and moved to new locations beyond the reach of the rising lake. Their translocation remains an extraordinary feat, with Ramses II's temples at Abu Simbel being the poster child. Here the entire complex was excavated, recorded and then cut up into separate blocks before being reassembled 65 metres higher and 200 metres further inland from the Nile. New hills had to be built to replicate the original cliff setting, one of which contained a vast concrete dome to give space for the interior of the temple. The entire project had to be delivered to within 5 millimetres accuracy of the original, and on the same alignment, because of the importance of the interplay of the sun on the temple's interiors. The cost was around $40 million. Such theatricality and technical endeavour would surely have appealed to the man who entered the temple some 150 years earlier, the 'Great Belzoni', who originally travelled to Egypt seeking to persuade its ruler, Muhammud Ali Pasha, to invest in his invention for raising the waters of the Nile.

The other examples of translocation were equally innovative, each in their own way.

The temple at Amada, built by Thutmose III (r. 1479–1426 BCE), is one of the oldest Egyptian temples in Nubia. Dedicated to the gods Amun-Ra and Ra-Horakhty, it is filled with highly coloured reliefs on its interior, including two important early inscriptions. Unlike Abu Simbel, the extent and rarity of the decorated interiors combined with issues of structural instability prevented the monument being cut up and dismantled piecemeal; instead, the entire temple was secured in a cradle comprising a concrete base framed by steel bands, and lifted hydraulically onto rails to be slowly moved 2.5 kilometres away to its current location. The rails were simply moved from behind the monument and relaid in front of it. Such techniques were not so very different from those adopted by the ancient Egyptians in their construction and relocation of monuments; for example, the temples of Pi-Ramesses in the Nile Delta were moved downstream to a new site at Tanis in about 1000 BCE, when the course of the river shifted and the harbour of Ramses II's former capital silted up, rending its location unusable.

Philae Island, the focus of several Belzoni interventions, was the last major complex to be relocated, being between the new dam and the old, and therefore not subject to the same new issue

Fig. 67 Coffer dam around Philae Island constructed in advance of the temple's relocation to Agilkia, 1 January 1974.

of rising water. Here a large coffer dam was constructed in 1972 around the original island site and the water pumped out to allow the main monuments to be cleaned of silt, cut up and moved to higher ground. The operation involved disaggregating the temples into 40,000 separate blocks, each of around two tons. The new site, 500 metres away, was on Agilkia Island, which was levelled off to give it the same appearance as the original location. The 'new' Philae was reopened to the general public in 1980.

A different approach was required at the temple of Kalabsha, a Roman place of worship (*c.* 30 BCE) constructed over an earlier sanctuary of Amenhotep II (r. *c.* 1426–1 BCE). Here German engineers made the most of the site's location in an area of the Nile that was already flooding, waiting until the river's flood was at its height before dismantling the submerged temple from the top down, using boats moored in the river. In a subsequent gesture of thanks, Egypt gave one of the temple's *pylons* (ceremonial gateways) to the German nation. This was transferred to the Neues Museum in Berlin in 1971

AMONGST THE RUINS

and will form the gateway to the fourth wing of the reconfigured Pergamon Museum to be completed in 2025–6.

The Kalabsha pylon was not the only gift made by Egypt to other nations. An ancient rock-cut temple of Ellesyia, built by Thutmose III (r. 1479–1426 BCE), went to Turin in Italy, while the Roman temple of Taffa is now on display in a specially designed building in the Rijksmuseum van Oudheden in Leiden, the Netherlands. Similarly, New York's Metropolitan Museum houses the Roman temple of Dendur after the building was offered to the US in 1965. Its pending arrival sparked what the press declared to be the 'Dendur Derby', in which museums across the country competed for the gift: New York's gain was Boston's, Memphis's and Washington's loss.[40]

Spain too benefited from the temple of Debod, gifted in 1968 and reconstructed in the Parque del Oeste in Madrid. The structure, which dates from the late-third–early-second century BCE, comprised three massive entrance pylons through which people would approach an enclosed sanctuary. Unfortunately, the gates were reassembled in Spain in a different order than the originals, and recent criticism

Fig. 68 The temple of Debod in its original Egyptian location, now reassembled in the Parque del Oeste, Madrid. The photograph was taken by English photographer Francis Frith in around 1862. It clearly shows the collapse of the front facade and the pylon closest to the temple.

by the Egyptologist Zahi Hawass on the state of the monument led to the Madrid city authority agreeing to build an appropriate cover to protect it from the elements.

Perhaps the most significant gesture of thanks was not the translocation of ancient buildings from Egypt *to* foreign soil, but rather the honouring of the Soviet support *on* Egyptian soil: the 70-metre Soviet-Egyptian Friendship Monument, which stands overlooking the Aswan Dam. The Soviet contribution towards its construction was enormous. Once the US, UK and World Bank withdrew funding, the USSR stepped in with finance, equipment and expertise. President Nasser and Soviet Premier Khrushchev marked the first stage of the project with a ceremony in 1964, while their successors, respectively President Sadat and President Podgorny, officially celebrated its completion in 1970. The project was an opportunity to extend Soviet influence in the Arab world.

The UNESCO-led programme to excavate, record and relocate the monuments of Nubia ended on 10 March 1980 and was declared 'a complete and spectacular success'.[41] Indeed, such a success that the relocated sites from Abu Simbel to Philae were inscribed as a World Heritage Site in 1979.

Not everything was saved, nor was that either possible or the intention. Many of the relocated monuments left orphans behind. The freestanding elements of the temple Gerf Husein, dedicated to Ramses II, were moved, but the rock-cut sanctuary and its statues now rest underwater, no longer blackened and infested with bats, as one early-twentieth-century inspector found it, but with silt and fish.[42] The Roman settlement of Qasr Ibrim and its later churches survive as a partially submerged island in the lake. The fortress on the high ground at the heart of the settlement is defended against the water, but the suburbs beyond are gradually eroding and disappearing under lake sediment.

Some places were simply too big and not deemed important enough to warrant relocation. A string of fourteen fortresses and their towns, mostly established in the Twelfth Dynasty (1991–1802 BCE) to protect Egypt's southern border with the Nubian Kingdom of Kush, were excavated during the campaign. Many of these mud-brick structures now lie disintegrating in the lake, but at Buhen, Semna East and Semna West the temples were surgically extracted

Fig. 69 The interior of the temple Gerf Husein by David Roberts.

and placed in Sudan's National Museum: 'it has been possible to dismantle the stone temples and transport them to Khartoum, but the lofty constructions which commanded the noble and savage beauty of Batn-El-Haggar have disappeared forever'.[43]

While the UNESCO campaign to record and save the Nubian monuments was indeed a 'spectacular success', there was also much that was lost which went largely unrecognized at the time. The campaign's eye was naturally drawn to the imposing and monumental, and so the subsequent narrative is predominantly about Ancient Egyptian and classical antiquity and, within that, about rulers and gods, temples and fortresses. Later and earlier periods are missing; the region has been shown to have a rich prehistory, but its ephemeral nature will be guaranteed destruction under the lake waters. As significantly, there was a clear separation between the stone-built monumental ruins and the living heritage of existing settlements. In the latter, the accumulation of distinctive and long-lived building styles, combined with social traditions, food, dress, art and other aspects of intangible cultural heritage, were largely disregarded by the rescue programme. Today, such an approach feels wholly disconnected, separating the living inheritors of Nubian culture from the cultural remains of their past.

Wadi Halfa in northern Sudan, a nineteenth-century town overlying settlement dating back to the earliest Nubian peoples (8000 BCE), was completely destroyed by Lake Nasser, alongside 27 nearby villages, displacing 52,000 people. Ironically, it was Wadi Halfa that was the base for many of the nineteenth-century adventurers and twentieth-century archaeologists who did much to rediscover the nearby monuments. The worst affected, however, were the Nubian people themselves, leading to protest and campaigns. In total, 90,000 Egyptian fellahin and Sudanese Nubians were relocated, mainly to Nubaria in Egypt's Kawn Umbu valley or to Khashm al-Qirbah in Sudan.

These decisions were the product of their time, and 2020 marked efforts by the Egyptian government to compensate those unfairly treated through the loss of land and livelihoods because of the dam. But the debate remains a live one, and history has a nasty habit of repeating itself. Construction of the Merowe Dam, 600 kilometres further south of Aswan on the fourth cataract of the Nile and north of Khartoum in Sudan, started in 2004 and was complete by 2009. Instead of the USSR as principal funders as at Aswan, it was China who made the largest investment, although the motivations to extend influence remain the same. There are further echoes of UNESCO's Nubian campaign, when in 2003 Sudan's National Corporation for Antiquities and Museums launched a global appeal to support the Merowe Dam Archaeological Salvage Project and ten international missions responded, working in the region until 2008. At the same time, up to 70,000 people were displaced and, yet again, an unfortunate distinction was made between archaeological sites, which warranted excavation, and living villages, which didn't, as if to value the dead over the living. Many from the Manasir, Haadab and Amri tribes refused to relocate and now live by the reservoir shore.

More dams are proposed on the Nile, each understandably contentious. One – currently on hold – located at the third cataract at Kajbar would displace 10,000 people, submerge 90 villages, and destroy around 500 archaeological sites. The commercial opportunities presented by the mighty Nile and the subsequent loss of historic monuments and drowning of communities are, and have been, echoed in countless other river catchments across the world. Reminders of a lost Atlantis can be glimpsed through the murky underwater photographs of submerged cities at Shi Cheng in China and Potosi in Venezuela, or poignantly come into view during times of drought, as with villages such as Vilarinho da Furna in Portugal and Mardale Green in the English Lake District, ironic siren calls for both more and less water at the same time.

Here then is the sacrifice of heritage, from monumental archaeological remains to living communities, for the greater 'progress' of nations: in this case to create electricity for power and water for agriculture and drinking. Was it worth it? Opinion on Aswan is deeply divided. It brought new industries and the industrialization of Egyptian agriculture. The controlled management of water from the dam allowed far greater crop production – but at a cost. The annual Nile floodwaters used to naturally enrich farmland downstream by depositing 40 million tons of silt onto the fields. Today, that silt is trapped behind the dams, and to replace it Egypt uses over 1 million tons of artificial fertilizer as a poor substitute (see Humberstone above). On the Mediterranean coast, the ancient Nile Delta is slowly receding without the stabilizing replenishment of its sediments, exposing archaeological material as it is washed away by a rising sea. In addition, changes to the water table have resulted in increased salinity, again requiring more intensive management (see chapter 3, Girsu). For some, the Aswan Dam project raised the quality of life for millions and represents a proud symbol of modern Egypt. For those in its path, living and dead, it brought nothing but destruction or enforced migration.

CONCLUSION

So far, we have focused on seventeen stories of disappearance and collapse. But, returning to our theme of history repeating itself, each of these places tells us something of what has happened elsewhere in the world. In this concluding chapter we will first explore the themes that link our chosen historic buildings, cities and landscapes to others, before returning to the fundamental question posed by this book – is it possible to learn from past collapse?

Understanding Loss and Renewal on a Global Stage

CLIMATE CHANGE

The destructive power of a changing climate is written large across many abandoned communities and lost civilizations, and in different ways. But to understand it requires the unpicking of a large knot of causes, effects, false friends and real relationships.

A recurring theme of this book is that the reason for decline is rarely singular, a rule that certainly applies to climate change. Human decision-making has caused climate to change *and* has been influenced by it. Natural hazards, particularly those brought about by an increasing intensity and frequency of storm events, can be traced back to long-term trends in weather patterns. A warming or cooling climate can impact upon the spread of disease or invasive species, while reducing resources, especially water and therefore liveable, fertile places, can lead to conflict and war.

There are other complexities too, such as unravelling the impact of climatic change from the impact of the weather. A severe hurricane can devastate communities and turn a historic town into splintered timber and rubble, but it may simply be a single extreme event. In this context climate change is usefully defined as long-term changes to weather, as illustrated by the slow drying of Libya's Fazzān region (see chapter 1). Fazzān's example also demonstrates another need for forensic disentanglement, and that is to determine the difference between naturally occurring climate change and that directly resulting from human action. The long-term changes which influenced both the growth and decline of the Garamantes were the result of a natural drying cycle as the region transitioned from a water-rich area of lakes to one where the precious liquid is increasingly out of reach. In the Sperrin Mountains and at Dunwich the stories have been about people's response to the attrition of big, long-term and inevitable changes to their environment, rather than being the root cause of that change (see chapter 1).

Conversely, the current acceleration of global warming seen from the twentieth century into the twenty-first is the result of anthropogenic climate change, in particular the impact of greenhouse gas emissions. The burning of fossil fuels for industry, transport and energy is the primary culprit, but so too is land-use change, especially the clearing of forest to replace it with rubber, tobacco, palm oil or cattle.

The impact of climate change accelerated by humans is clearly visible in the polar regions and across great swathes of permafrost, where it is literally disrupting the foundations of historic villages in places such as Canada's Herschel Island (Qikiqtaruk) and along the Mackenzie Delta (see chapter 1). This is a story repeated throughout the northern hemisphere. Four-thousand-year-old permanently frozen wood excavated from middens in Qujaa, Greenland, appeared as fresh as if it were discarded yesterday, but that which had thawed out over the course of a few years had already lost 25 per cent of its mass. At the opposite end of the earth, the temporary huts built by explorers such as Amundsen, Hillary, Mawson, Scott and Shackleton have, remarkably, survived, mainly because they were preserved under an accumulation of snow in conditions where humidity is low. Once the snow is removed or starts to melt because of changing climatic conditions, these ephemeral structures become vulnerable to freeze-thawing and increased fungal damage. While small in number and visited annually by fewer people than climb Mount Everest, these structures are the rarest and earliest traces of human survival from the Antarctic mainland.

We tend to think of climate change in terms of big impacts: polar icecaps melting and releasing millions of litres into the world's oceans, sea-level rises that will submerge whole islands, increased storms and winds which will wreak havoc, and unbearable temperature rises causing drought and starvation. These are real enough, but it is the small changes that underpin the damage. Humans can withstand a significant range of temperatures as illustrated by communities who live in deserts, mountains or polar regions. In mild, temperate

Fig. 70 The interior of Nimrod Hut at Cape Royds, Antarctica, after conservation. Equipment, provisions and clothing remain on shelves from the 1907–9 Nimrod Expedition of British explorer Ernest Shackleton.

Greenwich in London, the average low temperature in January for the last thirty years was 3.36 degrees Celsius, while the average high temperature in July for the same period was 23.75 degrees. That's a 20-degree temperature range in a gentle climate, one that extends considerably when extremes are taken into account. In the Saharan region of Fazzān, that range can span 40 degrees. Yet water simply needs a one-degree difference to transform it from liquid to solid, and in that single degree lies a significant and at times hugely destructive change, including the melting of glaciers and icecaps. That one degree sits behind the sea-level rises that we see today and are predicted in the future. It will therefore be responsible for the loss of individual buildings, settlements and, potentially, nations, especially those that are small island states or larger low-lying countries. Bangladesh is predicted to have over 20 million climate-change refugees over the coming decades.

Climate change sits as a root cause precipitating the decline of empires, such as that of the Garamantes, and smaller historic communities, like the town of Dunwich. Its role as a major sponsor of collapse can be seen across the world and throughout different periods. Too hot or cold, wet or dry are the typical limiting bookends to successful human settlement, with hurricanes, windstorms and rising seas being definitive moments in between. Persistent years of drought were contributory factors that led to or accelerated the demise of the Indus Valley civilization in Central Asia after 2000 BCE, the Mayans in Central America after 800 CE and the Tiwanaku in the Central Andes after 1000 CE, to name but a few. Conversely, the colder conditions of the Little Ice Age forced Norse settlers to abandon Greenland by the sixteenth century. It is possible to connect the big roller-coaster changes of global temperature with the rise and demise of empires, sometimes as a root cause, sometimes as an exacerbating factor.

We have also travelled to places where a changing climate threatens the evidence of past civilizations; that is to say, places which have already been abandoned and are slowly disappearing from the physical landscape. Herschel Island (Qikiqtaruk) is one such example, but there are many others, some suffering from the double whammy of collapsing because of climate change and then their ruined places being erased from the human record by the same forces. The Ancestral

Puebloans of the southwest United States emerged in the twelfth century BCE, establishing a long and complex series of settlements, of which perhaps the most famous are the cliff dwellings of the Mesa Verde. The history of the Puebloans is deeply connected to the climate, with their towns and villages populated and depopulated in synch with weather extremes and drought conditions. Spruce Tree House, one of the largest of the iconic cliff dwellings, was abandoned in the decades after 1280 CE along with many other villages. It's probable that this evacuation was a response to a prolonged period of colder, drier weather, combined with food shortages and signs of increased conflict – all of which are likely to go hand in hand.[1] Seven hundred years later and the climate continues to have a deleterious effect on the now abandoned ruins, a popular visitor destination (Chaco Canyon and Taos are other famous Ancestral Puebloan settlements, each just an hour north of Route 66; see chapter 5). Rockfalls caused by the increased freeze/thaw cycle on the cliffs have closed the site to the public, while colder, wetter winters combined with hotter, drier summers have left the area increasingly vulnerable to wildfires. These burn off the tree cover, scorching the earth, putting further stress on the environment.

We've explored the global impact of the single degree of separation between ice and liquid water – small changes that make entire landscapes untenable, either directly in the polar regions or indirectly due to the melting of icecaps causing sea-level rise in a distant world, such as at Dunwich. But seemingly modest changes with big impacts can also be viewed from the microscale. For example, each time water freezes in the porous sandstone of the cliffs and buildings of Mesa Verde's Cliff House complex, it results in a minute, repetitive expansion and contraction. This, by turn, leads to spalling, cracking, splitting: a metronomic attrition that ends with mechanical failure and collapse. The greater the frequency of the freeze/thaw cycle, or the quantities of moisture within the stone, each of which is linked to a changing climate, the greater the speed of decay. The same process takes place in the historic building materials across the world, from mud and brick to plaster and wood. It is the contrast between hard, frozen foundations in the permafrost versus a boggy decaying mass. Similar non-linear tipping points occur throughout the environment as a result of a changing climate, for example the

Fig. 71 Crépissage at Djenné, Mali. The Great Mosque and old town are part of a World Heritage Site established in 1988 for its remarkable use of earthen architecture.

few degrees of difference that might separate a 10 per cent success rate for the hatching insects versus a 90 per cent success rate. The more bugs there are, the greater their consumption of the fabric of a timber building, or its contents. Temperature changes aside, every aspect of climate change can intensify damage: take wind for example, where an increase in intensity can more quickly sandblast a Numidian pyramid, drive rain into the fabric of a Scottish black-house, desiccate the Canadian permafrost, or flatten a Barbadian chattel house. Climatic changes can alter the timing or duration of seasons, the intensity of rainfall, the direction and power of ocean currents, the humidity in the atmosphere, even the amount of direct sunlight, and each will have a knock-on effect on historic structures, both now and in the past.

Buildings are primarily designed to shelter us from the sun, rain, cold and wind, and so we expect them to take the weight of what the weather throws at them, anticipating the need to replace roofs, fix windows, repaint doors and reapply render. The rhythm of repair varies according to tradition and material – the 20-metre-high mud-brick walls of Djenné's Great Mosque in Mali are replastered during

AMONGST THE RUINS

one day in April, the Crépissage (plastering) – in a festival which involves the whole community. This protects the mosque from the fierce deluge of the short rainy season that follows. By contrast, a country mansion, such as that at Plas Newydd in Wales (see chapter 5), might have been reroofed just a handful of times in its 500-year-old history. The need for maintenance should be factored into a building's lifecycle, or that of a managed ruin. But climate change dramatically disrupts such a cycle, accelerating or occasionally slowing down the need for repair. And sometimes the acceleration is so great and so unmanageable that the only consequence is abandonment by people and of place.

NATURAL HAZARDS

Historically, natural hazards can be a trigger for decline, the final nail in the coffin, or, after an initial period of shock and pain, the opportunity for a fresh start. Lisbon's 1755 earthquake and tsunami devastated the city, directly absorbing between 32 and 48 per cent of Portugal's GDP and contributing towards the country's decline as a global colonial power.[2] It also led to economic reform, a loosening of the dependency on Great Britain, and profoundly influenced several writers and philosophers of the Age of Enlightenment, including Voltaire, Rousseau and Kant.

The impact of natural hazards – earthquake, hurricane, flooding, volcanic eruption and more – is quick, dramatic and devastating. Port Royal's 1692 quake and tsunami lasted a little over three minutes, by which time the Caribbean's busy trading capital had been reduced to a macabre new landscape of twisted timber-frames, collapsed brick and ruined lives (see chapter 2). There might have been warnings of the unsettled state of Montserrat's Soufrière Hills volcano pending its major eruption in July 1995, but once the pyroclastic flows and lahars began to head towards the former capital of Plymouth, the town was swiftly abandoned and its population evacuated (see chapter 2). In 79 CE Mount Vesuvius erupted, sending an ash cloud 30 kilometres into the air which fell as a deadly, suffocating black rain, followed by fast-moving pyroclastic flows which destroyed the towns of Pompeii and Herculaneum. The event lasted less than twenty hours. The most powerful earthquake ever recorded was centred on Lumaco on Chile's coast. Of 9.4–9.6 magnitude, it took place over 10 minutes on 22 May 1960, destroying the town of Valdivia, and sending 10-metre waves as far as Hawaii.

While the initial shock of a naturally occurring event is both immediate and carries with it a high death toll, the longer-term consequences can be equally damaging to societies. Montserrat's 1997 volcanic eruption led to nineteen deaths, but also resulted in 8,000 people leaving the island. The current population is just under 5,000. Some who chose to stay and be relocated rather than emigrate to the UK are still living in temporary housing, itself vulnerable to the hurricanes which frequent the region. The situation is compounded by a shortage of land on which to build new homes and to produce home-grown food – unsurprising since two-thirds of Montserrat remains an exclusion zone. It is estimated that 140,000 people drowned during the first months of the calamitous floods of China's Yangtse and Huai Rivers in 1931,[3] but at least four times as many died of starvation and disease the following year, possibly more; some commentators estimate a death toll of 4 million.[4]

A commonplace reaction to such stories of disaster is why would anyone choose to live on an active tectonic fault, or within sight of a smoking volcano? One answer, of course, is that most people don't select where they are raised, and do not have the luxury of being able to move elsewhere. Or worse: when the Soufrière volcano on St Vincent, 500 kilometres to the south of Montserrat's volcano of the same name, erupted in 1812, the people who suffered the most were the indigenous population who lived on the coast prior to the arrival of white colonists, but had since been forced inland. Later, after emancipation, the area around both the Soufrière volcanoes on St Vincent and Montserrat were largely populated by the poorest in society, in particular formerly enslaved people living a subsistence lifestyle on its more difficult and inaccessible terrain. When the explosions came, they were the most vulnerable.

There are benefits to living in places where the threat of danger seems overwhelming (especially after the event). Volcanoes can mean rich, fertile soils, or great mineral wealth. For ancient peoples they may indicate the presence of gods, such as Pele on Hawaii, while in the present day, they offer new opportunities for thermal energy.

Volcanoes may conjure mesmerizing images of molten orange lava – images that tourists pay to see, alongside bathing in the thermal springs often found nearby. Similarly, living in an earthquake zone may seem counterintuitive, but the same geological DNA might also correspond to the place where a mountain range butts up with the desert, and hence is the logical (or only) route for trade to pass along. Many of the Silk Roads balance on the same course of faults running between high mountains and dry deserts. Ani, Armenia's ancient capital, benefited from being part of that trade network, and was substantially damaged by at least five major earthquakes. Recent attempts to conserve the abandoned city's remains continue to be hampered by the same destructive powers (see chapter 2).

The village of Sefidabeh on Iran's eastern border with Afghanistan was flattened by an earthquake in 1994. It lies on a tectonic fault between Dasht-e-Margo ('desert of death') and Dasht-e-Lut ('barren desert'). The names are graphically expressive of the remoteness and inhospitableness of the area, so why choose to live there? The answer is also in a name: Sefidabeh means 'white water',[5] and it's located close to an underground aquifer created by the very same geological conditions that later led to the village's destruction. This relationship between water and dynamic geological conditions is commonplace, but is made more fraught in places where there is little water in the first place.

There are other positives. Part of Montserrat's future will almost certainly involve tapping into the geothermal energy that its destructive volcanic underlay offers. Historically, the island's geography has made it less competitive than its bigger, flatter, more trade-convenient neighbours. It sits at the long end of an ever-increasingly expensive chain of imported diesel needed for power, resulting in high electricity costs. The use of underground high temperature reservoirs, alongside solar power, is a key element in Montserrat's ambition for cheap, clean energy to power its economy.

Iceland may not share the Caribbean sun, but five geothermal plants contribute a quarter of its energy use, nearly all the rest coming from hydropower. Only 0.1 per cent of the country's power derives from fossil fuels. Hellisheidi, near Reykjavik, is among the ten largest geothermal power stations in the world. Sixty kilometres away lies Hekla, one of Iceland's most active volcanoes, which was first

recorded erupting in the twelfth century CE by monks who sought
to use it as proof of the existence of hell.[6] But Hekla is also very
visible in the archaeological record because of the plume of rock,
ash and dust, or tephra, that it sent into the atmosphere each time it
had a major eruption. Tephra from Hekla and from other Icelandic
volcanoes has been identified in peat bogs across northern Europe,
including those in the Sperrin Hills of Northern Ireland.[7] When
Hekla 3 erupted in 950 BCE it sent a plume of rock and dust 7.3
kilometres into the atmosphere, blocking the sun and resulting in a
period of global cooling. The 1815 CE eruption of Mount Tambora
in Indonesia, the most powerful recorded in history, led to 'a year
without summer'. The eruptions of Ilopango in El Salvador in 536
and 539–40 CE killed up to 80,000 people in the local area, with ash
polluting water supplies and rendering agricultural land redundant.
Globally, its impact, possibly combined with that of Krakatoa in
Indonesia which erupted at the same time, was felt as far away as
northern Europe where it can be seen in tree-ring data which illustrates a decade-long period of a meagre growth indicative of a colder
climate. Procopius, a contemporary Greek Byzantine chronicler, wrote

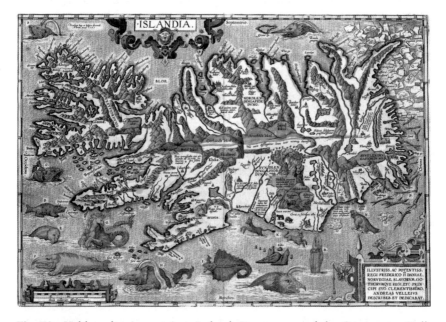

Fig. 72 Hekla volcanic eruption, Iceland. Drawn map of the Gateway to Hell,
Hekla, from 1585, by A. Ortelius.

AMONGST THE RUINS

that 'the sun gave forth its light without brightness', a mysterious darkness that shrouded Constantinople for over a year. The event has been linked to famine, crop failure and a range of other crises across the world.[8]

Regardless of the merits and demerits in living in an area prone to natural hazards, the reality is that there is no risk-free location on this planet. It is all a matter of degree. Small island states take up the top rankings in a World Risk Report produced by the United Nations Institute for Environment and Human Security in 2016.[9] People living on Vanuatu in the Pacific in 2016 had a 36 per cent chance of being a victim of earthquake, volcanic eruption, storms or sea-level rise. Those living in the more populous nations of the Philippines, Guatemala and Bangladesh were faced with a risk of over 19 per cent, compared to 0.08 per cent for Qatar and around 2 per cent for Sweden, Norway and Finland. The whole of Japan, the eleventh most populated country in the world (Bangladesh and the Philippines are the eighth and thirteenth respectively), is an earthquake zone. Therefore relocation, while an option with plenty of historical precedent, is not the most helpful lesson to learn from the past. What is? The answer lies in how people have designed their lives to accommodate the risks that natural hazards pose to them. Here solutions may lie in local or regional architectural traditions, a theme to which we shall return.

HUMAN DISASTER

Great Civilisations are not murdered, they take their own lives.

ARNOLD TOYNBEE

All of the stories of collapse in this book are marked by a thick stripe of poor human decision-making, some deliberate, such as the choice to go to war, others, such as in these chapters, unforeseen consequences of our own invention.

At the heart of several of these stories is the 'tragedy of the commons'. This is a battle between short-term economic gain and long-term social disaster, the decisions of the individual versus those of the collective. The theory was first put forward by the English economist William Forster Lloyd, in a pamphlet using the example of farmers who put more of their own cattle out to graze on shared common land, leading to overgrazing. If the same area of land had been fenced and subdivided with each farmer managing their own parcel, then the impact of overgrazing would have been personal and prudence should have prevailed. We have seen something of this in Girsu where the success of irrigation combined with the increasing demands of a growing population eventually led to overwatering and death by salt (see chapter 3). Those same salts continue to eat away at the relict archaeological remains of one of the world's first civilizations, and are a persistent problem where water, salt and historic buildings meet anywhere in the world.

In Sumer, it was human 'overgrazing', born by invention and population growth, that threatened and ultimately destroyed the common resource of healthy, productive soil. There are echoes of the same theme at Rapa Nui, where the native tree cover disappeared as the indigenous Rapanui made space for growing crops and later European settlers partitioned the island for sheep ranching (see chapter 3). We have observed that the cause of Rapa Nui's population collapse was primarily related to slavery and disease, but these catastrophes were preceded by a slow loss of the island's native palm trees, which must have introduced stress into the system, forcing the indigenous population to change and adapt. Today that population has risen significantly from the low point of 111 recorded in 1877. In 2020 there were approximately 5,000 people living on Rapa Nui, 3,000 of whom were indigenous people.[10] By contrast, up until 2020, the place was visited by between 80,000–100,000 tourists each year. In March 2020 the local government locked down Rapa Nui in response to the Covid-19 pandemic. The island remained closed to tourists until summer 2022.

Prompted by Rapa Nui's response to a time of pandemic, it is worth briefly dwelling on the calamitous impact of disease on past civilizations, and on the role of humans as vectors. The Black Death of the fourteenth century caused up to 200 million deaths across Eurasia and North Africa. The generally accepted theory is that the bubonic plague was carried as *Yersinia pestis* bacteria by rats, and transmitted by fleas. Its rapid growth and repeating cycles may have been facilitated by climate change which reduced the rodent populations, forcing fleas to find new hosts in humans and other animals. Once present within large human populations, particularly the cities of Europe, its pneumonic and septicaemic forms accelerated its devastating impact. And what an impact it had, the most lasting of which was that it spurred on the slow breakdown of feudal society and heralded the emergence of the modern world. For the artisans and peasants who survived, the bindings of fealty between master and commoner that had previously governed life began to fracture. In England, the Black Death's impact on the countryside and Church were harbingers of the enclosure of the former and the reformation of the latter.

The Black Death changed the course of history. It was the worst demographic disaster the world has witnessed, but there were plenty of others that have shaped nations and society. The 'Spanish Flu' (1918–20), Plague of Justinian (541–9) and the HIV/AIDS epidemic (1981–present) were responsible for millions of deaths. The introduction by European colonizers of smallpox, cocoliztli, typhus and a lethal cocktail of other infectious diseases to the American continent and Caribbean, caused the stripping out of indigenous peoples from the arctic north to the South American highlands by way of the great plains and Aztec cities. The population of Mexico dropped from around 22 million in 1520 to under two million by 1580, prompted at least in part by repeated epidemics. The abandonment of St Kilda in Scotland shares some of the same story of the sudden exposure of those with little natural immunity to incomers who have had the already accumulated morose luxury of reliance, but played out in miniature (see chapter 3).

Sadly, the Covid-19 pandemic is set to join such a tragic list.

WAR

In January 2020 the President of the United States threatened to target fifty-two sites, 'some . . . important to Iran and Iranian culture', as a warning against retaliation for the killing of Qasem Soleimani, the Islamic Revolutionary Guard general.

Would US missiles fall on Isfahan's famous Naqsh-e Jahan Square or destroy the remains of Darius's great city of Persepolis? Such threats, had they been carried out, are against international law and could constitute a war crime, but they are also part of a long history of warfare against heritage and cultural identity.

Fortunately, President Trump did not press the button, but history tells us that there are plenty who did, including Alexander at Persepolis in 300 CE, possibly in revenge for Xerxes' destruction of the Acropolis in Athens during the second Persian invasion of Greece 180 years earlier.

As we have seen at Nimrud, the deliberate targeting of ancient buildings and architecture during times of conflict is often used to mark the final subjugation of one rule by another, a symbolic moment of dominance and change of authority (see chapter 4). By destroying the cultural institutions of an enemy – their palaces, temples, kings and gods – the aggressor wishes to assign a definitive transfer of power. We see this not once, but twice in the capital cities of the Neo-Assyrian Empire. First when the Babylonians and Medes turned Nimrud and Nineveh into 'a ruin heap',[11] smashing temples, defacing the carved panels that lined the palace walls which celebrated the achievements of those they had vanquished, and neutering their protective genies. It happened again over 2,600 years later when ISIS wished to clear their newly conquered territories in Iraq and Syria of idolatrous earlier histories, imposing their extremist interpretation of the Islamic faith which had no room for an alternative version, or for other faiths, or for the pre-Islamic religions. In 2014 Abu Bakr al-Baghdadi, the secretive leader of ISIS, chose to proclaim the creation of a new Islamic State at the al Nuri Mosque in Mosul, a site of great significance to Sunni extremists, as well as to many others of the Islamic faith. Three years later ISIS packed the mosque and its al-Hadba minaret with explosives, effectively scuttling the ship of a revered place, rather than let it fall into the hands of the approaching Iraqi forces, and allowing them to claim a symbolic victory. Such is the importance of historic places, their monuments and all they represent.

We see deliberate ruination everywhere, coursing a chaotic journey to the twenty-first century by way of the destruction of Babylon in 539 BCE (just over seventy years after the fall of the Nimrud and the Neo-Assyrian Empire that the Babylonians precipitated), of the Somnath Temple in India in 1024 CE (and again in 1299 and 1665 CE), and the burning of the Tuileries Palace in 1871 during the Paris Commune. As we have seen with ISIS in Iraq, at Palmyra in Syria and earlier with the Taliban's destruction of the Buddhas at Bamiyan, modern times are not immune. Unfortunately, examples from the twentieth and twenty-first centuries are many and include the destruction of the Ghetto in Warsaw and the bombing campaigns that targeted both Allied and Axis historic cities as a means with which to break civilian morale during the Second World War (Guernica, the Blitz and Dresden), the damage done by the Khmer Rouge in Cambodia, at places such as Angkor Wat, and the devastating impact of the Balkan conflict, characterized by many lost churches and mosques and symbolized by the shelling (and reconstruction) of the Stari Most in Mostar (1993). The Russian invasion of Ukraine will doubtless add further examples to that list.

Targeting cultural icons is at the symbolic apex of the impact on heritage of conflict, but a greater loss results from the subjugation or erasure of civilizations, communities or culture after defeat. War hollows out society. When Carthage was sacked by Rome in 146 BCE, not only was the city set alight and its buildings destroyed, but the whole framework of Carthaginian power was dismantled and replaced by that of Rome. Some 55,000 Carthaginians were sold into slavery, the land around the city was declared *ager publicus* (public land) and distributed among those loyal to Rome, and Carthaginian territory was subsumed into the new Roman Province of *Africa Proconsularis*, with Utica as its capital. While those who died or were enslaved were directly impacted by the new world order, those who survived were no longer in control, and thus the cultural narrative transferred to those now in power. Carthage re-emerges but as an important Roman city not a Punic one, influenced and dictated to by a foreign authority.

Not all battles are fought among the rubble of wartime: the erasure of cultural heritage during China's Cultural Revolution continues the same theme but played out under different circumstances (see chapter 4). Looting too is a less obvious but pernicious impact of the consequence of war. The wholesale stripping and transfer overseas of the Old Summer Palace by British and French troops during the Opium War is just one example of the way in which the

Fig. 73 The ancient city of Dura-Europos, Syria, in 2014. The dark shadows of thousands of robber trenches can be seen both inside (right) and outside (left) the city walls.

treasures of other cultures are stolen (see chapter 4). Again, history tells us that there is nothing new in this. There are examples where state-sanctioned looting is celebrated, such as wall reliefs at Nimrud depicting Ashurnasirpal II's troops returning from Babylon with booty, or in the Roman carvings of triumphal procession and redistribution of *spoila* on the Arch of Titus in Rome (82 CE). Sometimes the activity was legitimized as a means of paying for conflict and effecting compensation, as at the Old Summer Palace.

Elsewhere, it is the conditions of war that have led to systematic looting of archaeological sites and museums, often on a vast scale, which is every bit as destructive as the actions of fundamentalists which catch the headlines. Over a period of thirty-six hours in 2003, a mob ransacked more than 13,000 artefacts from the National Museum of Iraq in the aftermath of the US invasion. Satellite images of Dura-Europas in Syria show how the Greco-Roman city has been perforated by thousands of robber trenches during the first years of the Syrian War, diminishing its archaeological integrity.

While some looting is systematic and state approved, in other cases it may simply be the result of farmers who turn to harvesting antiquities when left with no other source of income and in the absence of a protective state infrastructure. Regardless of the motive, looting represents the slow erosion of culture, one in which the artefact is removed from the surroundings that give it part of its value, severing the connection between people and place. One of the reasons that the Old Summer Palace is such a lightning rod for Chinese people is because it has become a humiliating symbol of subjugation by outside powers:

> Ironically its very power as a symbol rests in its physical invisibility – there is almost nothing to see except the ruins of European palaces that formed one part of the entire garden. Although there is 'no there there', the Yuanmingyuan is everywhere in the Chinese national consciousness.[12]

By returning looted art back to China, the connection between people and place is also restored, and pride is assuaged.

ECONOMIC DISASTER

The natural and human resources of our planet are unevenly distributed. Such inequality can be physical or economic. For example, access to water, the world's most precious resource, is determined by where precipitation occurs *and* by the economic capacity to satisfy demand. It is perfectly possible to live in a water-rich country, such as many nations in sub-Saharan Africa, which are also water-scarce because of poor infrastructure or inequitable distribution. By contrast, central Arizona in the United States is a desert region but is not (relatively) water-scarce due to the Central Arizona Project (CAP), which provides for 80 per cent of the state's population. This massive 336-mile infrastructure programme diverted water from the Colorado River via aqueducts and was constructed over twenty years from 1973 at a cost of about $4 billion.

The possession of rich natural resources is not a guarantee of economic affluence. Many resource-rich countries remain poor: this is for a variety of reasons that range from political structure and corruption through to a lack of diversification, weak institutions and a flow of money beyond borders. Chile possessed most of the global market for saltpetre in the nineteenth century, and that wealth spread across the nation, but not evenly, as illustrated by the struggles of those at the dirty end of extraction (see chapter 5). Conversely, Japan ranks low in terms of its share of global natural resources and is highly dependent on energy imports, but it has the third largest economy in the world. Geography is an advantage, but not a necessity. Interestingly, history – particularly that touched by those nations who successfully industrialized first – is probably as important. The uneven legacy of imperialism in which empire-building nations exploited the raw materials and cheap labour of new territories remains self-evident in the contrasting architecture of our towns and cities today.

Over-reliance on a single industry, as illustrated at Humberstone, is a common theme. Here the vulnerability is threefold, the first implicit in the mining of a finite resource, which will run out or reach the limit of viability. The second is in susceptibility to alternatives being found elsewhere, and the third is new technologies superseding the old. In Humberstone's case it was the invention of artificial saltpetre for chemical fertilizers and explosives in Germany which dramatically challenged Chile's monopoly, and eventually rendered it valueless. The nineteenth-century whalers who used Herschel Island as a base from which to catch bowhead whales for lamp oil and dressmaking bone were put out of business both by diminishing stocks and by the discovery of mineral oils and technological advances in refining practice. Today in the Gulf those petrostates with foresight are seeking to diversify away from their time-limited reliance on black gold into tourism, technology, transport or overseas investment, the latter effectively a nest egg for when the oil runs out. The lesson from history for others who are comfortably content to live in the finite riches of the moment is the near certainty of social and political unrest as well as economic collapse in the future.

The economic costs of maintaining an empire are often part of the story of downfall. Empires require a large and expensive military and civil infrastructure: for example, the Seven Years War (1754–63) nearly bankrupted both Britain and France, and ultimately sowed the seeds of both the American and French Revolutions. The World Wars of the twentieth century drained Britain of its reserves and its colonies. War requires money, both in its execution and in the aftermath of reconstruction, so conflict, economy and the loss of heritage are often inextricably linked. This is one of the threads that runs through the Beaudesert Hall story, in which a past way of life became unsustainable because the old economic model no longer calibrated with a new social reality, and because of the taxation demands made by the British government to fund war debt (see chapter 5). The consequence: communities, in this case the landed gentry, could no longer afford to keep the staff- and upkeep-heavy historic buildings of the past.

Another recurring and related theme underpinning economically driven collapse is the result of moving patterns of trade, which by turn can be caused by innovation, changing tastes and demands, or result from the impact of war.

Route 66 is the perfect example of some of these pressures, in which it became so popular that it rendered itself redundant (see chapter 5). Demand was driven (literally) by innovation, including the rise of the motor vehicle as a means of transport for the many. It was also fuelled by the US wartime policy which required the efficient movement of people and arms across the country, and established military magnets that drew traffic to the western seaboard. But Route 66 was challenged by an inbuilt design flaw whereby it ended up trying to serve two masters. On one hand it was 'America's Main Street', deliberately routed to connect all the towns and villages that lay on its path, helping farmers to get their pigs to market, workers to park up at the office and residents to purchase breakfast in the local diner. On the other, it was the principal highway between the cities of the Great Lakes and those in the Californian sun. The need for local connectivity argued against the need for quick US-wide travel, and as demand increased, the consequences were slower journey times, traffic jams and potholes. One solution was to widen the road, easily done in the bare countryside, but impossible to achieve when physically hemmed in by the settlements it served. Instead, a new network of multiple highways was created, some distant from the original Route 66. At first glance both local and transnational users would win: the new highways would serve the former, while the old route remained in place for the latter, but the reality for many businesses on Route 66 was that they relied on its ability to slow and capture passing traffic that was no longer there.

The Silk Road reveals something of the same story, but at a different scale. Here war, regional geopolitics and innovation played into the rise and demise of major towns and settlements that lay on its course. This braided network of trading routes emerged when China's Han Dynasty started to face outwards in 130 BCE. It lasted until the fifteenth century CE when the new Ottoman rulers of Constantinople began to limit control of European traders to the western Silk Routes and, by turn, new sea routes were found connecting Europe to Southeast Asia. Within such a chronological overview there were multiple shifts and changes. Ani's virtual abandonment in the fourteenth century was largely the result of changes of rulership, with the various new overlords of the former Armenian capital favouring other capitals and networks, and so dragging their political and trading focus elsewhere.

Transport and trade are major drivers of economic activity, and if the dynamics change, then backwaters can emerge to prominence and once thriving places disappear. There is, then, a destructive power to shifting trade patterns and in the battle for resources, and one that is not restricted to the contemporary. The Abu Simbel story represents a world in which the evidence of past generations, as well as living heritage, is lost because of more recent economic demands, in this case water (see chapter 5). The construction of the Aswan Dam and its successors highlights a global phenomenon of drowned historic towns and villages.

Economic development, whether an infrastructure project such as a dam, or through the construction of new houses, the extraction of raw materials or turning over land to different agricultural practises, has always been the most destructive force contributing towards the loss of remains of the past.

Learning the Lessons of the Past

Finally, we return to the question that opened this book. Is it possible to learn from past collapse, and if so, what lessons can we usefully draw from ancient Sumer, Rapa Nui or the peoples of Canada's Arctic coast that will help us in the future?

'Let me through, I'm an archaeologist', is not a phrase that is often heard, but those with an interest in studying, conserving and managing heritage have a unique perspective on our prospects. It's partly to do with the timescales with which we work. Take, for example, a politician, those that we look to for leadership. A politician has a natural body-clock. Every four or five years, perhaps sooner, a klaxon goes off announcing the next general election. Everything then synchs to that timeframe: decisions are reached, budgets are announced, campaigns launched and results paraded in front of a grateful/resentful (delete according to political view) public. Their world calibrates to that cycle, and, if the politician is successful, the four-year unit becomes a building block on which longer, more thoughtful plans can be realized. If unsuccessful, they are placed outside, with the brief to undo the plans of the fresh-faced incumbent.

Archaeologists have a very different body-clock. We work less to years, more to centuries and millennia. When you are calibrated to such a long view, all you see is change. This is ironic, because as custodians of the past there is often a misconception that we champion the preservation of the world in aspic, to freeze it in a moment in time – nothing could be further from the truth. Instead, conservation is all about the careful management of change, a theme to which we shall return at the very end of this book.

So, what are the lessons learned from either the abrupt loss or slow decline of past civilizations due to climate change, natural hazards, economic collapse, war or other human frailties of decision-making? History alongside its much, much older parent, prehistory, truly does repeat itself. Humans have been residents on this planet for 300,000 years, during which the environment has constantly changed. In that time, we have been part of millions of spectacular failures and extraordinary adaptations. That is a vast but confusing library. As a form of archaeological librarian, here are nine lessons, a highly personal and selective synthesis both of the approach necessary and practical applications that can be gleaned from its deep shelves.

LESSON 1: SIMPLE OR SINGLE CAUSES FOR COLLAPSE ARE RARE

I have tried throughout this book to identify some specific reasons for the collapse of civilizations but recognize from the outset that these are hardly ever singular. Humberstone was abandoned because new chemical technology made the extraction of saltpetre in Chile uneconomic; but one of the causes for Germany's rise as the new centre of manufacture was that war excluded it from Chile's monopoly and it had to find alternative ways to feed its own demand for gunpowder and fertilizer. Conflict, moving trade routes and earthquakes all contributed towards Ani's fall from power and abandonment. Overexploitation of the land, political change, and then a colder, wetter climate hastened the disappearance of the Bronze Age cultural landscape under the Sperrin Mountain peat. Climate change can lead to scarcity of resources, to economic and political tension, to mass migration, and then to war. The two World Wars had a profoundly damaging effect on British country houses, completely changing the social structure of the UK, devastating a generation of heirs and workers alike, making a life in service far less attractive or affordable, and requiring massive tax hikes to contribute towards the costs of war and reconstruction. The lesson from these examples is not to consider the loss of civilizations or historic communities as a result of a binary cause, but as an accumulation of triggers and accelerators each of which feeds off and exacerbates the others. There are exceptions, most of which fall under the 'natural hazards' category: Port Royal never truly recovered its pre-eminence as the first city of Jamaica after the 1692 earthquake – Kingston was founded in 1693; the southern half of Montserrat remains largely uninhabitable, with the old capital, Plymouth, now temporarily housed at Brades as a new capital is built at Little Bay in the north of the island. These, however, are exceptions to the rule.

While the causes of collapse are rarely singular, we must be cautious of evidence that presents it as such. There are filters that we should be aware of as we draw conclusions from the evidence: 'The so-called lessons of history are for the most part the rationalizations of the victors. History is written by the survivors' (Max Lerner).

This is particularly true of change that has happened because of conflict. Where is the voice of the vanquished or the deceased? Ani, now in Turkey, is today presented as a multicultural site, with equal weighting given to Zoroastrian, Christian and Muslim faiths – and to the restoration of their buildings of worship – but the reality is that this former Armenian capital was the head seat of the Armenian Orthodox Church for almost half a century, and access to it for Armenians is extremely difficult, despite its location within metres of the Turkish border.

And what of those who are mute or unrepresented? The Nubian voices in the story of the flooding of the Nile are a good example. Here the loss is twofold, firstly for the Nubian people forced to relocate to new homes, and often a new way of life, to make way for the rising water; and secondly in the loss of heritage, in particular that of historic but living villages, which received scant record compared with the magnificent showpieces of the pharaonic elite. If a culture is underrepresented, it is at far greater risk of destruction.

Both of these imbalances – the winner writing their own history, or the invisibility of the unrepresented – demand the reader of the past be critical of the former and curious about the latter.

LESSON 2: CHANGE IS INEVITABLE, IT ALWAYS HAS BEEN

Regardless of why civilizations collapse, there is one guaranteed certainty: change is inevitable. It always has been. Take a geologist's perspective, noting that they have an even slower body-clock than archaeologists. Look back 5 billion years into the past and our world simply did not exist. Some 4,540,000,000 years ago the earth was formed as a bundle of solar debris and dust in the same protoplanetary disk as the sun, moon and the rest of our solar system. Like a growing snowball rolling down a wintery hill, the first phase of our planet's gathering, clumping and consolidation took between 10 and 20 million years to complete. Permanent oceans and continents began to appear from 4 billion years ago, followed by life on earth in its very simplest form. It's not until around 300,000 BCE that recognizable humans first walk its surface.

If the earth's journey from formation to the current day took place over the duration of an hour, we would only be present in the last quarter of a second. The planet is in its fifth Ice Age, the Quaternary Glaciation, which began over 2.6 million years ago. The first Ice Age, the Huronian, lasted for 3 million years from 2.4 to 2.1 billion years ago.

Our dynamic planet has therefore constantly and dramatically changed from the time it was a dusty twinkling in the solar nebular to the present. Geomorphological and climatic changes have continually shaped our landscapes and limited where humans could live. We have already seen that for Palaeolithic humans, Libya's Fazzān region in the Sahara was a landscape of lakes. Now it is largely desert, created by an ever-drying cycle which commenced in 3000 BCE, and which continues to this day. The difference between the long past and the last 270 years is that this time, *we* are the cause of accelerating global changes to the environment. The negative legacy of industrialization, particularly through the burning of fossil fuels, is solely down to us. If we accept the inevitability of change due to climate and our role in it, then we must face its challenges and find the solutions.

Solutions have been found in the past. Again, in Fazzān, the human response to a diminishing water supply was at first to build foggaras, then when they began to fail, to dig deeper wells, and now it is to search at still greater depth with modern artesian technologies. In the long term it is unlikely that such solutions will be sustainable, and so humankind will have to adapt, probably by abandoning the Libyan desert landscape. This is nothing new. Our foray into the peat-covered fringes of Northern Ireland's Sperrin Mountains revealed Bronze Age occupation that lasted for hundreds of years. The slow farewell to the early occupation of that landscape was likely a culmination of human tree clearance to create space for domesticated cows and sheep which fundamentally changed the structure of the soil, and a climate that was becoming wetter and colder. That population migrated elsewhere, as surely will that of Fazzān. These two responses – technological development and migration – offer up countless examples of what hindsight offers foresight.

LESSON 3: 'REDUCE, REUSE AND RECYCLE' MEANS OUR BUILDINGS TOO

An archaeologist's search for solutions is likely to begin not by looking forward, but by looking back. Creative processes aside, it is perverse to start with a completely blank piece of paper when seeking technological solutions to climate change or to avert the risk of natural hazards. Much of what we want to do has been done before. In this context we should not reject old technologies, particularly from a time when we were less hermetically sealed from the natural world.

'Reduce, reuse and recycle' refers to our buildings too. New buildings made of concrete and steel command vast amounts of energy, and pump large quantities of CO_2 into the atmosphere in terms of material production. An old building is already constructed, the carbon taken to put it together is embedded. It might be made from materials such as timber, lime, clay or stone, often acquired locally, which can be carbon neutral. Once constructed, a new building should have an excellent energy performance, but old ones can be retrofitted to accommodate modern needs for light, sanitation, connectivity and energy use. There are many good reasons to adapt them rather than tear the buildings down and start again, and the result can be more beautiful, cheaper and interesting too.

This is not backwards looking: the same applies to the reuse and recycling of ideas and traditional materials. It is now possible to build skyscrapers in timber and bamboo, and we've been insulating our homes with sheep wool, as on St Kilda, or straw for thousands of years.

Many architectural traditions contain solutions that are designed to protect from the sun, capture the natural ventilation of the wind, rise above the water, insulate from the cold or ensure our buildings do not flood or collapse during an earthquake. We must learn from these.

Buildings in hot climates across the world use tried and tested techniques to keep their interiors cool. Building underground, maximizing shade, making the most of the wind or water, or using the walls of a structure to insulate or retain heat are common attributes of traditional desert architecture. In India, particularly Rajasthan, *jaali* screens limit direct sunlight but allow a breeze to pass through their beautiful geometric tracery while at the same time keeping the interior well lit, without glare and private. The passing of air through the smaller perforations of the jaali also compresses, cools and diffuses it. The same technology has been applied in modern buildings, for example Manit Rasogi's design for the Pearl Academy of Fashion in Jaipur clad the entire exterior with a skin of jaali set a metre away from the main walls, creating a thermal buffer, filtering both light and air.

Projecting *mashrabiya* windows seen high on many old buildings in the Middle East and North Africa were used to catch the wind from several directions, and served a similar function as the jaali. Smaller perforations at the base of the window would be balanced by larger ones at the top, meaning that the breeze would flow into the room at differential speeds, causing it to mix comfortably and refreshingly. Jars of water placed by the window would further enhance the cooling impact through evaporation, while the usual placement of the mashrabiya on the narrower, darker street side of the building would draw colder air through the house to the sunnier open side.

Fig. 74 Wind-catchers or cooling towers and the Jame Mosque in Yazd, Iran. These towers, alongside *qanats*, courtyards, thick earthen walls, underground water cisterns and covered walkways, articulate a traditional architecture adapted to a hot desert climate.

Buildings incorporating water-cooling techniques are prevalent across the whole of the world: in Iran, wind towers catch the breeze and vent it down to a cooler basement which may contain a reservoir, or pull colder air from water flowing in a *qanat* (the Iranian equivalent of the North African *foggara*) running underneath the building, adding an evaporative cooling effect. In Egypt, triangular windcatchers called *malqaf* on the roofs of buildings draw in the wind from the prevailing direction and vent it out the leeward side. Such architectural devices are present on paintings and models dating from 3000 BCE, and can still be seen in Cairo today. Stepwells in India and Pakistan were in operation from as early as the Indus Valley Civilization (3300–1300 BCE); they comprise a deep well, where the water level is accessible by steps. Some are covered, many are highly decorated with space at the base in which people can socialize in the depths of the water-cooled shade.

The use of thick walls that act as heat reservoirs, soaking up the hottest of the daytime sun and then releasing it during the evening, can be remarkably effective. The low conductivity and high-energy storage capacity of adobe, for example, can absorb 80 per cent of exterior heat, transmitting just 20 per cent to the interior.[13] Narrow, tall courtyards offer not just shade, but capture the colder nighttime air of the summer, protecting a micro-climate from a dusty, hot daytime buffeting. The larger surface area of curved domes is more easily cooled, and, when combined with an air vent at their apex, can quickly draw internal hot air out, hence their effectiveness in thousands of hammams across West Asia. The list goes on, literally hundreds of regional architectural variations that have helped people survive in extremely hot climates, all making the most of shade, wind and water well before the advent of the ubiquitous air-conditioning unit.

A similar argument can be made in favour of traditional architecture designed for cold climates. Here, the ambition is the opposite of our desert examples, maximizing solar gain and minimizing heat loss. South-facing windows and doors, copious amounts of insulation, fireplaces and chimneys, are easily identified attributes that can be seen across cultures, including the blackhouses of St Kilda. These squat, low examples from the most remote of Scottish islands, with their thick stone walls, small openings and heavily insulated turf roofs, also reflect the requirement made of architecture by frequent high winds and fierce Atlantic storms. The placing of animal byres next door to the living accommodation, or on the ground floor beneath it, would have brought heat and a distinctly aromatic ambiance to many mountain farmsteads, as it did to the buildings of the St Kildans.

A rich vein of learning can be found in places where people have designed their lives to accommodate the risks that natural hazards pose to them too. Here solutions may lie in local or regional architectural traditions. Stilt houses are present across eras of the world, from Bronze Age lake-edge settlements in Switzerland, Germany or Austria through to the *palafitos* that line the Amazon and Orinoco rivers, and the *bahay kubos* of the Philippines, which are still in use today. These buildings make space for flooding, but also have the advantage of keeping vermin at bay, or even offering a degree of defence. Modern 'Hurricane proof' houses are being constructed in the Gulf of Mexico using alternative materials, but copying old designs. Some traditional architecture fares far better than modern techniques in withstanding the impact of earthquakes, in particular timber-framed buildings which can soak up the stress of movement, while other more rigid structures fail. A study into the after-effects of earthquakes in Srinagar, Kashmir, India, showed that old buildings made using the traditional *taq* and *dhajji dewari* methods were far more likely to survive than solid load-bearing masonry walls, or more recent concrete and steel constructions.[14] Both the earlier techniques introduced flexibility into the structure, either in the form of horizontal laced floors (*taq*) or an infilled timber frame (*dhajji dewari*). The devastating 2010 earthquake in Haiti took over a quarter of a million lives, most tragically crushed in concrete buildings. Nearly half the structures in the capital fell, with the majority of the surviving ones being over a hundred years old, and mostly timber-framed. Less than 5 per cent of Haiti's historic 'gingerbread houses' collapsed. Pagodas in Japan are traditionally designed around a *shinbashira*, a central, flexible pole, around which the rest of the wooden building can slide and flex during earthquake. Wide eaves add a balancing-pole benefit, dampening the impact of any abrupt shake. The 55-metre, five-story To-ji

Fig. 75 The To-ji Pagoda in Kyoto utilizes earthquake-resistance technologies, such as wide eaves for gravity loading, floating floors and a central *shinbashira* pillar.

Pagoda in Kyoto is the tallest in Japan, but has survived in one of the most seismically prone countries since it was rebuilt in the mid-seventeenth century.

Not all building designs from the past are universally wonderful and offer a magic solution for our future needs. Traditional approaches were largely born of the requirements of place – shelter from cold, heat, rain, sun, wind – the social needs of the local community, the proximity of raw materials – wood, stone, reeds, brick, lime, mud, even skin and bone – and cost. While timber buildings perform well during earthquakes because of their relative lightness, flexibility and tensile strength, traditional adobe or mud constructions do not. Such buildings may be cheap, easy to build and provide excellent insulation against temperature extremes, but they are also weak in shear, tension and compression, which means that they are especially prone to collapse. The past may be a library, but it doesn't mean that all the books within it are pertinent to the present. We should be frequent, but discerning readers.

'Restore', 'repair' and 'repurpose' might usefully be added to the well-known climate change mantra of 'reduce, reuse and recycle', and not only because to do so is good for the planet's environment. The restoration of old buildings after war or natural events, for example, can have a cathartic effect, both as a sign of a return to normality and as a symbol of pride and resilience in the face of an attack on cultural identity.

One of the most infamous images of the conflict with ISIS in the Middle East was a 2015 film of extremists smashing ancient Assyrian statues with sledgehammers in Mosul Museum, northern Iraq (see Fig. 43). The museum, itself an important modernist building by the architect Mohamed Makiya, was designed to display monumental statues and artefacts from the region, including those from the old Neo-Assyrian capitals of Nimrud and nearby Nineveh. The film also showed jihadists using power tools to deface an eighth-century lamassu that guarded Nineveh's Nirgal Gate. The same three-year drive against 'idolatry' resulted in destruction at Nimrud, including the bulldozing of its great Ziggurat, the ruin of countless Yezidi shrines in the nearby Bashiqa and Sinjar areas, and concluded in 2017 with ISIS's last, desperate act, which was to blow up the mosque of al-Nuri in Mosul along with al-Hadba, its famous leaning minaret.

The great Mosque of al-Nuri, alongside the Syriac al-Tahera church and Roman Catholic al-Saa'a monastery and the wider historic urban townscape of Mosul, is now part of a multi-million-dollar city-wide 'Revive the Spirit of Mosul' restoration programme led by UNESCO. The programme, largely funded by the United Arab Emirates and the EU with the Iraqi government, announced in April 2021 that the mosque would be reconstructed by a consortium of Egyptian architects led by Salah El Din Hareedy. There is even controversy here, with the new designs widely criticized as being inspired by modernist Gulf cityscapes rather than rooted in the traditions of Mosul. The arguments demonstrated how deeply people care about the restoration of their cultural identity and the importance of getting it right. Elsewhere in Mosul, a consortium comprising the Aliph Foundation, the Louvre, the Smithsonian and World Monuments

Fund is busy restoring Makiya's 1974 museum, bringing it back to life as a place of memory and celebration of culture for the people of Iraq's second city.

In the countryside southeast of Mosul, some of the many shrines targeted by ISIS in its systematic campaign of genocide against the Yezidis, are being restored:

> The enemies of the Yazidi people wanted to destroy the Yazidi religion, but they did not know that the Yazidis are the seeds of the earth, and the seeds cannot be destroyed. They do not die and do not disappear, so the Yazidis returned to the places of their centuries-old residence and began to restore their shrines.[15]

Such work is important, not simply in terms of putting back the bricks and mortar of a cherished historic structure, but as significantly in restoring a place for worship to take place in. If many Yezidis define themselves by their faith, then that connection to their faith is ruptured when the spaces in which religious practices are no longer available – either through physical destruction, or because the people are in refugee camps, or have emigrated. The impact is made worse for younger people: 'If you don't have shrines, if you don't have places to worship . . . the children are growing up in the last three years knowing nothing about their religion, their heritage, their culture.'[16] Interestingly, however, the rebuilding of these cultural emblems appears to have a strong element of youth leadership to it, as well as a generous thread of community funding.

What of Nimrud? It is unlikely that anyone will reconstruct the Great Ziggurat, but efforts to protect the ancient capital, to make it safe, to record and store the artefacts and monumental statuary that are scattered across the site, are already taking place, led by the Iraqi State Board of Antiquities, supported by international partners. A key lesson here, and elsewhere across the world in areas of post-conflict heritage recovery, is the importance of building local capacity. One of the many negative impacts of war is the loss of knowledge – through death, through the collapse of educational institutions, through flight or through a lack of resources. International heritage agencies can parachute in, deliver wonderful conservation projects, and then leave. A more sustainable approach, as seen with the Smithsonian's partnership at Nimrud, the British Museum's *Iraq Scheme* or World Monument's work to train Syrian refugees to become conservation stonemasons, is to give local people the skills needed to look after their own heritage.

All of the stories in this book on the loss of cultural heritage due to conflict underpin the value and importance of conservation after the dust of war has settled. Sometimes that conservation means physical restoration: China wants its looted heritage back from the ransacking of the Old Summer Palace, and is prepared to use the might of the state to ensure its return. Any recovered zodiac fountain heads will be rehoused alongside others in the Poly Art Museum in Beijing 25 kilometres southeast of the former garden. Sometimes conservation means preservation as a ruin, such as at the site itself, where a recent ruling in 2020 by China's National Cultural Heritage Administration (NCHA) rejected a proposal by a National People's Congress deputy to reconstruct the palace as a symbol of national rejuvenation. Instead, while 10 per cent of the site may be reconstructed to give visitors an impression of its former glory, the remainder should be conserved as a ruin and 'as a warning to our descendants that they shall never forget the national humiliation'.[17]

Here is conservation as a cautionary tale for future generations, and a political statement about nationhood. The other China story in this book – the Temple of Confucius and Kong Mansion – also has a political dimension, in that it is all about the attempted redaction of the past by Mao's Red Guards. Fortunately, conservation won out in the end, and now the temple, mansion and cemetery are a World Heritage Site, valued for much more positive reasons:

> The Temple of Confucius, the Cemetery of Confucius, and the Kong Family Mansion are not only outstanding representatives of oriental architectural skills, but they also have a deep historical content and are an important part of the cultural heritage of mankind. The enduring and rich cultural heritage of Confucianism will assuredly bring valuable enlightenment to bear on global development and the social advancement of mankind.[18]

The restoration of cultural heritage, both tangible and intangible, is therefore a powerful tool for healing the wounds of conflict, for fostering reconciliation, for marking a return to normality, and for restoring pride in both our differences and our similarities.

LESSON 5: WORK WITH NATURE, NOT AGAINST IT

The fifth lesson from past failures is that humans have been most successful in adapting to a changing environment when they have gone with the flow of nature. Canute, the eleventh-century King of England, Denmark and Norway, famously failed to turn back the sea's tide. Back then the apocryphal story was a demonstration to the king's fawning courtiers of his mortality in the face of God's omnipotence. Today the same is true of the natural world, with history littered with examples of humankind battling against the forces of nature and losing. Historically, where humans have been effective in the face of dramatic environmental change is when we work with the rhythm of nature, not against it. Making space by allowing farmland to flood, as our predecessors did using water meadows, is just one small example; replanting mangroves on the coast of Tanzania (or Puerto Rico) to protect against coastal erosion is another.

This theme links to our increasing disconnect with nature, particularly those of us privileged to live in rich Western societies where our homes allow us to control every detail of our micro-environment. We can effectively seal off the outside world, regulating temperature, excluding draughts, bugs and mosquitos, turning on lights in the dead of night, swapping the sounds of wind or traffic with something more ambient, even banishing unwanted smells via extractor fans and replacing them with designer aromas of our choosing. Again, this is not a plea for us all to revert to living in medieval smoke-filled halls and defecating down garderobes, more an observation about how our environment can sustain a false narrative about our ability to control nature.

Aside from utilizing traditional designs that make space for nature, such as buildings which allow water to flow under them or hunker low and warm in wind-blasted landscapes, the past is full of solutions where it was essential to nurture nature rather than overcome it. Farming subsidies in the UK and elsewhere now reward centuries-old management techniques, such as hedge-laying, pollarding or even the planting of winter cover crops, as ways in which to restore the wild-life value of the countryside, and to protect its soil. Forest creation, active woodland management, peatland restoration and watercourse protection are common weapons in the armoury of environmental protection, and each has many historical precedents. As does the concept of local, seasonal organic food – it is only in the last twenty years that we have been able to enjoy a cellophane-wrapped avocado in the middle of December.

LESSON 6: YOU CAN TAKE IT WITH YOU

At first glance, it might appear that picking heritage up and moving it, particularly before, during or after crisis is not an option. This is incorrect; indeed, sometimes it is the only option.

If we are learning lessons from the past, then large numbers of the world's population used to be nomadic pastoralists. Today, there are still an estimated thirty million people in society who live such a lifestyle and carry their own architecture with them, be it the reed huts of the Arbore people in southern Ethiopia, the black tents of the Tekna Berbers, the felt and willow yurts of Kyrgyz, the chooms of Siberian reindeer herders or Romany caravans. Approximately 1.2 million Mongolians are still nomadic, 40 per cent of the population. As a percentage of the world's population, however, they are a diminishing group. Such peoples may be able to transport their homes via camel, sled or truck, but their heritage is vulnerable in different ways, most notably from state disruption, loss of access to traditional pastoral lands and the impact of climate change.

What of heritage that is, at first glance at least, firmly rooted in the earth in which it sits? There are technical solutions, for example it is possible to physically pick up a historic building or archaeological site and move it to higher ground. The heroic examples of extreme conservation, epitomized by the saving of the pharaonic temples of Abu Simbel from the rising waters of the High Aswan Dam, illustrate the art of the possible.

Lighthouses, by their very nature, are positioned at the junction of land and sea, and are therefore often the canary in the coalmine warning of the impact of coastal climate change. The lighthouse complex at Rubjerg Knude on Denmark's northern tip, was completed in 1900, and comprised a tower, keepers' accommodation, kitchen gardens and a gasworks which provided power for the light and to the site. Coastal erosion and shifting sand dunes have been a consistent narrative for the Jutland peninsula. The medieval church at Mårup (*c.* 1250), about 300 metres north of the lighthouse, was originally 1 kilometre from the sea. It was closed for worship in 1926 and finally dismantled in 2016 with the ocean just metres away. The same coastal encroachment took place opposite the lighthouse, which was originally 200 metres from the sea, but the most damaging aspect was less the attrition of waves, more the impact of growing sand dunes. When it was constructed the 23-metre lighthouse tower stood on top of a 60-metre-high cliff, but this became obscured by a growing sand-dune system caused by changing patterns of coastal erosion, therefore rendering the lantern invisible from the coast and the lighthouse redundant. The growing pressure of sand against and around the buildings threatened them structurally too. By 1968 Rubjerg Lighthouse was decommissioned, and the complex turned

Fig. 76 Relocating Rubjerg Lighthouse. Located between Lonstrup and Lokken, Jutland, Denmark, the lighthouse was moved away from the coastline on 22 October 2019.

into a museum . . . on the topic of sand drift. This too was closed by 2002 – because of drifting sand!

With the entire complex predicted to fall into the sea by 2023, the local council relocated the lighthouse tower, moving its entire 720 tons to a new position of relative safety, 70 metres further inland. Beams were inserted at the base of the structure, which was then lifted on rails and edged towards its current location at 8 mph. The cost of the project, which was completed over three months in 2019, was 700,000 euros, and should ensure the lighthouse's safety for a further forty years.

However, nomadic peoples aside, relocation is not a cheap option. The 1854 Gay Head lighthouse at Martha's Vineyard, Massachusetts, was similarly moved back from its cliff edge location in 2015 at a cost of $2 million. The 4,800-ton lighthouse at Cape Hatteras on the treacherous Outer Banks of North Carolina was moved over twenty-three days in 1999. The price of its 2,900-foot journey was $11.8 million. Relocating the two temples at Abu Simbel required $40 million. Clearly moving heritage in advance of a pending disaster resulting from climate change, or for any reason, is an option that is only available to the tiniest percentage of heritage at risk.

What are the alternatives? One is to seek to slow down the passage of time. This conservation approach might include armouring the piece of coast that the heritage site sits upon to deflect the damaging impact of storms, or to prevent the ground being eaten away. Tree planting, such as the mangroves in Tanzania, is a softer, more natural solution. But, these too cost money, and while more feasible for more heritage than the translocation solution, will not be possible for a vast range of sites across the globe.

Another solution is for people moving from one country to another to take their traditional architecture with them, albeit as ideas to execute in a new city, town or village rather than the original physical entity. We see it all the time in colonialism, as soldiers, governors and traders bring with them the familiarity of home, such as the balconies, *balcãos* and *saquãos* of Portugese-inspired architecture in Goa, India, or the steep roofs, half-timbering and dormer windows of German influence in Luderitz, Namibia. It is possible to see British, Dutch, French and Spanish buildings in every part of their former empires. And earlier influences too: Ani illustrates several different architectural traditions reflecting the alternating ruling empires that have washed over it, from Persian through Byzantine to Islamic. Humberstone might be a functional, stripped-back working settlement, but the coastal city homes of the industrialists who ran it are entirely European in style. The 'board houses' of Sierra Leone's capital would not look out of place along America's eastern seaboard or the Caribbean, because that is where the architectural style originated from, brought to Freetown by formerly enslaved peoples.

Often, this new architecture is a blend, shaped by the climatic conditions and materials available, and by local vernacular traditions. In India, a mixture of British Gothic and Mughal styles can be seen in many governmental and public buildings, such as the Madras High Court and the Chhatrapati Shivaji Terminus in Mumbai. Christchurch Cathedral in Zanzibar's Stone Town was completed in 1879, commemorating the closure of the last purpose-built slave market in East Africa. Built by British missionaries out of the local coral stone, it has a large, vaulted nave and rose window straight out of the northern European Gothic playbook, but this is combined with decoration that clearly reflects the island's indigenous Swahili heritage, and that taken from its past as a Portuguese colony and an important Gulf trading post. A parapet made of the local white 'Neeru' plaster made from crushed marble dust was polished to gleam in the sun, boriti timber mangrove poles hold up the organ loft, and crenellations cap the walls with cusped niche decorative arches below, both reflecting the region's Islamic architectural traditions.

Similar hybridizations can be seen across the world, and not simply with the grand buildings of state or worship, but with vernacular architecture too; for example, the black and white houses of Singapore built to accommodate British service personnel combined Tudor and Jacobean revival styles that would not look out of place in the English Home Counties, with local Malay traditions. These included raising the building on pillars to improve air circulation and protect against flash flooding, large overhanging eaves to give shade, steeply pitched roofs to draw the heat up through the house and tiled floors, again to promote coolness in the fierce heat of the tropical sun. Sometimes, where there is no attempt by the incomer to marry local knowledge and tradition with their own, things can go horribly wrong. The tall, heavy brick and stone buildings that once lined the streets of Jamaica's Port Royal would have mirrored those in a seventeenth-century English port. However, such designs were completely incapable of surviving the earthquake and subsequent events of 1692. And, occasionally, there is a reverse flow of tradition. The bungalow, for example, first appeared in India – in Bengal, hence '*bengala*' – as a British military solution to provide quickly erected, standardized and cheap accommodation for officials working in trade, plantations and factories of the East India Company, and later during the Raj. Commonly low, single-story buildings with a veranda for shade, positioned in its own plot of land, the bungalow spread wherever the British Empire extended, and remains a popular housing type in the United Kingdom, as well as elsewhere across the world.

But none of these examples reflect the issue of lost heritage for those who are most negatively affected by it, namely the refugees or economic migrants escaping catastrophe, poverty or both. Here the most commonplace buildings to be transported from the old home to the new are places of worship, the churches, mosques, synagogues and temples of belief. Next come buildings or more typically areas of trade: there are thirty-five recognized Chinatowns in nineteen countries, most distinguished by their *paifang* arches and range of Chinese shops, restaurants and services. Chinese script, colours and decoration clearly mark such places from their surrounding neighbourhoods.

This neatly illustrates a point that, for many, the most portable and resilient reminders of cultural identity are not bricks and mortar, but a rich myriad of intangible traditions; food, music, dance, art, festivals and ways of celebrating, language, names. It is strongest where people of the same identity coalesce, be it in the distinctive inner-city areas of the world's cities where migrants first arrive, or ghettos where familiarity and tolerance through critical mass combine.

LESSON 7: MIGRATION CONTRIBUTES TO HERITAGE

A commonplace image of the architecture of those forced to move is the blue canvas or semi-permanent huts of UNHCR. These are not constructed as permanent residencies, more as waiting rooms for hundreds of thousands of refugees who either wish to return home or move on to a settled life elsewhere. One refugee camp, Dheisheh near Bethlehem in Palestine, constructed in 1949, is proposed as a World Heritage Site to highlight the permanent temporariness of those who live there, and to explore refugee heritage beyond the narrative of suffering and displacement.

The future points to more and more migration – or attempted migration – driven by a warming climate, pressure on global resources, especially water and land on which to live and grow food, the (relative) ease of travel, alongside the push of war and natural hazards, the pull of economic opportunity and digital networks that facilitate a global workplace. Parag Khanna in his book *Move* argues that we are entering a new age of mass migrations, one in which movement could be the new normality, and where populations will transfer en masse from the increasingly inhospitable parts of the world to areas that have capacity, such as Canada and Siberia:

> The future of human mobility points in just one direction: *more*. The coming decades could witness *billions* of people on the move, shifting from south to north, from coast to inland, from low-lying to higher elevation, from overpriced to affordable, from failing to stable societies.[19]

It is the physical heritage of these future migrants that is most likely to get left behind; their historic buildings and richly layered landscapes, their temples and palaces, farms and factories, their burial grounds and places of entertainment; all will be abandoned to water, salt, wind or fire, left without purpose or the resources to maintain them. Instead, it is the portable heritage of migrants that has the best chance of survival, and if we learn from the past, that survival might be in the form of the physical reproduction of architectural ideas, but in a hybridized form, blending new home with old home, and it will be the intangible cultural traditions that require no packing case.

There are two further observations on this theme: the first is that the people most likely and able to move are the young. Khanna writes, 'To know the future, then, we must follow the next generation into it.' So, what from their past will they take with them?

Secondly, the history of migration has taught us that 'belonging' is important, and that belonging can mean to more than one place. Historically, the New York City area has enclaves favoured by many different nationalities or beliefs: Little Italy, Hell's Kitchen, Chinatown, Koreatown; one in four residents of Brooklyn is Jewish. There are now six official Chinatowns in New York, with Flushing being the largest, and another three emerging. A map of the new 'littles' in the city includes Little Mexico, Little Syria and Little Odessa. To be Irish-American, Ghanaian-American, Indian American or Puerto Rican-American is not to choose between family background and home, but to celebrate both, and in so doing change the definition of the current and future city. More global migration, forced or chosen freely, will mean a continuing blend of heritages, sometimes in the form of a homogenizing melting pot, sometimes as a salad bowl where the constituent parts are still identifiable. And, lest we forget, we are all offspring – somewhere, someplace, sometime – of migrants.

LESSON 8: IF CHANGE IS INEVITABLE, THEN SO IS LOSS

Perhaps the most difficult but liberating lesson we can learn from the past is that if change is inevitable, then so too is loss. All the stories in this book have illustrated the forfeiture of heritage that has taken place gradually over years, decades, centuries even, hastened by extreme events: the medieval city of Dunwich has slowly shrunk from its heyday in the thirteenth century to become a village of 200 people. Its measured disappearance and relocation over 800 years was punctuated by disastrous storms in which whole parishes were lost. The thawing of the Arctic icesheets and permafrost on Canada's northern coast has led to the disappearance of Inuvialuit settlements and those of later western whalers and trappers. The physical remains of their presence are being blasted away by increased coastal storms, or being mulched as the ground loses its frozen stability and turns into a stew of moving earth and rock.

The Maldives is the lowest-lying country in the world; its most mountainous point is a 2.4-metre sand dune – that is, just above the height of a door. This archipelago of 1,200 islands has a population of 400,000 but was visited by 1.7 million people in 2019 in search of white coral beaches and rich marine wildlife. It has a fascinating heritage too, resulting from its position as a transit point between traders moving between east and west across the Indian Ocean. Its mosques, which were constructed out of Porite coral boulders removed from the surrounding reefs, are a wonderful fusion of Buddhist, African Swahili and Islamic decorative craft traditions, and are a tentative World Heritage Site. And yet, graveyards next to the sea are already becoming swallowed up by sand as tidal surges encroach further and further inland. Global warming of the seas, and an enhanced El Niño effect has, alongside the impact of increasing pollution, significantly damaged the coral reefs that the archipelago is founded on, threatening the two primary economic drivers of the country: tourism and fishing. The sad fact is that people born on the Maldives today are likely to be witnesses to their country's disappearance because of sea-level rise and increased storms.

The same threat of inevitable loss applies to many populations globally, particularly those currently living on the limits of land, water, ice, high mountain or dry desert. The scale of heritage loss across the world has been and will be enormous – far greater than that which is preserved. Future environmental, economic, social and political change will cause millions more heritage sites and historic buildings to disappear. Most will vanish without a trace: no acknowledgement, ceremony or record. A smaller proportion may be immortalized not as conserved bricks and mortar, but in a photograph, archaeological excavation archive or through the selective distillation of its contents in a museum cabinet. These acts are a eulogy of past achievement, a wake for dead historic buildings: worthwhile and necessary, but a shadow of the original. Preservation by record, as it is known in the heritage business, is acknowledged as a best-case last resort.

There is another consideration on the theme of heritage loss, which is not to think of it as loss at all, merely a change from one state and use to another. This returns us to the theme that heritage isn't static in the first place: it is not representative of a single point in time except the current. Today Beaudesert Hall is largely remembered as an elaborate eighteenth-century adaptation of a fine Tudor mansion. In the word 'adaptation', or its architectural allies, 'addition', 'update' and 'improvement', we already have sight of one major phase of loss at the Pagets' Staffordshire seat in which the remodelling by Wyatt substantially destroyed much of the interior of the 1573 house and completely changed the approach to it. By turn, the Elizabethan builders of the hall swept away most of its medieval predecessor to create their 'very fair brick house', a second major phase of loss. A third phase, probably dating to the fifteenth century, followed major improvements to create a hunting lodge out of the original twelfth-century monastery. A Cistercian monk would no more recognize Beaudesert in its Tudor or eighteenth-century forms than we would his church, dormitory or refectory today. Ironically, at Beaudesert, the most enduring modern survival of any of the halls is the stone stump of the medieval building, a resilient structure that has stubbornly survived within the cladding of later centuries.

Beaudesert is a single example of the norm. There are countless others: for a large number of medieval stone-built castles in England and Wales, there is likely to be an eleventh- or twelfth-century wooden predecessor. Virtually all the surviving medieval churches in the UK will illustrate multiple phases of expansion or contraction, from the addition of new aisles and chapels to the heightening of the nave for a clerestory to throw light onto the worshippers below. Thin Norman lancet windows blocked up for new expanses in Early English, decorated or perpendicular styles; the stripping back of the Restoration period, or the muscular 'restoration' of the nineteenth century. Each of these is a story of successive alteration, addition or destruction of what went before.

And, among these major changes taking place over time, there are a thousand small ones, each of which alter the physical appearance of a historic building. These range from the replacement of casement windows with sash and then double-glazed variants, to the application of a new coat of paint over layers of the old. It may be a change of use that substantially alters the spirit of a place with little tangible manifestation: think of the difference between a lived-in party house versus the place curated as a museum, a hotel or not lived in at all. Same structure, entirely different purpose and feel.

Caitlin Desilvey in her book *Curated Decay* (2017) takes this theme of permanently changing states a step further. In it she convincingly argues that a building's return to nature is just another part of its story – it changes from a place of shelter for humans to a habitat for insects and animals.

If we consider the cultural remains of the past in this way, as a rich but ever-changing resource, then it frees us from our natural response – particularly in the West – which is to try to preserve it. Graham Fairclough, quoted by Desilvey, observed:

> The obsession with physical conservation became so embedded in twentieth century mentalities that it is no longer easy to separate an attempt to understand the past and its meaning from agonizing about which bits of it to protect and keep. It is almost as if one is not allowed to be interested in the past without wanting to keep or restore it. So enmeshed in the conservation idea are we that 'significance' and value' seem to be the only legitimated way to describe the remains of the past which seems to exist only to be preserved.[20]

Letting go has to be an option, probably the default option. It's a case of how, not when.

These ideas are often amplified by the long timescale over which loss can occur and begin to question the doom-laden concept of collapse. Seen through such a lens, the loss of civilizations and historic communities becomes less about failure, and more about stories of human adaptation, ingenuity and resilience.

LESSON 9: CONSERVATION IS THE CAREFUL MANAGEMENT OF CHANGE

The idea for this book started with my obsession with ruinous, abandoned places. Some were impossibly romantic, dramatic and distant, sites such as Petra, Machu Picchu and Persepolis, seen first through glossy pictures and later, gratefully, in the flesh (where I learned that they might have been abandoned long ago by their builders, but not by us tourists). Others were much more commonplace, forming a backdrop to life – the corrugated landscape of medieval field systems seen from a passing train, a walk by the grassy tump of a Bronze Age burial mound or a visit up the twisting stairs of a redundant castle.

I wanted to group some of these places into stories to try to understand the drivers for the disappearance of cultural heritage at a large and small scale, and at different speeds, in order to discern the future. That aim still resonates, and hopefully has been illustrated here. But exploring historic places which have disappeared around the world has also challenged me to reflect on the nature of loss, and on the foundations of my personal motivation and that of my profession.

I have always seen my role to be about helping others to conserve historic buildings, ancient monuments and cultural landscapes that they and the wider world value. I do this because I believe such places are the building blocks of character and distinctiveness that surround our lives – I don't want Blackpool to look like Bhutan – and the warp and weft of the past shape such differences. I do it because such places are *our* story, they are paeans to our creativity, our greatest works of art. I do it because they are our memory and light where we might go in the future.

But there is an apparent contradiction in this, as illustrated by the stories told here, in that change is inevitable. To fix a building to a particular date or century is impossible. A seventeenth-century building is no longer a contemporary building in its own century, it is a 400-year-old building in the twenty-first century. Notwithstanding that it might already be an amalgam of different phases of build and adaptation, its function has changed, the context of its use has changed, many of its 'seventeenth-century' elements have been replaced through maintenance or fashion (roof, doors, floors, decoration), its furnishings will be long sold, it is likely to have bathrooms and toilets, and these, thankfully, now connect to the mains as opposed to being emptied by a gongfermour. It may possess the simple accoutrements of modern health and safety, be lit and powered by electricity and sit within a garden containing plants never seen by those who originally lived there. Even if it had none of such modern accessories, and was a living museum of the type where the actors feign startlement at mobile phones and ask, 'What be that curious jewel on thine wrist . . .?' (a watch, always a watch . . .), it is a visitor attraction not a residence, and the actors go home at the end of the day to watch TV in comfort.

It's also a decaying building. If we return to the long-term timescale of the geologist, then the physical entity will erode, whether through the microscopic loss of the grains of mica or seashell that make up the stone, or the weathering of wood, or the washing away of adobe. It may be possible to slow down the rate of decay, but it is not possible to stop it.

Not only is it not possible to 'fix' a building or landscape, it is also not desirable. Freezing a cultural asset in time – in our century, but supposedly of another – makes it something it has never been. Remove the 'living' element of a place, and it dies. Museums are fabulous and necessary places, but our landscapes and buildings should not be museums, they need a different kind of freedom to adapt and change and be relevant to the present.

And, as we have seen, if change is inevitable, then so too is loss. That is where conservation comes in, and the apparent contradiction between preservation and change disappears. It recognizes the pain of loss and seeks to address it by managing the transition between the treasured heritage we have in the present, and its altered form in the future. *Conservation is the careful management of change*: as much a philosophy as action, giving people and places time to physically move, to adapt or to mourn and celebrate. It can be about temporal physical retention, but not always; it is more about retaining the character or soul of a place, a distillation of the special elements of the past that people treasure today and may value in the future, knowing full well that change will happen. These are the tangible components of materials and architecture, and they are the intangible activities that find a home there. If we manage change in such a way as to align it with and enhance the historic *spirit of a place*, then we retain those important connections with the past in a liberating, forward-looking way. Our seventeenth-century building doesn't need to be 'fixed' in the time of Newton, Descartes or Aurangzeb, it can be a multi-phase structure, some of which is 400 years old and modern at the same time. In this way it remains relevant and used: it contributes and has a future.

And where did the idea of a 'spirit of place' come from?

In the oldest story in this book, Girsu's lion-headed eagle, the White Thunderbird, was the divine, semi-mythical representation of the god Ningirsu. It was the avatar not only of the god and his temple but also the protective spirit of the city and its people. Two thousand years later, the same god (now known as Ninurta) was the patron deity of the Neo-Assyrian city of Nimrud. The two most frequently recurring sculptural motifs of Nimrud and the Assyrian Empire are the lamassu and the winged genie. The former combines the body of a lion or bull with a human head and usually stands either side of the entrance to palaces and temples or was engraved on clay tablets and buried under the threshold of ordinary houses. Lamassus too are guardian spirits, protective of all life within their portals. The genie features on the carved relief panels, usually as bearded men with wings and caps decorated with horns or diadem crowns, or with a bird's head and human bodies. These are also protective deities, guarding kings, people and places – as we have seen to destroy them is to break the bond. The Romans too had a similar concept, with a *genius* being a personal guiding spirit and a *genius loci* being a protective *spirit of place*.

It seems fitting to end this book with a concept that originated in the distant past, but still feels to me as relevant today as it did to the ancient Mesopotamian wishing to protect their home, or the Roman praying at the altar of their *genius loci*.

Fig. 77 Mace-head from Girsu, showing the White Thunderbird, a lion-headed eagle, holding two lions in its talons. This ceremonial device has three figures on the back.

AMONGST THE RUINS

ACKNOWLEDGEMENTS

The writing of this book has been a solo effort, by which I mean I have no one to blame but myself, but that does not mean that I have not had help. I am extremely appreciative of all those who have contributed, including Jonathan Bell and an unknown peer reviewer, each offering a genuinely constructive challenge; to Professor David Mattingly, Professor Maamoun Abdulkarim, Edward Johnson, Sebastien Rey and Kaisa Barthuli, who helped me refine certain stories and source illustrations; and to Yiannis Avramides, Stephen Battle, Ben Cowell and Alessandra Peruzzetto from World Monuments Fund, who either commented or cajoled. My own small team at World Monuments in the UK, Charlotte Matthews and Emma Sweeney, were often the unwitting recipients of the testing of ideas, and they put up with my occasional obsession with strange places across the world.

The team at Yale were also wonderfully supportive, including Sophie Neve, Richard Mason, Lucy Buchan and Felicity Maunder. Susannah Stone once again worked her magic, finding exactly the right illustrations and often sourcing far better alternatives than my originals. Ann Chapman Daniel has been incredibly generous in her support for the illustrations, without which this book would simply not work.

Finally, I have to acknowledge the support of friends and family, especially since I have borrowed time from them during holidays, evenings and weekends, so a heartfelt thanks to all of them, but especially Brennie, Flo, Jay . . . and Pin (but can I have my shoes back?).

NOTES

Introduction

1 Bowersock, 1996, p. 32
2 Toynbee, 1934–61
3 Pirenne, 1937

Chapter 1

1 Xu et al., 2018, pp. 134–40
2 Gearey et al., 2010, p. 5
3 McDermott, 2007, pp. 17–30
4 Barnett, 1965
5 Burl, 1976, p. 246
6 Foley, 1983, pp. 146–8
7 Burl, 1976, pp. 242–53
8 Burl, 1976, p. 247
9 Evans, 1966, p. 4
10 Burl, 1976, p. 248
11 Thom, 1980, pp. 15–19
12 Foley and Macdonagh, 1998, p. 28
13 Curran et al., 2002, pp. 153–4
14 Betts, 2007, p. 129
15 Fleming, 2001
16 Franklin, 2012 reprint of 1828, p. 119
17 Stone, 1981, p. 103
18 Bockstoce, 1977, p. 40
19 Stone, 1981, p. 110, quoting a letter from Skinner to his bishop in 1894
20 Usher, 1971, p. 175
21 *Dawson Daily News*, quoted in Piggott, 2011, p. 99
22 Usher, 1971, p. 180
23 Riedlinger, 1999, p. 430
24 Inuvialuit Regional Corporation, 2016
25 Jones et al., 2008, pp. 367–70
26 Hollesen et al., 2018; and a significant underestimation of the true numbers
27 From the entry for land held by Robert Malet, Tenant in Chief, Suffolk Folio 32, 1086

28 Comfort, 1994, p. vi
29 Comfort, 1994, p. 74
30 Comfort, 1994, p. 71
31 Comfort, 1994, pp. 77–8
32 Comfort, 1994, p. 90
33 Sear et al., 2012, p. 97
34 Defoe, 1724, pp. 54–5
35 Sear et al., 2012
36 East Suffolk Council, 1996, Suffolk Shoreline Management Plan 7
37 Defoe, 1724, p. 54
38 Mattingly, 2003, p. 72
39 Mattingly, 2003, p. 342
40 Herodotus 4.183
41 Murray, 1981, in Mattingly, 2003, p. 346
42 Mattingly, 2003
43 Mattingly, 2022, pp. 13–16
44 Mattingly, 2003, p. 237
45 Mattingly, personal communication
46 Lethielleux in Mattingly, 2003, p. 270
47 Mattingly, 2003, p. 351
48 *Sahara Italiano*, 1937, pp. 403–15

Chapter 2

1 'The Great Earthquake of Port Royal', *Chambers Journal*, vol. 60, 1883, p. 663
2 Link, 1960, pp. 178–81
3 Heath, 1692, letter 9 September
4 Heath, 1692, letter 9 September
5 Sloane and de Toledo, 1694
6 Zahedieh, 1986, p. 570
7 Mulcahy, 2008, p. 403
8 Mulachy, 2008, p. 399
9 Mulachy, 2008, p. 398
10 Wiggins-Grandison, 2005, p. 4
11 Letter to Hans Sloane dated 23 September 1692, in Sloane and de Toledo, 1694
12 Heath, 1692
13 Ward, 1698, p. 14
14 From the Spanish *cimarron*, referring to enslaved Africans who ran from the plantations and often banded with local Taino to fight the Spanish and British
15 Zahedieh, 1986, p. 578
16 Zahedieh, 1986, p. 589
17 Zahedieh, 1986, p. 571
18 Hanson, 1683
19 Zahedieh, 1986, p. 570
20 Hanson, 1683
21 Heath, 1692
22 The Great Earthquake: Acts of William and Mary AD 1693, An Act for Establishing a Perpetual Anniversary Fast on the Seventh of June
23 Ward, 1698, p. 16

24 *The Journey of William of Rubruck to the Eastern Parts of the World, 1253–55, as narrated by himself.* Translated from the Latin and edited by Rockhill, William Woodville, 1900. London: Bedford Press
25 Anadolu Agency, 14 March 2018
26 Watenpaugh, 2014, pp. 534–5
27 Anadolu Agency, 24 June 2020
28 Anadolu Agency, 27 May 2021
29 Watenpaugh, 2014, p. 535
30 World Heritage Nomination File, 2015
31 Watenpaugh, 2014, p. 542
32 Sinclair, 1987
33 Casadevall, Tormey and Roberts, 2019
34 Petersen and Watters, 1991, p. 286
35 Gwynn, 1929, pp. 278–9
36 Berleant-Schiller, 1989, p. 545
37 Berleant-Schiller, 1989, p. 541
38 Ryzewski and Cherry, 2015, p. 359
39 Akenson, 1997, pp. 154–70
40 Richard, 1864, p. 140
41 Watters and Norton, 2007, p. 51
42 Sadler, 2015, p. 9
43 From the website of the Alliouagana Singers, a London-based choral group https://www.alliouaganasingers.com
44 Mott Macdonald, 2018, p. 22
45 Anne Marie Dewar quoted in Shotte, 2007, p. 59
46 Government of Montserrat, 2019
47 Lea, 2010

Chapter 3

1 Barlow, 1994; Harari, 2014, p. 122
2 Ray, 2016, p. 69
3 Sand, 2018, pp. 98–9
4 Translation of EANATUM (Stela of the Vultures) in *Sources from the Ancient Near East* (SANE), vol. 2, fascicle 1, 'Reconstructing History from Ancient Inscriptions: The Lagash-Umma Border Conflict', pp. 45–6, by Jerrold S. Cooper, 1983. Revised third printing. Malibu, CA: Undena Publications
5 Rey, 2016, pp. 6–7
6 Weiss, 2020, p. 42
7 The ETCSL project, 2003, translation of Ninurta's exploits, t.1.6.1, paras 334–46
8 The ETCSL project, 2003, translation of Ninurta's exploits, t.1.6.1, paras 347–67
9 Rost, 2017, p. 3
10 Schrakamp, 2018, p. 120
11 Rost, 2017, pp. 5–6
12 Schrakamp, 2018, pp. 175–6
13 Westenholz, 2002, p. 26
14 Jacobsen and Adams, 1958, p. 1251
15 Jacobsen and Adams, 1958, pp. 1251–2
16 Thompson, 2004, pp. 612–52

17 Geddes, 2018, p. 16
18 Macaulay, 1764, p. 53
19 Maclean, 1972, p. 34
20 Martin, 1703, pp. 280–99
21 Gaskell, 2000, p. 142
22 Martin, 1703, pp. 283–4
23 NRS Scotland, 1764: NRAS Survey 4360/7/2
24 Martin, 1749, p. 7
25 Mackenzie, 1911, p. 20
26 Gannon and Geddes, 2015, p. 112
27 Gannon and Geddes, 2015, p. 89
28 Gannon and Geddes, 2015, p. 67
29 Martin, 1703, p. 284
30 Maclean, 1972, p. 69
31 Mackenzie, 1904, p. 399
32 Stride, 2008
33 Richards, 1992, p. 138
34 Richards, 1992, p. 148
35 Meharg et al., 2006, pp. 1818–28
36 10 May 1930, National Records of Scotland AF57/26/3
37 National Trust for Scotland, 2012
38 Office for National Statistics UK House Price Index https://www.ons.gov.uk
39 Plumber, 2021
40 Lee, 1989
41 Martinsson-Walling and Crockford, 2001, p. 256
42 Martinsson-Walling and Crockford, 2001, pp. 259–60
43 Routledge, 1919, p. 181
44 Lipo et al., 2013
45 Diamond, 2005; Flenley and Bahn, 2002; Kirch, 2000, McCoy, 1979
46 Hunt and Lipo, 2011; Mulrooney, 2012; Rainbird, 2002; Peiser, 2005
47 Roggeveen and Sharp, 1970
48 Chamisso, 1836, pp. 116–17
49 McGall, 1976, p. 96
50 Heyerdahl and Ferdon, 1961, p. 76
51 Anguita, 1988, pp. 21–39
52 Maziere, 1964, p. 35, quoted in Peiser, 2005, p. 534
53 Davidson, 2021

Chapter 4

1 Keeley, 1996, p. 28
2 Oppenheim, 1969, pp. 558–61
3 Reade, 2002, pp. 156–67
4 Gadd, 1923, p. 40
5 Simpson, 2021, p. 2
6 Simpson, 2021, p. 2
7 Simpson, 2021, p. 3
8 Reade in Curtis et al., 2008, p. 3
9 Bahn, 1996, p. 104

10 Waterfield, 1963, p. 171
11 Li, 2016
12 Barmé, 1996, p. 126 – extrapolated from 1996 figures
13 Barmé, 1996, p. 125
14 Barmé, 1996, p. 113
15 Attiret, 1749, pp. 124–5
16 Li, 2016
17 Attiret, 1982, pp. 8–10
18 Attiret, 1982, p. 12
19 Wong, undated
20 Sullivan, 1973, p. 68
21 Varin, 1862, pp. 240–1
22 *Encyclopaedia Britannica*, 2008
23 Wolseley, 1862, pp. 224–7
24 Reprinted in Treue, 1960, pp. 205–6
25 D'Hérrison, 1901, p. 625
26 Knollys, 1875, pp. 226–7, and *The Illustrated London News*, no. 1068, 5 January
    1861, p. 7
27 Heathcote, 1974, pp. 110, 128
28 Hevia, 2003
29 Barmé, 1996, p. 131
30 Wolseley, 1862, p. 280
31 Requoted in Hevia, 2003, p. 108
32 Hugo, 1861
33 Barmé, 1996, p. 141
34 Tythacott, 2015, p. 469
35 Shen, 2012
36 Wang, 1988, p. 71
37 MacFarquhar and Schoenhals, 2008, pp. 114–15
38 Zhou, 2011, p. 84
39 Foshan shi dang'anju, 1991, p. 116
40 MacFarquhar and Schoenhals, 2008, p. 120
41 Zhou, 2011, pp. 100–1
42 The term 'Confucius Family Shop' is an expression used to describe Confucian
    ideology, tradition and institution; Zhou, 2011, p. 9
43 MacFarquhar and Schoenhals, 2008, p. 119
44 Ye and Barmé, 2009
45 Zhou, 2011, p. 144
46 Zhou, 2011, p. 197
47 Zhou, 2011, p. 220
48 Zhou, 2011, p. 229
49 MacFarquhar and Schoenhals, 2008, p. 118

Chapter 5

1 Wisniak and Garcés, 2001, p. 434
2 Bermúdez, 1987, quoted in UNESCO, 2005, p. 47
3 Darwin, 1839, pp. 442–3
4 UNESCO, 2005, p. 50

5 Wisniak, 2001, p. 526
6 *New World Encyclopedia* contributors, 2020
7 Foster and Clark, 2004, p. 191
8 Wisniak and Garcés, 2001, p. 428
9 Soil Association Website, https://www.soilassociation.org/causes-campaigns/fixing-nitrogen-the-challenge-for-climate-nature-and-health/the-impacts-of-nitrogen-pollution, accessed 19 October 2020
10 Jefferson, 1849, pamphlet
11 Bike League, https://www.bikeleague.org/content/mission-and-history, accessed 3 May 2022
12 Ford, 1922
13 Delong, 1997
14 Steinbeck, 2017, p. 119
15 National Park Service, 1995, p. 8
16 Connolly, 2011
17 Eisenhower, 1963, p. 548
18 Eisenhower, 1967, ch. XI
19 TRB, 1956, p. 2
20 Kelly and Scott, 1988, p. 182
21 Cassity, 2004, p. 252
22 Listokin et al., 2011, vol. 1., p. 8
23 Hess, 2000, p. 59
24 Kaisa Barthuli, US National Park Service, personal communication
25 Worsley, 2002, p. 7
26 Repton, 1816, p. 41
27 Repton, 1816, p. 42
28 Repton, 1816, p. 48
29 A note by J. Robson in *The Journal of Horticulture, Cottage Gardener and Country Gentleman*, 9 May 1872, p. 387
30 The Gardens Trust, 2019
31 Mandler, 1997, pp. 255–8
32 Parliamentary Debates, 1894
33 *Lichfield Mercury*, 28 June 1935
34 HMSO, 1950
35 Shelley, 1826, p. 100
36 Burckhardt, 1819, p. 88
37 Burckhardt, 1819, pp. 90–1
38 Belzoni, 1820, p. 357
39 Tamborrino and Wendrich, 2017, p. 170
40 Rockett, 1980, pp. 30–8
41 UNESCO, https://whc.unesco.org/en/activities/172, accessed 11 December 2020
42 Weigall, 1919, p. 319
43 Vercoutter, 1980, p. 65

Conclusion

1 Cordell et al., 2007, pp. 379–405
2 Pereira, 2009, p. 477
3 National Flood Relief Commission, 1932, foreword and p. 6

4 Courtney, 2018, p. 6
5 Jackson, 2006, p. 1914
6 Thorarinsson, 1970, p. 4
7 Larsen and Thordarson, 2019
8 Toohey et al., 2016, p. 401
9 Toohey et al., 2016, p. 401
10 Davidson, 2021
11 Gadd, 1923, p. 40
12 Li, 2016
13 Alp, 1991, p. 810
14 Langenbach, 2010, pp. 1–25
15 Cultural Center of Caucasian Yazidis, March 2021
16 Isakhan and Shahab, 2020, p. 15
17 French and Holland, March 2021
18 ICOMOS Advisory Body Evaluation, 1994
19 Khanna, 2021, p. 16
20 Fairclough, 2005, p. 158

BIBLIOGRAPHY

Akenson, Donald H., 1997, *If the Irish Ran the World: Montserrat 1630–1730*. Montreal: McGill-Queen's University Press

Alp, Ahmet Vefik, 1991, 'Vernacular Climate Control in Desert Architecture', in *Energy and Buildings*, vol. 16, nos. 3–4 (1990/91), pp. 809–15

Anadolu Agency, 2018, 'Beautiful Year-Round, Ani Ruins a Spectacular Tourist Destination in Turkey', *Daily Sabah*. https://www.dailysabah.com/travel/2018/03/14/beautiful-year-round-ani-ruins-a-spectacular-tourist-destination-in-turkey, accessed 8 March 2022

Anadolu Agency, 2020, 'Anatolia's 1st Turkish Mosque to Open to Worship after Restoration', *Daily Sabah*. https://www.dailysabah.com/life/history/anatolias-1st-turkish-mosque-to-open-to-worship-after-restoration, accessed 22 April 2022

Anadolu Agency, 2021, 'Excavations to Reveal Hidden History of Eastern Turkey's Ani Ruins', *Daily Sabah*. https://www.dailysabah.com/life/history/excavations-to-reveal-hidden-history-of-eastern-turkeys-ani-ruins, accessed 22 April 2022

Anguita, Patricia, 1988, 'L'insertion des Rapanui à Tahiti et Moorea 1871–1920', *Bulletin de la Société des Etudes Océaniennes*, vol. 20, no. 8, pp. 21–39

Attiret, Jean Denis, 1749, From *Lettres édifiantes et curieuses: Ecrite des Missions Etrangères*, vol. 27 (1749 edn), in Sirén, *Gardens of China*, pp. 124–5

Attiret, Jean Denis, 1982 (reprint of 1753), *A Particular Account of the Emperor of China's Gardens Near Pekin*, trans. Sir Harry Beaumont. London: Garland

Bahn, Paul G. (ed.), 1996, *The Cambridge Illustrated History of Archaeology*. Cambridge: Cambridge University Press

Barlow, John Perry, 1994, 'The Economy of Ideas: Selling Wine without Bottles on the Global Net', *Wired Magazine*, vol. 2, no. 3

Barmé, Geremie R., 1996, 'The Garden of Perfect Brightness, a Life in Ruins', in *East Asian History*, vol. 11, June, pp. 111–58 (Institute of Advanced Studies, Australian National University)

Barnett, George, 1965, 'The Beaghmore Stone Circles', from *The Wee Black Tin* (poems), in Ballinascreen Historical Society 1980, compiled by Graham Mawhinney and Jennifer Johnston, Draperstown, Co. Londonderry

Belzoni, Giovanni Battista, 1820, *Narrative of the Operations and Recent Discoveries within the Pyramids, Temples, Tombs, and Excavations, in Egypt and Nubia; and of a Journey to the Coast of the Red Sea, in Search of the Ancient Berenice, and of another to the Oasis of Jupiter Ammon*. London: John Murray

Berleant-Schiller, Riva, 1989, 'Free Labor and the Economy in Seventeenth-Century Montserrat', *The William and Mary Quarterly*, vol. 46, no. 3, pp. 539–64

Bermúdez, Oscar, 1987, *Brief History of Saltpeter; Historical Synthesis from its Origins up to the Middle of the 20th Century*. Iquique: Pampa Desnuda Publications

Betts, Matthew W., 2007, 'The Mackenzie Inuit Whale Bone Industry: Raw Material, Tool Manufacture, and Trade', *Arctic*, vol. 60, no. 2, pp. 129–44

Bockstoce, John R., 1977, *Steam Whaling in the Western Arctic*. New Bedford: Old Dartmouth Historical Society

Bowersock, Glen W., 1996, 'The Vanishing Paradigm of the Fall of Rome', *Bulletin of the American Academy of Arts and Sciences*, vol. 49, no. 8, pp. 29–43

Buisseret, David, 2008, *Jamaica in 1687: The Taylor Manuscript at the National Library of Jamaica*. Kingston: University of the West Indies Press

Burckhardt, Johan, 1819, *Travels in Nubia*. London: John Murray

Burckhardt, Johan, 1822, *Travels in Syria and the Holy Land*. London: John Murray

Burl, Aubrey, 1976, *The Stone Circles of the British Isles*. New Haven and London: Yale University Press

Casadevall, Thomas J., Daniel Tormey and Jessica Roberts, 2019, *World Heritage Volcanoes: Classification, Gap Analysis, and Recommendations for Future Listings*, vol. 8. Gland, Switzerland: IUCN

Cassity, Michael, 2004, *Route 66 Corridor National Historic Context Study*. Report for the Route 66 Corridor Preservation Program, National Park Service

Chamisso, Adelbert von, 1836, *Reise um die Welt mit der Romanzoffischen Entdeckungs-Expedition in den Jahren 1815–18 auf der Brigg Rurik Kapitain Otto v. Kotzebue*. Adelbert von Chamisso's Werke. vol. 1. Leipzig: Weidmann'sche Buchhandlung

Comfort, Nicholas, 1994, *The Lost City of Dunwich*. Lavenham: Terence Dalton

Connolly, Billy, 2011, *Billy Connolly's Route 66: The Big Yin on the Ultimate American Road Trip*. Hachette Digital UK

Cordell, Linda S. et al., 2007, 'Mesa Verde Settlement History and Relocation: Climate Change, Social Networks, and Ancestral Pueblo Migration', *Kiva,* vol. 72

Courtney, Chris, 2018, *The Nature of Disaster: The 1931 Yangzi River Flood*. Cambridge: Cambridge University Press

Cultural Center of Caucasian Yazidis, 2021, 'Reconstruction and Opening of Sheikh Hassan Shrine in Kabar Village Shangal' (6 May 2021). https://yazidis.info/en/news/2564/reconstruction-and-opening-of-sheikh-hassan-shrine-in-kabar-village-shangal, accessed 10 June 2022

Curran, Joanne, Bernard Smith, and Patricia Warke, 2002, 'Weathering of Igneous Rocks during Shallow Burial in an Upland Peat Environment: Observations from the Bronze Age Copney Stone Circle Complex, Northern Ireland', *Catena*, vol. 49, pp. 139–55

Curtis, J. E., H. McCall, D. Collon and L. al-Gailani Werr (eds), 2008, 'New Light on Nimrud', *Proceedings of the Nimrud Conference*, 11–13 March 2002, British Institute for the Study of Iraq in association with The British Museum, London

Darwin, Charles, 1839, *Journal of Researches into the Geology and Natural History of the Various Countries Visited by H.M.S. Beagle under the Command of Captain Fitzroy, R.N. from 1832 to 1836*. London: Henry Colburn

Davidson, Charlie, 2021, 'How Many Tourists Visit Easter Island Yearly?', *Pursuant Media*, 2 May. https://www.pursuantmedia.com/2021/02/05/how-many-tourists-visit-easter-island-yearly, accessed 10 June 2022

Defoe, Daniel, 1724, *A Tour Thro' the Whole Island of Great Britain, divided into circuits or journeys*, vol. 1. London: G. Strahan et al.

Delong, J. Bradford, 1997, *Slouching Towards Utopia?: The Economic History of the Twentieth Century – XIII. The Roaring Twenties*. https://web.archive.org/web/20140520220920/http:/www.j-bradford-delong.net/tceh/slouch_roaring13.html, accessed 17 April 2022

Desilvey, Caitlin, 2017, *Curated Decay: Heritage Beyond Saving*. Minneapolis: University of Minnesota Press

D'Hérrison, Count, 1901, 'The Loot of the Imperial Summer Palace at Peking', translated from a reprint of an extract of D'Hérrison's memoirs in *Journal d'un Interprète en Chine, par le Comte D'Hérrison*. Washington DC: Smithsonian Institution

Diamond, Jared, 2005, *Collapse: How Societies Choose to Fail or Succeed*. New York: Viking.

East Suffolk Council, 1996, *Suffolk Shoreline Management Plan 7 – Lowestoft Ness to Languard Point* (reviewed 2006)

Eisenhower, Dwight D., 1963, *The White House Years: Waging Peace, 1956–1961*. London: Doubleday

Eisenhower, Dwight D., 1967, 'Through Darkest America with Truck and Tank', in *At Ease: Stories I Tell to Friends*, ch. XI, pp. 155–68. New York: Doubleday and Company

Encyclopaedia Britannica, 2008, 'opium trade'. Retrieved February 2008 from *Encyclopaedia Britannica Online*. http://www.britannica.com/eb/article-9105757

The ETCSL project, 2003, translation of t.1.6.2, 'Ninurta's Exploits: A *cir-sud* (?) to Ninurta', Faculty of Oriental Studies, University of Oxford. Updated 19 December 2006 by JE, https://etcsl.orinst.ox.ac.uk/cgi-bin/etcsl.cgi?text=t.1.6.2&charenc=j#

Evans, E. Estyn, 1966, 'George Barnett: An Appreciation', *Ulster Journal of Archaeology*, Third Series, vol. 29, pp. 1–5

Fairclough, Graham, 2009, 'n.d. Conservation and the British', in John Schofield (ed.), 'Defining Moments: Dramatic Archaeologies of the Twentieth Century', in *Studies in Contemporary and Historical Archaeology*, vol. 5, pp. 157–64, BAR International Series 2005

Fleming, Fergus, 2001, *Barrow's Boys: The Original Extreme Adventurers: A Stirring Story of Daring Fortitude and Outright Lunacy*. Cambridge: Granta

Flenley, John, and Paul Bahn, 2002, *The Enigmas of Easter Island: Island on the Edge*. Oxford: Oxford University Press

Foley, Claire, 1983, 'A Stone Circle Complex at Copney Hill, County Tyrone', *Ulster Journal of Archaeology*, Third Series, vol. 46, pp. 146–8

Foley, Claire, and Michael Macdonagh, 1998, 'Copney Stone Circles: A County Tyrone Enigma', *Archaeology Ireland*, Spring 1998, vol. 12, no. 1, pp. 24–8

Ford, Henry and Samuel Crowther, 1922, *My Life and Work*. New York: Garden City

Foshan shi dang'anju, ed., 1991, *Foshan shi dashiji (1949–1989) (Chronology of Major Events in Foshan City [1949–1989])*. Foshan: n.p.

Foster, John Bellamy, and Brett Clark, 2004, 'Ecological Imperialism: The Curse of Capitalism', in *Socialist Register*, pp. 186–201

Franklin, John and John Richardson, 2012, *Narrative of a Second Expedition to the Shores of the Polar Sea, in the Years 1825, 1826, and 1827*, [1828] (Cambridge Library Collection – Polar Exploration). Cambridge: Cambridge University Press

French, Paul and Oscar Holland, 2021, 'Debates over Beijing's Derelict Old Summer

Palace Are About More Than History', CNN. https://edition.cnn.com/style/article/china-old-summer-palace-intl-hnk-dst/index.html, accessed 13 June 2022

Gadd, C.J., 1923, *The Fall of Nineveh: The Newly Discovered Babylonian Chronicle, No. 21,901*. London: British Museum, p. 40

Gannon, Angela, and George Geddes, 2015, *St Kilda the Last and Outmost Isle*. Edinburgh: Historic Environment Scotland

The Gardens Trust, 2019, *Beaudesert: 'a desert beautified'* blog. https://thegardenstrust.blog/2019/07/27/beaudesert-a-desert-beautified, accessed 17 April 2022

Garschagen, Matthias et al., 2016, *World Risk Report 2016*. Bündnis Entwicklung Hilft and UNU-EHS

Gaskell, Jeremy, 2000, *Who Killed the Great Auk?* Oxford: Oxford University Press

Gearey, Ben et al., 2010, 'Peatlands and the Historic Environment', a scientific review commissioned by the IUCN UK Peatland Programme's Commission of Inquiry on Peatlands, pp. 1–42

Geddes, George, F., 2018, *The Landscape Archaeology of St Kilda*. Research by publication for Doctor of Philosophy, University of Edinburgh

Gibbon, Edward, 1776–89, *The History of the Decline and Fall of the Roman Empire*, six vols. London: Strahan and Cadell

Government of Montserrat, 2019, *Montserrat Tourism Strategy*. Brades, Montserrat: Government of Montserrat

Gwynn, Aubrey, 1929, 'Early Irish Emigration to the West Indies (1612–1643)', *Studies: An Irish Quarterly Review*, vol. 18, no. 71, pp. 377–93

Hanson, Francis, 1683, *The Laws of Jamaica, Passed by the Assembly, and Confirmed by his Majesty in Council, February 23, 1683*, Preface. London: H. Hills

Harari, Yuval Noah, 2014, *Sapiens: A Brief History of Humankind*. New York: Harper

Heath, E. Rev., 1692. *A full account of the late dreadful earthquake at Port-Royal in Jamaica, written in two letters from the minister of that place, from aboard the Granada in Port-Royal Harbour, June 22, 1692*. Edinburgh. Reprinted by John Reid, to be sold at his house in Bells-Wynd. https://www.proquest.com/books/full-account-late-dreadful-earthquake-at-port/docview/2240855190/se-2?accountid=133442, accessed 13 June 2022

Heathcote, T. A., *The Indian Army: The Garrison of British Imperial India, 1822–1922*, Historic Armies and Navies Series, plates. Newton Abbot: David and Charles, 1974, p. 215

Hess, Alan, 2000, 'Route Structure', *Architecture*, vol. 89, issue 9, pp. 58–9

Hevia, James, 2003, *English Lessons: The Pedagogy of Imperialism in Nineteenth-Century China*. Durham, NC: Duke University Press

Heyerdahl, Thor and Edward N. Ferdon, 1961, 'The Archaeology of Easter Island: Reports of the Norwegian Archaeological Expedition to Easter Island and the East Pacific', Monograph 24, vol. 1. Santa Fe: School for American Research and Museum of New Mexico

HMSO, 1950, *Report of the Committee on Houses of Outstanding Historic or Architectural Interest*. London

Hollesen, Jørgen et al., 2018, 'Climate Change and the Deteriorating Archaeological and Environmental Archives of the Arctic', *Antiquity*, vol. 92, issue 363, pp. 573–86

Hugo, Victor, 1861, Letter to Captain Butler, Hauteville House, 25 November 1861

Hunt Terry L. and Carl P. Lipo, 2011, *The Statues that Walked: Unraveling the Mystery of Easter Island*. New York: Free Press

ICOMOS, 1994, 'World Heritage List. The Temple of Confucius. No. 704', Advisory Body Evaluation, October

Inuvialuit Regional Corporation, 2016, *Inuvialuit on the Frontline of Climate Change: Development of a Regional Climate Change Adaptation Strategy*. https://irc.inuvialuit.com/sites/default/files/ISR_Climate_Change_Strategy.pdf, accessed 13 June 2022

Isakhan, Benjamin and Sofya Shahab, 2020, 'The Islamic State's Destruction of Yezidi Heritage: Responses, Resilience and Reconstruction after Genocide', *Journal of Social Archaeology*, vol. 20, no. 1, pp. 3–25

Jackson, James, 2006, 'Fatal Attraction: Living with Earthquakes, the Growth of Villages into Megacities, and Earthquake Vulnerability in the Modern World', *Philosophical Transactions: Mathematical, Physical and Engineering Sciences*, 15 August, vol. 364, no. 1845, Extreme Natural Hazards, pp. 1911–25

Jacobsen, Thorkild and Robert M. Adams, 1958, 'Salt and Silt in Ancient Mesopotamian Agriculture', *Science*, 21 November, New Series, vol. 128, no. 3334, pp. 1251–8

Jamie, Kathleen, 2012, *Sightlines*. London: Sort of Books

Jefferson, T. H., 1849, *Brief Practical Advice to the Emigrant or Traveller, published as an Accompaniment to the Map of the Emigrant Road from Independence, MO to St. Francisco, California*. New York: T. H. Jefferson

Jones, Benjamin M. et al., 2008. 'Modern Erosion Rates and Loss of Coastal Features and Sites, Beaufort Sea Coastline, Alaska', *Arctic*, vol. 61, pp. 361–72

Keeley, Lawrence, H., 1996, *War Before Civilization: The Myth of the Peaceful Savage*. Oxford: Oxford University Press

Kelly, Susan Croce, and Quinta Scott, 1988, *Route 66: The Highway and Its People*. Norman: University of Oklahoma Press

Khanna, Parag, 2021, *Move: The Forces Uprooting Us*. New York: Simon & Schuster

Kirch, Patrick V., 1984, *The Evolution of Polynesian Chiefdoms*. Cambridge: Cambridge University Press

Knollys, Henry, 1875, *Incidents in the China War of 1860, Comp. From the Private Journals of General Sir Hope Grant*. Edinburgh and London: Blackwood and Sons

Kotzebue, Otto von, 1821, *Voyage of Discovery in the South Sea, and to Behring's Straits, in Search of a North-East Passage, Undertaken in the Years 1815, 16, 17, and 18, in the Ship Rurick*. Part 1. London: Sir Richard Phillips

Langenbach, Randolph, 2010, '"Earthquake Resistant Traditional Construction" is Not an Oxymoron: The Resilience of Timber and Masonry Structures in the Himalayan Region and Beyond, and its Relevance to Heritage Preservation in Bhutan', a paper from *Living in Harmony with the Four Elements*, The Royal Government of Bhutan International Conference on Disaster Management and Cultural Heritage, 12–14 December. https://www.conservationtech.com/RL's%20resume&%20pub's/RL-publications/Eq-pubs/2010-Kingdom-Of-Bhutan/Langenbach-BHUTAN.pdf

Larsen, Guðrún and Thor Thordarson, 2019, 'Hekla', in B. Oladottir, G. Larsen and M. T. Guðmundsson, *Catalogue of Icelandic Volcanoes*. IMO, UI and CPD-NCIP. https://icelandicvolcanoes.is//?volcano=HEK, accessed 25 June 2022

Lea, David, 2010, Videographer speaking in a video: *The Rebirth of Montserrat Part 2*, Future History Films. https://www.youtube.com/watch?v=Mis8pQX4PF0, accessed 13 June 2022

Lee, Georgia, 1989, *An Uncommon Guide to Easter Island*. International Resources, Booklink Distributors, California

Li, Lillian, 2016, 'The Garden of Perfect Brightness – 1: The Yuanmingyuan as Imperial Paradise (1700–1860)', *MIT Visualizing Cultures*. Massachusetts Institute of Technology. https://visualizingcultures.mit.edu/garden_perfect_brightness/ymy1_visnav05.html, accessed 8 January 2021

Link, Marion Clayton, 1960, 'Exploring the Drowned City of Port Royal', *National Geographic Magazine*, vol. 117, February, pp. 179–80

Lipo, Carl Philipp, Terry L. Hunt and Sergio Rapu Haoa, 2013, 'The "Walking" Megalithic Statues (*Moai*) of Easter Island', *Journal of Archaeological Science*, vol. 40, issue 6, June, pp. 2859–66

Listokin, David et al., 2011, *Route 66 Economic Impact Study, Technical Report, Vol. 1. History, Characteristics, and Economic Contributions*, a study conducted by Rutgers, The State University of New Jersey

Listokin, David et al., 2011, *Route 66 Economic Impact Study, Technical Report, Vol. II. Tales from the Mother Road: Case Studies of the People and Places of Route 66*, a study conducted by Rutgers, The State University of New Jersey

Macaulay, Kenneth, 1764, *The History of St Kilda*. London: James Thin

Macdonald, Mott, 2018, *Economic Growth Strategy and Delivery Plan for Montserrat*, Government of Montserrat, Final Report, June. http://finance.gov.ms/wp-content/uploads/2018/12/Economic-Growth-Strategy-Delivery-Plan.pdf, accessed 5 May 2022

MacFarquhar, Roderick, and Michael Schoenhals, 2008, *Mao's Last Revolution*. Cambridge, MA: Harvard University Press

Mackenzie, J. B., 1904, 'Antiquities and Old Customs in St Kilda, compiled from Notes made by Rev. Neil Mackenzie, Minister of St Kilda, 1829–48', *Proceedings of the Society of Antiquaries of Scotland*, vol. 39, pp. 397–402

Mackenzie, J. B. (ed.), 1911, *Episode in the Life of the Rev. Neil Mackenzie at St Kilda from 1829 to 1843*. Privately printed

Maclean, Charles, 1972, *Island of the Edge of the World: The Story of St. Kilda*. Edinburgh: Canongate

MacLean, Lachlan, 1838, *Sketches on the Island of St Kilda*. Glasgow: McPhun

Mandler, Peter, 1997, *The Fall and Rise of the Stately Home*. New Haven and London: Yale University Press, pp. 255–8

Martin, Martin, 1698, *A Late Voyage to St Kilda*, 1986 edn. Edinburgh: The Mercat Press

Martin, Martin, 1703, *A Description of the Western Isles of Scotland*. London, Printed for Andrew Bell, at the Cross-Keys and Bible, in Cornhil, near Stocks-Market

Martin, Martin, 1749, *A Voyage to St Kilda*. London: R. Griffith

Martinsson-Walling, Helène, and Susan J. Crockford, 2001, 'Early Settlement of Rapa Nui (Easter Island)', *Asian Perspectives*, vol. 40, no. 2 (Fall), pp. 244–78

Marx, Robert, 1973, *Port Royal Rediscovered*. London: New English Library

Mattingly, David J., 2022, 'The Garamantes in North Africa in the Roman Period', *Oxford Research Encyclopedias, African History*, 24 February. https://doi.org/10.1093/acrefore/9780190277734.013.1197, accessed 13 June 2022

Mattingly, David J. (ed.), 2003, *The Archaeology of Fazzan, Volume 1, Synthesis*. Society for Libyan Studies Monograph 5. The Department of Antiquities, Tripoli, and The Society for Libyan Studies

May, Andrew Maclean and G. F. Mitchell, 1953, 'Neolithic Habitation Site, Stone Circles and Alignments at Beaghmore, Co. Tyrone', *The Journal of the Royal Society of Antiquaries of Ireland*, vol. 83, no. 2, pp. 174–97

McCall, Grant, 1976, 'European Impact on Easter Island: Response, Recruitment and the Polynesian Experience in Peru', *The Journal of Pacific History*, vol. 11, no. 2, Labour Trade (Part 2), pp. 90–105

McCoy, Patrick C., 1979, 'Easter Island', in *The Prehistory of Polynesia*, ed. J. Jennings. Canberra: Australian National University Press, pp. 135–66

McDermott, Conor, 2007, 'Plain and Bog, Bog and Wood, Wood and Bog, Bog and Plain!: Peatland Archaeology in Ireland. Archaeology from the Wetlands: Recent Perspectives', *Proceedings of the 11th WARP Conference*, Edinburgh 2005 (WARP Occasional Paper 18), eds J. Barber, et al., pp. 17–30. Edinburgh: Society of Antiquaries Scotland

M'Ghee, Robert James Leslie, 1862, *How We Got into Pekin: A Narrative of the Campaign in China of 1860*. London: R. Bentley

Meharg, Andrew, et al., 2006, 'Ancient Manuring Practices Pollute Arable Soils at the St Kilda World Heritage Site, Scottish North Atlantic', *Chemosphere*, vol. 64, issue 11, pp. 1818–28

Méndez, Patricio Garcia, 2018, *The Reinvention of the Saltpeter Industry*. Santiago: SQM Department of Communications

Messenger, John, 1967, 'The Influence of the Irish in Montserrat', *Caribbean Quarterly*, vol. 13, no. 2, pp. 3–26

Mulcahy, Matthew, 2008, 'The Port Royal Earthquake and the World of Wonders in Seventeenth-Century Jamaica', *Early American Studies*, vol. 6, no. 2 (Fall 2008), pp. 391–421

Mulrooney, M. A., 2012, *Continuity or Collapse? Diachronic Settlement and Land Use in Hanga Ho'onu, Rapa Nui (Easter Island)*. PhD dissertation, University of Auckland

National Flood Relief Commission, 1932, *Report of The National Flood Relief Commission 1931*. Shanghai

National Park Service, 1995, *Route 66 Special Resource Study*. New Mexico: Santa Fe

National Trust for Scotland, 2012, *St Kilda World Heritage Management Plan 2012–17*. Edinburgh

New World Encyclopedia contributors, 2020, 'War of the Pacific', *New World Encyclopedia*. https://www.newworldencyclopedia.org/p/index.php?title=War_of_the_Pacific&oldid=1037877, accessed 2 May 2022

Oppenheim, A. Leo, 1969, 'The Banquet of Ashurnasirpal II', *Ancient Near Eastern Texts Relating to the Old Testament*, 3rd ed. with Supplement, ed. James B. Pritchard, pp. 558–61. Princeton: Princeton University Press

Peiser, Benny, 2005, 'From Genocide to Ecocide: The Rape of "Rapa Nui"', *Energy & Environment*, vol. 16, no. 3/4, Special Issue: 'Institutions, Progress, Affluence, Technology and the Environment', pp. 513–39

Pereira, Alvaro S., 2009, 'The Opportunity of a Disaster: The Economic Impact of the 1755 Lisbon Earthquake', *The Journal of Economic History*, vol. 69, no. 2 (June), pp. 466–99

Petersen, James B. and David R. Watters, 1991, 'Archaeological Testing at the Early Saladoid Trants Site, Montserrat, West Indies', *Proceedings of the Fourteenth Congress of the International Association for Caribbean Archaeology*, eds. Alissandra Cummins and Phillipa King, pp. 286–305

Piggott, Peter, 2011, *From Far and Wide: A History of Canada's Arctic Sovereignty*. Toronto: Dundurn Press

Pilcher, J. R., 1969, 'Archaeology, Palaeoecology, and 14C Dating of the Beaghmore Stone Circle Site', *Ulster Journal of Archaeology*, Third Series, vol. 32, pp. 73–91

Pirenne, Henri, 1937, *Mohammed and Charlemagne*. London: George Allen and Unwin

Plumber, Robert, 2021, 'UK Holiday Boom: Bookings "coming in thick and fast"'. BBC, 28 January. https://www.bbc.co.uk/news/business-55826646, accessed 9 March 2022

Rainbird, Paul, 2002, 'A Message for our Future? The Rapa Nui (Easter Island) Ecodisaster and Pacific Island Environments', *World Archaeology*, vol. 33, no. 3, pp. 436–51

Ray, Sébastien, 2016, *For the Gods of Girsu, City-State Formation in Ancient Sumer*. Oxford: Archaeopress

Reade, J. E., 2002, 'The Ziggurrat and Temples of Nimrud', *Iraq*, vol. 64, pp. 135–216.

Repton, Humphry, with the assistance of J. A. Repton, 1816, *Fragments on the Theory and Practice of Landscape Gardening*. London: Bensley and Sons. https://archive.org/details/mobot31753002820014/page/n1/mode/2up?q=beaudesert, accessed 22 July 2021

Richard, Henry, 1864, *Memoirs of Joseph Sturge*. London: S. W. Partridge

Richards, Eric, 1992, 'St Kilda and Australia: Emigrants at Peril, 1852–3', *The Scottish Historical Review*, vol. 71, no. 191/192, JSTOR, pp. 129–55. www.jstor.org/stable/25530537, accessed 24 December 2020

Riedlinger, Dyanna, 1999, 'Climate Change and the Inuvialuit of Banks Island, NWT: Using Traditional Environmental Knowledge to Complement Western Science', *Arctic*, vol. 52, no. 4, December, pp. 430–2

Rockett, William H., 1980, 'A Temple at the Met', *Aramco World*, vol 31, no. 3

Roggeveen, Jacob and Andrew Sharp, 1970, *The Journal of Jacob Roggeveen*, ed. (and trans. from the Dutch ms.) by Andrew Sharp. Oxford: Clarendon Press

Rost, Stephanie, 2017, 'Water Management in Mesopotamia from the Sixth till the First Millennium B.C.', *WIREs Water*, 4:e1230. doi: 10.1002/wat2.1230, pp. 1–23

Routledge, Katherine, 1919, *The Mystery of Easter Island, the story of an expedition*, 2nd edn (1920). London and Aylesbury: Hazell, Watson and Viney. https://archive.org/details/mysteryofeaster00rout/page/n22/mode/2up, accessed 13 June 2022

Ryzewski, Krysta and John F. Cherry, 2015, 'Struggles of a Sugar Society: Surveying Plantation-Era Montserrat, 1650–1850', *International Journal of Historical Archaeology*, vol. 19, no. 2, pp. 356–83

Sadler, Nigel, 2015, 'Endangered Archives Programme 769: Montserrat in written records and photographs: preserving the archive for the nation and the Montserrat diaspora', EAP Report prepared by the Montserrat National Trust

Sahara Italiano, 1937, *Il Sahara Italiano. Fezzan e oasi di Ga!* Rome: Reale Societil Geographica Italiana

Sand, Peter H., 2018, 'Mesopotamia 2550 B.C.: The Earliest Boundary Water Treaty', *Global Journal of Archaeology & Anthropology*, vol. 5, issue 4

Schrakamp, Ingo, 2018, 'Irrigation in 3rd Millennium Southern Mesopotamia: Cuneiform Evidence from the Early Dynastic IIIb City-State of Lagash (2475–2315 BC)', in Jonas Berking (ed.), 'Water Management in Ancient Civilizations', *Berlin Studies of the Ancient World*, vol. 53

Sculle, Keith A., 1994, 'A Sign of the Times: Commentary on the Route 66 Revival in Illinois', *Material Culture*, vol. 26, no. 2, pp. 1–14 (International Society for Landscape, Place & Material Culture)

Sear, David, Andy Murdock, Tim LeBas, Paul Baggaley, and Gemma Gubbins, 2012, *Dunwich Project 5883 Final Report*, English Heritage, GeoData Institute, National Oceanography Centre and Wessex Archaeology

Shelley, Percy Bysshe, 1826, 'Ozymandias', in *Miscellaneous and Posthumous Poems of Percy Bysshe Shelley*. London: William Benbow

Shen, Aviva, 2012, 'Ai WeiWei's Giant Animal Heads at the Hirshhorn Fountain', *Smithsonian Magazine*, 26 April 2012. https://www.smithsonianmag.com/smithsonian-institution/ai-weiweis-giant-animal-heads-at-the-hirshhorn-fountain-76826788, accessed 3 May 2022

Shotte, Gertrude, 2007, 'Diasporic Transnationalism: Relocated Montserratians in the UK', *Caribbean Quarterly*, vol. 53, no. 3. pp. 41–69

Simpson, S. John, 2021. 'The Haunting of Assyria: A Chilling New Detail from the Sack of Nimrud', *Academia Letters*, Article 1389. https://doi.org/10.20935/AL1389, accessed 25 August 2021

Sinclair, T. A., 1987, *Eastern Turkey: An Architectural and Archaeological Survey*. London: Pindar Press

Sloane, Hans and Alvarez de Toledo, 1694, 'A Letter from Hans Sloane, M. D. and S. R. S. with Several Accounts of the Earthquakes in Peru October the 20th 1687. And at Jamaica, February 19th. 1687/8 and June the 7th. 1692', *Philosophical Transactions* (1683–1775), vol. 18 (1694), pp. 78–100

Steinbeck, John, 1997, *The Grapes of Wrath*. New York: Penguin Books

Stell, Geoffrey and Mary Harman, 1988, *Buildings of St Kilda*. Edinburgh: The Royal Commission on the Ancient and Historical Monuments of Scotland

Stone, Thomas, 1981, 'Whalers and Missionaries at Herschel Island', *Ethnohistory*, vol. 28, no. 2 (Spring 1981), pp. 101–24

Stride, P., 2008, 'St Kilda, the Neonatal Tetanus Tragedy of the Nineteenth Century and Some Twenty-First Century Answers', *Journal of the Royal College of Physicians Edinburgh*, vol. 38, pp. 70–7

Sullivan, Michael, 1973, *The Meeting of Eastern and Western Arts*. London: Thames & Hudson

Tamborrino, Rosa and Willeke Wendrich, 2017, 'Cultural Heritage in Context: The Temples of Nubia, Digital Technologies and the Future of Conservation', *Journal of the Institute of Conservation*, vol. 40, no. 2, pp. 168–82

Thom, A. S., 1980, 'The Stone Rings of Beaghmore: Geometry and Astronomy', *Ulster Journal of Archaeology*, Third Series, vol. 43, pp. 15–19

Thompson, William, R., 2004, 'Complexity, Diminishing Marginal Returns, and Serial Mesopotamian Fragmentation', *Journal of World-Systems Research*, vol. X (Fall), pp. 613–52

Thorarinsson, Sigurdur, 1970, *Hekla: A Notorious Volcano*, trans. Johann Hanneson and Petur Karlsson. Reykjavik: Almenna Bókafélagid

Toohey, M., K. Krüger, M. Sigl, F. Stordal, and H. Svensen, 2016, 'Climatic and Societal Impacts of a Volcanic Double Event at the Dawn of the Middle Ages', *Climatic Change*, vol. 136, pp. 401–12

Toynbee, Arnold J., 1934–61, *A Study of History*. Oxford: Oxford University Press

TRB (Richard L. Strout), 1956, 'Washington Wire', *The New Republic*, vol. 135 (6 August), p. 2

Treue, William, 1960, *Art Plunder: The Fate of Works of Art in War, Revolution and Peace*. London: Methuen

Tythacott, Louise, 2015, 'Trophies of War: Representing "Summer Palace" Loot in Military Museums in the UK', *Museum & Society*, vol. 13, no. 4, pp. 469–88

UNESCO, 2005, *Humberstone and Santa Laura Saltpeter Works Nomination for Inclusion on the World Heritage List/UNESCO* (Republic of Chile)

UNESCO, 2009, *The Underwater City of Port Royal. Tentative List nomination by the Jamaica National Heritage Trust*. http://whc.unesco.org/en/tentativelists/5430/, accessed 6 June 2021

Usher, Peter, 1971, 'The Canadian Western Arctic: A Century of Change', *Anthropologica*, New Series, vol. 13, no. 1/2, 'Pilot, Not Commander: Essays in Memory of Diamond Jenness (1971)', pp. 169–83

Varin, Paul (actually Charles Dupin), 1862, *Expédition de Chine*. Paris: Michel Lévy Frères

Vercoutter, Jean, 1980, 'The Flooded Fortresses of Nubia', *The Unesco Courier*, (February/March)

Waterfield, Gordon, *Layard of Nineveh*. London: John Murray, 1963

Watters, D. R. and G. E. Norton, 2007, 'Volcanically Induced Loss of Archaeological Sites in Montserrat', in B. Reid, H. Petitjean Roget and A. Curet, eds, *Proceedings of the Twenty-First Congress of the International Association for Caribbean Archaeology*, vol. 1., pp. 48–55

Wang, Nianyi, 1988, *Da dongluande niandai (A Decade of Great Upheaval)*. Zhengzhou: Henan renmin chubanshe

Ward, Edward, 1698, *A Trip to Jamaica: With a True Character of the People and Island*, 3rd edn. London: n.p.

Watenpaugh, Heghnar Zeitlian, 2014, 'Preserving the Medieval City of Ani: Cultural Heritage between Contest and Reconciliation', *Journal of the Society of Architectural Historians*, vol. 73, no. 4 (December), pp. 528–55

Weigall, Arthur, P. E., 1910, *Guide to the Antiquities of Upper Egypt from Abydos to the Sudan Frontier*. London: Methuen

Weiss, Daniel, 2020, 'Temple of the White Thunderbird', *Archaeology* (January/February), pp. 38–45

Westenholz, Aage, 2002, 'The Sumerian City-State', in *A Comparative Study of Six City-State Cultures*, ed. M. Hansen. Copenhagen: Kgl. Danske Videnskabernes Selskab

Wiggins-Grandison, Margaret D., 2005, 'Tsunamis and Jamaica', an article by the Head, Earthquake Unit, University of the West Indies – Mona Campus Kingston 7, Jamaica

Wisniak, Jaime, 2001, 'The History of Iodine from Discovery to Commodity', *Indian Journal of Chemical Technology*, vol. 8, pp. 518–26

Wisniak, Jaime and Ingrid Garcés, 2001, 'The Rise and Fall of the Saltire (Sodium Nitrate) Industry', *Indian Journal of Chemical Technology*, vol. 8, pp. 427–38

Wolseley, Garnet Joseph, 1862, *Narrative of the War with China in 1860*. London: Longman

Wong, Young-tsu, undated, 'European Buildings with Chinese Characteristics: The Xiyanglou in the Imperial Garden Yuanming Yuan', accessed 7 January 2021

Worsley, Giles, 2002, *England's Lost Houses*. London: Aurum Press

Xu, Jiren et al., 2018, 'PEATMAP: Refining Estimates of Global Peatland Distribution Based on a Meta-Analysis', *CATENA*, vol. 160, pp. 134–40

Ye, Sang and Geremie Barmé, 2009, 'The Fate of the Confucius Temple, the Kong Mansion and King Cemetery', *China Heritage Quarterly*, no. 20 (December). http://www.chinaheritagequarterly.org/scholarship.php?searchterm=020_confucius.inc&issue=020, accessed 25 November 2019

Zahedieh, Nuala, 1986, 'The Merchants of Port Royal, Jamaica, and the Spanish Contraband Trade, 1655–1692', *The William and Mary Quarterly*, vol. 43, no. 4 (October), pp. 570–93

Zhou, Zehao, 2011, 'The Anti-Confucian Campaign during the Cultural Revolution, August 1966–January 1967', Dissertation submitted to the Faculty of the Graduate School of the University of Maryland

IMAGE CREDITS

Every effort has been made to trace copyright holders and to obtain their permission for the use of copyright material. The publisher would be grateful if notified of any corrections that should be incorporated in future reprints or editions of this book.

Chapter Openers

Introduction, p. x: Yale University Art Gallery

Chapter 1, p. 8: © Manchester Art Gallery/Mr James Thomas Blair bequest, 1917/Bridgeman Images

Chapter 2, p. 52: Royal Astronomical Society/Science Photo Library

Chapter 3, p. 86: Gavin Hellier/ Robert Harding

Chapter 4, p. 124: PjrArt/Alamy Stock Photo

Chapter 5, p. 164: Reitz/ullstein bild via Getty Images

Chapter 6, p. 214: Image courtesy of the New Bedford Whaling Museum

Endpapers

Front: The Metropolitan Museum of Art

Back: The Metropolitan Museum of Art. Harris Brisbane Dick Fund, 1937

All Other Images

Fig. 1: New York Historical Society

Fig. 2: © Mark Geddis Photography

Fig. 3: Colin William Photography

Fig. 4: © Crown DfC Historic Environment Division

Fig. 5: © Crown DfC Historic Environment Division

Fig. 6: Department of Anthropology, Smithsonian Institution (E2545-02A)

Fig. 7: Loetscher Chlaus/Alamy Stock Photo

Fig. 8: Photo © Maedward

Fig. 9: © Boris Radosavljevic

Fig. 10: © Giancarlo Costa/Paris, National Archive/Bridgeman Images

Fig. 11: © Professor David Sear/University of Southampton

Fig. 12: Graham Turner/Alamy Stock Photo

Fig. 13: Courtesy of the Trustees of the British Museum. © David Coulson/TARA

Fig. 14: Montage by Martin Sterry for the Trans-Sahara Project

Fig. 15: © Professor David Mattingly

Fig. 16: NASA, Johnson

Fig. 17: Artokoloro/Alamy Stock Photo

Fig. 18: © British Library Board. All Rights Reserved/Bridgeman Images

Fig. 19: Donny L. Hamilton, Nautical Archaeology Program, Texas A&M University.

Fig. 20 tl: Donny L. Hamilton, Nautical Archaeology Program, Texas A&M University.

Fig. 20 bl: Donny L. Hamilton, Nautical Archaeology Program, Texas A&M University

Fig. 20 br: Photo © Marion Link/John H. Evans Library Digital Collections

Fig. 21: Nur Photo/Getty Images

Fig. 22: Age fotostock/UNESCO/Photoshot

Fig. 23: Age fotostock/Martin Siepmann/ImageBROKER

Fig. 24: Yusuf Aslan/Alamy Stock Photo

Fig. 25: Martin Rietze/Westend61/Age fotostock

Fig. 26: Earth Observatory Nasa

Fig. 27: Science History Images/Alamy Stock Photo

Fig. 28: Photo Alain BUU/Gamma-Rapho via Getty Images

Fig. 29: Photo RMN, Paris/Scala, Florence

Fig. 30: S. Rey 2017 © The Girsu Project

Fig. 31: Private collection

Fig. 32: S. Rey 2017 © The Girsu Project

Fig. 33: © Crown copyright: HES (Canmore archive)

Fig. 34: Aberdeen G Washington Collection by Norman MacLeod

Fig. 35: © Crown copyright: HES (Canmore archive)

Fig. 36: UPPA/Photoshot/Age fotostock

Fig. 37: Asar Studios/Alamy Stock Photo

Fig. 38: © Cambridge University Library

Fig. 39: © Walter Weinberg

Fig. 40: The Miriam and Ira D. Wallach Division of Art, Prints and Photographs: Photography Collection, The New York Public Library

Fig. 41: © The British Institute for the Study of Iraq

Fig. 42: Bowdoin College Museum of Art collection. Gift of Dr Henri Byron Haskell, Medical School Class of 1855. Critical support for the Assyrian Collection at the Bowdoin College Museum of Art is provided by the Yadgar Family Endowment

Fig. 43: Pictures from History/ Universal Images Group via Getty Images

Fig. 44: Pictures from History/ Universal Images Group via Getty Images

Fig. 45: The Bibliothèque nationale de France, Paris

Fig. 46: Wikimedia

Fig. 47: DeA/Veneranda Biblioteca Ambrosiana, Milan/Age fotostock

Fig. 48: Royal Collection Trust/© His Majesty King Charles III 2023

Fig. 49: Photo by VCG/VCG via Getty Images

Fig. 50: Universal History Archive/ UIG via Getty Images

Fig. 51: National Archives, Kew

Fig. 52: International Institute of Social History collection (BG D29/184)

Fig. 53: China Heritage Quarterly and China Underground

Fig 54: PRISMA ARCHIVO/ Alamy Stock Photo

Fig. 55: © Jeremy Richards/Age fotostock

Fig. 56: Nico Stengert/Novarc Images RM/Age fotostock

Fig. 57: Martin Bernetti/Getty Images

Fig. 58: Private collection

Fig. 59: Oakland Museum of California/© Dorothea Lange

Fig. 60: Carol M. Highsmith Archive/Library of Congress, USA (original digital file) highsm 04005

Fig. 61: BDP/Alamy Stock Photo

Fig. 62: National Portrait Gallery, London

Fig. 63: © William Salt Library/ Bridgeman Images

Fig. 64: Country Life Picture Library/Future Publishing Ltd

Fig. 65: Wikipedia/Bs0u10e01

Fig. 66: Wellcome Collection, London

Fig. 67: © UNESCO

Fig. 68: John Paul Getty Museum

Fig. 69: The New York Public Library (b14293088)

Fig. 70: Chris Walker/Chicago Tribune/Tribune News Service via Getty Images

Fig. 71: © Paul de Roos

Fig. 72: Hum Historical/Alamy Stock Photo

Fig. 73: Image © 2014 DigitalGlobe, Inc.

Fig. 74: Ivan Vdovin/age fotostock

Fig. 75: Sean Pavone/Alamy Stock Photo

Fig. 76: Hans Ravn/Ritzau Scanpix/AFP via Getty Images

Fig. 77: © The Trustees of the British Museum

INDEX

Vilarinho da Furna, Portugal, 213
volcanoes: benefits of living near, 222–4; destructive power of, 54, 221–2, 224–5; in Iceland, 223–4; Montserrat (1995–97), 54–5, 76–7, 83–5, 221; Mount Vesuvius (79 CE), 221; St Vincent, Caribbean (1812), 222; and World Heritage Sites, 75

Wadi Halfa, 167, 212
Wadi Sebua, 167
Wang Youdun (calligrapher), 139
Wang Zhengxin, 158–9
war: economic costs of, 232–3; and the erasure of cultural heritage, 227–31; extent of over time, 125
Warner, Sir Thomas, 78
Warsaw ghetto, 229
Watenpaugh, Heghnar, 74
water: irrigation systems, 45–9; reduced supply of, 47, 49–50; reservoir building, 166–7, 201, 212–13

Watters, David, 83
whaling, 23–4, 26–7, 28
Wheeler, Sir Mortimer, 43
White, John, 56, 59
White Thunderbird (lion-headed eagle), 93, 259–60, *260*
Wilson, Woodrow, 183
Wolsley, Garnet, 144, 147
Woodruff, John, 183
World Risk Report (2016), 225
Wyatt, James, 194
Wynn, Steve, 150

Xenophon, 133
Xi Jinping, 163

Yezidi people, 245
Yongzheng Emperor, 138, 139
Yu, Madame, 162
Yuanmingyan summer palace *see* Old Summer Palace, China

Zahedieh, Nuala, 61–2
Zoroastrian faith, 67–8